Translated Texts for Historians

This series is designed to meet the needs of students of ancient and medieval history and others who wish to broaden their study by reading source material, but whose knowledge of Latin or Greek is not sufficient to allow them to do so in the original languages. Many important Late Imperial and Dark Age texts are currently unavailable in translation and it is hoped that TTH will help to fill this gap and to complement the secondary literature in English which already exists. The series relates principally to the period 300-800 AD and includes Late Imperial, Greek, Byzantine and Syriac texts as well as source books illustrating a particular period or theme. Each volume is a self-contained scholarly translation with an introductory essay on the text and its author and notes on the text indicating major problems of interpretation, including textual difficulties.

Editorial Committee
Sebastian Brock, Oriental Institute, University of Oxford
Averil Cameron, Keble College, Oxford
Henry Chadwick, Oxford
John Davies, University of Liverpool
Carlotta Dionisotti, King's College, London
Peter Heather, University College London
William E. Klingshirn, The Catholic University of America
Michael Lapidge, Clare College, Cambridge
Robert Markus, University of Nottingham
John Matthews, Yale University
Claudia Rapp, University of California, Los Angeles
Raymond Van Dam, University of Michigan
Michael Whitby, University of Warwick
Ian Wood, University of Leeds

General Editors
Gillian Clark, University of Liverpool
Mary Whitby, Oxford

A complete list of titles in the Translated Texts for Historians series is available on request. Recent titles are shown below.

Venantius Fortunatus: Personal and Political Poems
Translated with notes and introduction by JUDITH GEORGE
Volume 23: 192pp., 1995, ISBN 0-85323-179-6

Donatist Martyr Stories: The Church in Conflict in Roman North Africa
Translated with notes and introduction by MAUREEN A. TILLEY
Volume 24: 144pp., 1996, ISBN 0 85323 931 2

Hilary of Poitiers: Conflicts of Conscience and Law in the Fourth-Century Church
Translated with introduction and notes by LIONEL R. WICKHAM
Volume 25: 176pp., 1997, ISBN 0–85323–572–4

Lives of the Visigothic Fathers
Translated and edited by A. T. FEAR
Volume 26: 208pp., 1997, ISBN 0–85323–582–1

Optatus: Against the Donatists
Translated and edited by MARK EDWARDS
Volume 27: 220pp., 1997, ISBN 0–85323–752–2

Bede: A Biblical Miscellany
Translated with notes and introduction by W. TRENT FOLEY and ARTHUR G. HOLDER
Volume 28: 240pp., 1999, ISBN 0–85323–683–6

Bede: The Reckoning of Time
Translated with introduction, notes and commentary by FAITH WALLIS
Volume 29: 352pp., 1999, ISBN 0–85323–693–3

Ruricius of Limoges and Friends: A Collection of Letters from Visigothic Gaul
Translated with notes and introduction by RALPH W. MATHISEN
Volume 30: 272pp., 1999, ISBN 0–85323–703–4

The Armenian History attributed to Sebeos
Translated with notes by R. W. THOMSON. Historical Commentary by JAMES HOWARD-JOHNSTON. Assistance from TIM GREENWOOD
Volume 31: 464pp., 1999, ISBN 0–85323–564–3

For full information, please write to the following:
All countries, except the USA and Canada: Liverpool University Press, Senate House, Abercromby Square, Liverpool, L69 3BX, UK (*Tel* +44-[0]151-794 2233, *Fax* +44-[0]151-794 2235, *Email* J.M.Smith@liv.ac.uk.
USA & Canada: University of Pennsylvania Press, 4200 Pine Street, Philadelphia, PA 19104-6097, USA (*Tel* +1-215-898-6264, *Fax* +1-215-898-0404).

Chronicle of 754, caps. 57-63 (see pp. 133-6). MS London, British Library, Egerton 1934, fol. 2 (9th century, Visigothic script), showing the lower half of a folio page. By permission of the British Library.

Translated Texts for Historians
Volume 9

Second edition

Conquerors and Chroniclers of Early Medieval Spain

Translated with notes and introduction by
KENNETH BAXTER WOLF

Liverpool
University
Press

First published 1990 by
LIVERPOOL UNIVERSITY PRESS
4 Cambridge Street, Liverpool, L69 7ZU

Second edition published 1999

Copyright © 1990, 1999 Kenneth Baxter Wolf

British Library Cataloguing-in-Publication Data
A British Library CIP Record is available
ISBN 0–85323–554–6

Printed in the European Union by
Redwood Books, Trowbridge

CONTENTS

PREFACE ix

SOURCES AND ABBREVIATIONS x

MAP xiv

INTRODUCTION xv

ESSAYS:
    John of Biclaro and the Goths 1
    Isidore of Seville and the Goths... 11
    An Andalusian Chronicler and the Muslims 25
    An Asturian Chronicler and the Muslims.. 43

TEXTS:
    John of Biclaro, *Chronicle*.. 57
    Isidore of Seville, *History of the Kings of the Goths*........................... 79
    The Chronicle of 754 111
    The Chronicle of Alfonso III 161

LISTS OF RULERS 179

SELECT BIBLIOGRAPHY 183

INDEX 191

To my mother,

Ruth Elizabeth Stuart Adams Wolf.

Matris est filius.

PREFACE

A number of individuals and institutions contributed to this project. First and foremost I would like to thank Margaret Gibson, who not only recognized a 'diamond in the rough' when she first saw the manuscript, but patiently devoted her time and linguistic acuity to making it shine. In addition I am grateful to Giles Constable, who read the manuscript in one of its earlier stages; Glen Bowersock and Christopher Jones, whom I consulted in matters of ancient history; and James Powell and James Muldoon, who offered their expertise in things medieval. Finally, Dwayne Carpenter, with his appreciation of the value of textually-focused history, provided the perfect sounding board for the ideas generated by my research. My thanks to the Institute for Advanced Study for bringing all of these scholars together and giving me the opportunity to benefit from close contact with them. In this regard I would also like to acknowledge Robert Burns, S.J., Gavin Langmuir, and especially Teófilo Ruíz, for helping me get into the Institute in the first place.

On the home front, I would like to express my gratitude to Pomona College as well as to key members of its faculty, in particular Carl Ernst, J. William Whedbee, and Vincent Learnihan. Finally a special thanks to my children, Owen and Ellie, who, as always, helped me keep this project in perspective.

SOURCES AND ABBREVIATIONS

EDITIONS USED FOR TRANSLATIONS

John of Biclaro, *Chronicle*:
Campos, Julio. ed. *Juan de Biclaro, obispo de Gerona, su vida y obra* Madrid: 1960.
The numbering of the paragraphs in the translation is my own.

Isidore of Seville, *History of the Kings of the Goths*:
Rodríguez Alonso, Cristóbal. ed. *Las historias de los Godos, Vándalos, y Suevos de Isidoro de Sevilla: estudio, edición crítica, y traducción.* León: 1975.
I have translated the 'long version' of the *History of the Kings the Goths*, minus the appended histories of the Vandals and the Suevi.

Chronicle of 754:
López Pereira, Eduardo. ed. *Crónica mozárabe de 754: edición crítica y traducción.* Zaragoza: 1980.

Chronicle of Alfonso III:
Crónicas Asturianas. ed. Juan Gil Fernández, José L. Moralejo, Juan Ruíz de la Peña. Oviedo: 1985.
I have translated the Roda version.

ADDITIONAL SOURCES AND ABBREVIATIONS:

Akbar Majmu'a: Ajbar Machmua (colleción de tradiciones). tr. Emilio Lafuente y Alcántara. Madrid: 1867, 1984.

Ambrose, *De fide ad Gratianum Augustum*: ed. Otto Faller. *CSEL* 78.

Augustine, *City of God:* CCSL 47, 48.

Biclaro: John of Biclaro, *Chronicle* (see above).

Boniface, *Epistola:* MGH *Epistolae Merowingici et Karolini aevi* 1.

Bonnaz, Yves. ed. *Chroniques asturiennes (fin IXe siècle).* Paris: 1987.

Campos, Julio. ed. *Juan de Biclaro, obispo de Gerona, su vida y obra.* Madrid: 1960.

CCSL: *Corpus Christianorum, Series Latina.*

Chr741: *Chronicle of 741. ed. Juan Gil. Corpus scriptorum muzarabicorum.* 2 vol. 2:7-14.

Chr754: *Chronicle of 754* (see above).

ChrAlf: *Chronicle of Alfonso III* (see above).

Chronicle of Fredegar: The Fourth Book of the Chronicle of Fredegar and its Continuations. tr. J. M. Wallace-Hadrill. London: 1960.

Corpus scriptorum muzarabicorum. ed. Juan Gil. 2 vol. Madrid: 1973.

Crónicas Asturianas. ed. Juan Gil Fernández, José L. Moralejo, Juan Ruíz de la Peña. Oviedo: 1985.

CSEL: *Corpus Scriptorum Ecclesiasticorum Latinorum.*

Eusebius, *Ecclesiastical History:* SC 31, 41, 55, 73.

Eusebius-Jerome: *Eusebius Pamphili chronici canones, Latine vertit, adauxit, ad sua tempora produxit S. Eusebius Hieronymous.* ed. John K. Fotheringham. London: 1923.

Gregory, *Dialogues:* SC 251, 260, 265.

Gregory of Tours, *History of the Franks: MGH Scriptores rerum Merovingicarum 1.*

HistGoth: Isidore of Seville, *History of the Kings of the Goths* (see above).

Hydatius, *Chronicle: MGH AA* 11:13-36.

Ildephonsus, *De virginitate perpetua Sanctae Mariae: Santos Padres Españoles I: San Ildefonso de Toledo.* ed. V. Blanco and J. Campos. Madrid: 1971.

Ildephonsus, *De viris illustribus*: ed. C. Codoñer Merino. Salamanca: 1972.

Isidore, *Chronicle: MGH AA* 11:391-497.

Isidore, *De viris illustribus*: ed. C. Codoñer Merino. Salamanca: 1964.

Isidore, *Etymologies*: ed. W. M. Lindsay. 2 vol. Oxford: 1911.

Jerome, *Epistola: CSEL* 55.

Jerome, *Liber hebraicarum quaestionum in Genesim: CCSL* 72.

Julian of Toledo, *Apologeticum de tribus capitulis: CCSL* 115.

Julian of Toledo, *De sextae aetatis comprobatione: CCSL* 115.

Julian of Toledo, *History of King Wamba: CCSL* 115.

Leander, *De instructione virginum: De la instrucción de las vírgenes y desprecio del mundo.* ed. Jaime Velázquez. Madrid: 1979.

López Pereira, Eduardo. ed. *Crónica mozárabe de 754: edición crítica y traducción.* Zaragoza: 1980.

MGH AA: Monumenta Germaniae Historica, Auctores Antiquissimi.

Orosius: *Historiarum adversum paganos libri VII.* CSEL 5.

Pacatus, *Panegyric to the Emperor Theodosius*: tr. C. E. V. Nixon. Liverpool: 1987.

PL: Patrologia Latina.

Prosper of Aquitaine, *Chronicle: MGH AA* 9:385-485.

Rodríguez Alonso, Cristóbal. ed. *Las historias de los Godos, Vandalos, y Suevos de Isidoro de Sevilla: estudio, edición crítica, y traducción.* León: 1975.

Royal Frankish Annals: MGH Scriptores rerum germanicarum 13:3-178.

SC: Sources Chrétiennes.

Victor of Tunnuna, *Chronicle: MGH AA* 11:184-206.

Vitas sanctorum patrum Emeretensium: ed. Joseph N. Garvin. Dissertation. Catholic University of America. Washington, D.C.: 1946.

Vives, José. ed. *Concilios visigóticos e hispano-romanos.* Barcelona: 1963.

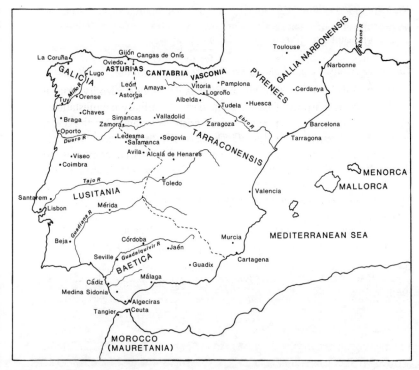

Map of 6th–8th century Spain

INTRODUCTION

Historians of Latin Christian views of Islam have traditionally limited the scope of their studies to the evolution of misconceptions about Muhammad and his teachings. Yet such an approach is based on something of a misconception of its own: that Islam was perceived by medieval Christians to be a strictly religious phenomenon. In fact, Islam was always more than a religion, both for those who participated in it as well as for those who perceived it from the outside. It constituted a community of believers with an unmistakeable political identity. And it was this political aspect of Islam, particularly its military manifestations, that first impressed itself upon the Latin Christians living in North Africa, Spain, and France, who found themselves face to face with the conquering Muslim armies. Once we recognize this, it comes as no surprise that the very earliest Latin Christian views of Islam—in the broad sense of the term—are to be found precisely in the chronicles that describe these conquests.[1] Though they reveal little about perceptions of Islam as a religion, they tell us a great deal about attitudes toward Islam as a Mediterranean power.

The earliest Latin chronicle to report on the progress of the Muslim armies in the east, across Africa, and into Europe was the so-called *Chronicle of Fredegar*, written and updated a number of times in seventh-century Burgundy.[2] But it was the chroniclers of Spain who, understandably, left behind the most extensive treatments of the arrival of Islam in the west. Their works fall into two categories: those written in the mid-eighth century by Christians living under Muslim rule, and those written in the late ninth century by Christians living just outside of Muslim jurisdiction in the mountain kingdom of Asturias. As it turns out, the chroniclers living within al-Andalus[3] saw things differently than did

---

[1] To date, Ron Barkai is the only student of Christian views of Islam to use such sources. *Cristianos y musulmanes en la España medieval: el enemigo en el espejo* (Madrid, 1984).
[2] *Chronicle of Fredegar*, pp. 54-5, 68-9, 90-1, 93-5, 113, 119.
[3] The Arabic word for 'Spain', used here as a synonym for 'Muslim Spain'.

their coreligionists in the Christian north. While the former recounted the Muslim invasion and settlement more or less matter-of-factly as a change of regime in Spain, the latter interpreted it in providential terms as a punishment for the sins of their forefathers.

This difference in the depiction of the conquest is in part a reflection of the political circumstances under which the chroniclers wrote. The Asturians, living at a time when Alfonso III (866-910) was enjoying unusual military success at the expense of the Muslims in the south, could permit themselves to see the conquerors as a scourge that they hoped was about to be lifted. On the other hand, the Andalusian[4] chroniclers, from their vantage point in the heart of Muslim territory, presumably had difficulty imagining that the occupation could be anything but permanent and so were wary of such providential speculation. But if the difference in political climate accounts for the basic difference in approach to the conquest, it was the way in which the chroniclers tapped into earlier works of Iberian history that determined the precise shape that their descriptions of the conquest would take.

The Andalusian and Asturian chroniclers alike regarded their task as one of continuing chronicles that had been written in Spain before the Muslim invasion, specifically those of John of Biclaro (c. 590) and Isidore of Seville (c. 625). These chronicles, written while the Visigoths were consolidating their hold on the peninsula, provided not only points of departure for historians of the Muslim conquest, but useful historiographical models for dealing with foreign invasion. For until their recasting at the hands of John and Isidore, the Visigoths were, from the perspective of imperial historians, antagonists. They were barbarian, heterodox invaders of a Catholic, Roman empire. The military success of the Visigoths and their conversion to catholicism in the late sixth century allowed John and Isidore to transform them into historical protagonists, the builders of a new 'Christian empire' in the west. As it turned out, the Gothic monarchy that these chroniclers eulogized ultimately proved

---

[4]'Andalusian', as the term is used here, refers to anyone living in al-Andalus (Muslim Spain).

incapable of withstanding the Muslim invasion of 711. But the works that John and Isidore left behind provided something of a model for those Christian historians who faced the significantly more complicated task of coming to terms with the new conquest. In short, much of what the Andalusian and Asturian chroniclers had to say about the Muslims was influenced by what John of Biclaro and Isidore of Seville had said about the Visigoths.

The purpose of this study is precisely to compare the Latin chronicles produced in the wake of these two successive invasions, asking not only how they depicted the invaders, but how their portraits were influenced by the work of their predecessors. The first two chapters focus on the *Chronicle* of John of Biclaro and Isidore of Seville's *History of the Kings of the Goths*, as examples of how the Visigothic kings were transformed from heretical barbarians into the legitimate heirs of Christian imperial rule in Spain. The third chapter treats an anonymous continuation of John of Biclaro's *Chronicle* written in the mid-eighth century by a Christian living under Muslim rule. The fourth looks at a chronicle attributed to Alfonso III, which was intended as a continuation of the *History of the Kings of the Goths*.

In each case, I have attempted to distill a 'view of the conquest' from the chronicle by asking three basic questions. First, what is the nature of the specific historical information about the conquest and the conquerors recorded by the chronicler? Second, what terms did he use to convey this information? And third, what, if any, narrative structures did he employ to 'make sense' out of the conquest? Though textual, these questions reveal something of the *mentalité* of the chronicler, because the selection of information for inclusion in the chronicle reflects his own criteria of noteworthiness, and the words and narrative patterns applied to the data reflect the interpretative structures of his own mind. When we compare these observations with what we know about the political, cultural, and historiographical context within which the author wrote, we have come as close as we can to understanding why the chronicler depicted the conquest as he did.

JOHN OF BICLARO AND THE GOTHS

In 589, King Reccared convened the Third Council of Toledo at which he repudiated the Arianism of his predecessors and embraced Catholicism. The modern debate about the political and religious significance of this royal volte-face has not been resolved. But the historiographical implications of Reccared's decision are clear. While the Goths were Arians, they, quite simply, had no history. The Catholic ecclesiastics who, beginning in the fourth century, monopolized the production of historical literature in the west, typically subscribed to the Eusebian notion of one empire and one church, and thus had no category but 'interloper' with which to pigeonhole the Goths. It was Reccared's conversion that allowed the Goths to be incorporated into Christian history as protagonists for the first time. Within a year of the council, John of Biclaro took it upon himself to do just that.

What little we know about John of Biclaro's life suggests that he was well-suited for the task. According to his younger contemporary Isidore,[1] John was born in the province of Lusitania[2] of Gothic parentage. Isidore's brief account does not tell us how it was, given John's ancestry, that he came to be a Catholic. Whatever the reason, we can perhaps safely assume that as a Catholic Goth John would have been attracted to the idea of a Catholic Gothic monarchy, especially in light of his treatment by the Arian King Leovigild. According to Isidore, John had returned to Spain after seventeen years of study in Constantinople (c.559-c.576)[3] only to be arrested as part of a royally-sponsored crackdown on the Catholic clergy. As a result, John spent the next ten years living in internal exile in Barcelona (c.576-586). For him, then, the accession of Reccared in 586 and the Toledan council of 589 meant freedom and vindication. It also opened the door to his preferment: he was appointed to the see of Gerona sometime between 589 and 592.[4] In the midst of this sudden transition

---

[1] Isidore, *De viris illustribus* 44.

[2] More specifically, in Scallabis (Santarem, Portugal), near the mouth of the Tajo River.

[3] Campos, pp. 17-25, and Roger Collins, *Early Medieval Spain: Unity in Diversity, 400-1000* (New York, 1983), p. 42, offer slightly different calculations of the dates of John's stay in Constantinople.

[4] Alicius, bishop of Gerona, attended the Third Council of Toledo in 589. John's name appears on the lists of those who attended the Second Council of Zaragoza (592), the

from *persona non grata* to prelate, John decided to record the history of the Gothic monarchy under Leovigild and Reccared.[5]

The format that John of Biclaro chose for this project was that of the universal chronicle, pioneered by Sextus Julius Africanus in the third century and made famous by Eusebius of Caesarea in the fourth.[6] The original purpose of the universal chronicle genre was apologetic: to demonstrate the relative antiquity of Hebrew history in comparison to the histories of Greece and Rome. Eusebius organized his data schematically, with parallel, synchronized chronologies that covered the history of the Mediterranean and the Near East from the birth of Abraham up into the reign of Constantine (325). Some fifty years later, Jerome took it upon himself to translate Eusebius's tables into Latin and to extend them up to the death of the emperor Valens (378). Jerome's efforts ultimately inspired a series of chronicles of Mediterranean history specifically written as continuations of the universal chronicle. Prosper of Aquitaine, after summarizing Eusebius and Jerome, brought the account up to 455. Victor of Tunnuna continued Prosper to the year 567. And John of Biclaro pushed the chronicle forward to 590.[7]

John was very explicit about his role as a continuator. In his preface, he applauded Eusebius, Jerome, Prosper and Victor, who 'have woven together the history of practically all peoples with the greatest brevity and diligence, bringing the accumulation of years up to our own age, and passing on, for our understanding, those events which happened in the world'.[8] John's stated goal was simply to extend their work: 'to record,

---

Council of Toledo (597), and the Second Council of Barcelona (599). Vives. pp. 138, 155, 157, 161.

[5] The most detailed study of John's *Chronicle* to date is to be found in Suzanne Teillet, *Des goths à la nation gothique: les origines de l'idée de nation en occident du Ve au VIIe siècle* (Paris, 1984), pp. 428-55.

[6] Indrikis Sterns, *The Greater Medieval Historians: An Interpretation and a Bibliography* (Lanham, Maryland, 1980), pp. 4-8. For a more detailed treatment, see: Alden A. Mosshammer, *The 'Chronicle' of Eusebius and Greek Chronographic Tradition* (Lewisburg, Pennsylvania, 1979).

[7] There were others who authored continuations that parallel those listed here. The fifth-century Galician bishop Hydatius, for example, apparently unaware of Prosper's chronicle, wrote a continuation of Jerome up to the year 469. I have limited my attention to the specific series of chronicles that John of Biclaro had in mind when he wrote his continuation.

[8] Biclaro, prologue.

using a concise format, those events which have occurred in our own times'. For our purposes, the important point is that John's chronicle is not, at face value, a history of the Gothic monarchy. What he recorded about the kings of Toledo he placed within the broader framework of the universal chronicle, of which he considered his own work to be no more than the most recent installment. In order to appreciate fully the process by which John gave the Goths a history, then, we must take a closer look at the genre within which he worked, specifically at the earlier segments of the universal chronicle that John had in mind when composing his own.

Though each of Eusebius' continuators regarded his own efforts simply as the extension of his predecessor's work, in fact each had his own particular preferences with regard to style and content. In addition to extending Eusebius' chronicle, Jerome took it upon himself to insert in the original chronicle events from Latin Roman history that Eusebius, with his more eastern orientation, had neglected to include.[9] Beyond this, the most significant difference between the two is the choice of ending. While Eusebius concluded his account on a positive note with the confluence of Greco-Roman and Judaeo-Christian history during the reign of Constantine, Jerome ended his continuation with the imperial defeat at the hands of the Goths at Adrianople in 378.[10] Jerome may have had apocalyptic reasons for ending on such a sombre note, or he may simply have never got around to adding to his account. In any case, his choice of ending signaled his continuators that barbarian history, at least insofar as it impinged on that of the empire, was worthy of record. In a sense Jerome opened the door for those who followed to treat the political successes and failures of the various barbarian *gentes* as new strands of history to be presented parallel to the history of the Christian empire, in a manner reminiscent of the multi-national scope of Eusebius' original work.

Prosper of Aquitaine summarized the Eusebius-Jerome chronicle and added his own continuation while serving as secretary to Pope Leo I in 455. He retained the sparseness of the yearly entries and organized his material according to the succession of consuls in Rome. The types of

---

[9] J. N. D. Kelly, *Jerome: His Life, Writings, and Controversies* (New York, 1975), pp. 72-5.
[10] Eusebius-Jerome, p. 331.

historical information that Prosper deemed worthy of record are very similar to those reported by Eusebius and Jerome. Imperial accessions, rebellions, and wars with barbarian peoples, dominate that portion of the chronicle dedicated to what we would call secular history. Entries such as these are irregularly punctuated with references to church matters: synods, papal successions, the deeds of outstanding churchmen, and, above all, struggles with heresy.

Prosper's continuation is full of references to barbarian incursions. It refers to the Lombards, Burgundians, Huns, Goths, and Vandals. The Vandals receive far and away the most attention—and the most antipathy—for two reasons. For one thing Prosper was probably in or around Rome at the time that it was sacked by the Vandal navy in 455. In fact the last entry in his chronicle is dedicated to this disaster. But from Prosper's perspective, the Vandals had already distinguished themselves from the other barbarians by threatening not only the empire but the church. Their Arian king Geiseric (428-77), alone among the barbarian leaders of the time, actively sought to 'replace the Catholic faith with Arian impiety', something that Prosper's sensitivity to things heretical would not permit him to treat briefly or dispassionately.[11] According to Prosper, Geiseric persecuted bishops by torturing them, depriving them of their churches, sending them into exile, even killing them. The account at this point reads much more like a selection from the Roman martyrology than a continuation of Eusebius, whose account of the earlier, imperial persecutions is more matter-of-fact.

Prosper focused so much on the barbarism of the Vandals that his references to the incursions of other peoples, specifically the Goths, seem perfunctory by comparison. He did repeat verbatim Jerome's account of the debacle at Adrianople. But, on the other hand, he showed no signs of being scandalized by Theodosius' treaty with the Goths and Athanaric's subsequent reception in Constantinople. Compared to his description of the sack of Rome in 455 by the Vandals, his one-line account of Alaric's sack in 410 is anaemic: 'Rome, once the conqueror of the world, is seized by the Goths under their leader Alaric'.[12] Later, King Athaulf carries off

---

[11] Prosper 1327.
[12] Prosper 1240. In fact, Prosper seemed more concerned about the effect of the sack on his chronological framework: henceforth he would be referring only to the consuls of the east. For *Roma victrix, capta*, compare Jerome, *Epistola* 127.12.

Placidia, the sister of the emperors Arcadius and Honorius, but after a short time she is honourably returned to Constantinople. At one point the Goths break a treaty and attack Narbonne, but on another occasion they ally with the empire against the Huns. In short, the little that Prosper tells us about the Goths does not place them in the same, unambiguously antagonistic category as the Vandals. They remain barbarians, though not particularly barbaric ones.

Victor of Tunnuna wrote his continuation of Prosper's chronicle from a monastery near Constantinople, where he had been confined in 565 by Justin II for his stance during the 'Three Chapters' controversy.[13] The content of Victor's chronicle reflects his personal involvement in such doctrinal matters. His selection of events leaned far more in the direction of ecclesiastical history than Prosper's, the imperial military campaigns receiving comparatively little attention. Moreover, while Prosper regularly recorded only the accession of the bishops of Rome, Victor covered the sees of Constantinople, Antioch, Jerusalem, and Alexandria as well. As far as the barbarians were concerned, it was predictably the Vandals, as persecutors of the church, that monopolized Victor's attention. He barely mentioned the Goths.

Though John of Biclaro wrote that his chronicle was meant simply to bring Victor's up to date, there is little to connect the two, apart from John's point of departure (567) and his use of the emperors rather than the consuls as chronological signposts.[14] For one thing, John restored the balance between secular and ecclesiastical affairs that Victor had upset with his emphasis on the church. Though John did begin with Justin II's enforcement of Chalcedon and essentially ended with the Third Council of Toledo, the bulk of the entries in between treat political successions and military campaigns. In terms of the relative weight of attention devoted to secular and religious history, John's chronicle is much more akin to Prosper's.

But even here the differences outweigh the similarities. For one thing, there is a marked shift in the chronicler's geographical focus. Prosper's concern was the empire and only insofar as other peoples affected the empire were they included in his account. In contrast, John devoted at

---

[13] See: Biclaro 2 and note.

[14] Though the bulk of Victor's chronicle follows Prosper's consular dating system, the last four entries refer to the imperial reign of Justin II.

least as much attention to the Gothic monarchy in Spain, giving his chronicle the distinct appearance of a parallel history of two powers on opposite sides of the Mediterranean. His use of headings that referred both to the year of the emperor and to that of the Visigothic kings is indicative of this dual focus.

This increase in attention to the Goths is matched by an increase in sympathy. John of Biclaro did not try very hard to hide his admiration for the kings of Toledo. His first reference to Leovigild, early in the chronicle, describes him as one who 'wonderfully restored to its former boundaries the province of the Goths, which by that time had been diminished by the rebellions of various men'.[15] The sentence leaves the impression that the author is describing a long-standing, legitimate Gothic power in Spain. Furthermore, Leovigild's exploits are treated not as conquests, but as campaigns aimed at the restoration of a Gothic realm legitimate enough for its challengers to be regarded as rebels. John adopted the same tone when, later in the chronicle, he summarized Leovigild's unblemished military record: 'With tyrants destroyed on all sides and the invaders of Spain overcome, King Leovigild had peace to reside with his own people'.[16] In short, John depicted Leovigild not as an aggressor but as a defender and a preserver.

This image of Leovigild as a 'restorer' and a 'defender of peace' is particularly interesting in light of the fact that he conducted his southern campaigns primarily at the expense of the empire, which, under Justinian, had reconquered the southeastern part of Spain fifteen years before Leovigild's accession. To avoid the difficulty of presenting Leovigild as a rebel challenging imperial authority over a Roman province, John of Biclaro simply neglected to mention that those who had unsuccessfully defended Málaga, Baza, Sidonia, and perhaps Córdoba, owed their

---

[15]Biclaro 10.
[16]Biclaro 51.

allegiance to Constantinople.[17] Nor did John disclose that the most important allies of Leovigild's rebellious son were imperial.[18]

Beyond Leovigild's success in establishing Gothic control over most of Spain, John also credited him with the building of cities. This was not an activity normally associated with barbarian rulers. Yet Leovigild founded Recopolis—named after his son—and, 'endowed it with splendid buildings, both within the walls and in the suburbs, and he established privileges for the people of the new city'.[19] Again, the impression left is one of a legitimate king spreading peace and civilization rather than a barbarian usurper sowing violence and discord.

Equally significant in this context is the depiction of Leovigild's Arianism, not so much for what John says about it as for what he does not say. Despite what Isidore revealed about the circumstances of John's exile, there is no mention in John's *Chronicle* of Leovigild's persecution of Catholics. Though Prosper and Victor had provided a perfectly good model of an Arian persecutor in their depiction of Geiseric, John chose not to follow their example. He simply reported that Leovigild convened a council of Arian bishops at which it was decided that converts to Arianism would receive the imposition of hands rather than undergo another baptism, thus removing a major obstacle for would-be converts to Arianism. 'By means of this seduction', observed John, 'many of our own inclined toward the Arian doctrine out of self-interest rather than a change of heart'.[20] Even this sounds more critical of the Catholics who became Arians than of the king who only made it easier for them to do so.

John also chose to ignore the religious dimensions of Hermenegild's rebellion against Leovigild. Though it is a matter of some debate whether or not Hermenegild, under the dual influence of his Frankish wife, Ingundis, and Leander of Seville, converted to Catholicism prior to his

---

[17]Biclaro 12, 17, 20. This apparent hesitation to set up the Goths and Romans as direct adversaries suggests that Teillet (pp. 434, 436) may have made too much of her distinction between Cassiodorus' reconciliation of the empire and Ostrogothic Italy and John's supposed treatment of the rise of the Visigoths (in Spain) at the expense of the empire. This step is more safely ascribed to Isidore whose feelings vis-à-vis the empire were less ambiguous.

[18]Biclaro 55, 65, 66, 69.

[19] Biclaro 51. The other city that Leovigild founded was Vitoriacum (Biclaro 61).

[20]Biclaro 58.

revolt in 579, he clearly had done so by the time he was finally captured in 584 and murdered a year later.[21] Writing five years after Hermenegild's death, John could have depicted the unfortunate prince as a Catholic martyr who had suffered at the hands of an Arian king. Gregory I did just that in his *Dialogues*, written about 594.[22] But John preferred to treat the incident simply as one of the many military obstacles that Leovigild had to overcome in his pursuit of peninsular hegemony.[23]

As if to make up for his reticence about Leovigild's Arianism, John was verbose, considering the constraints of the genre, in his description of Reccared's Catholicism:

> In the first year of his reign, in the tenth month, Reccared became a Catholic, with the help of God. He then approached the priests of the Arian sect with words of wisdom and converted them to the Catholic faith through reason rather than force. He thus restored all of the people of the Goths and the Suevi to the unity and peace of the Christian church.[24]

The subsequent account of Reccared's reign is deeply coloured by this conversion. He was a just king, having 'generously restored the property that had been seized by his predecessors'.[25] He was a pious king, founding and enriching churches and monasteries and holding church councils.[26] And he was a divinely assisted king, as evidenced by the victory of Reccared's general Claudius over the numerically superior Franks.

---

[21]J. N. Hillgarth, 'Coins and Chronicles: Propaganda in Sixth-Century Spain and the Byzantine Background', *Historia* 15 (1966), pp. 483-508. See especially the 'Additional Note' immediately following the reprinted article in Hillgarth, *Visigothic Spain, Byzantium and the Irish* (London, 1985). Collins, *Early Medieval Spain*, p. 47.

[22]Gregory, *Dialogues* 3.31. Compare Gregory of Tours' *History of the Franks*, 5.38, 8.28, 9.16.

[23]Biclaro 55.

[24]Biclaro 85.

[25]Biclaro 87.

[26]Ibid.

In this battle, divine grace and the Catholic faith—which King
Reccared along with the Goths had faithfully taken up—were at
work, since it is not a difficult thing for our God to give victory to a
few over the many.... Not unworthily is God praised in our own
times for having intervened in this battle. In a like manner, many
years ago, God is known to have destroyed, at the hand of the
general Gideon with only three hundred men, many thousands of
Midianites who were attacking the people of God.[27]

In short, Reccared, as described by John of Biclaro, had all of the
attributes of the perfect Christian ruler.

This was nowhere more apparent to John than when the king convened
the Third Council of Toledo.

Reccared was, as we have said, present at the holy council, reviving
in our own times the image of the ruler Constantine the Great,
whose presence illuminated the holy synod of Nicaea, or that of the
most Christian emperor Marcian, in whose presence the decrees of
the Council of Chalcedon were established.[28]

John, in fact, went so far as to claim the superiority of Reccared's council
over that of Constantine on the grounds that, while Arianism was first
denounced at Nicaea, the heresy continued to thrive until 'cut at its very
root' by the bishops assembled by royal order in Toledo.

These two entries, describing the victory over the Franks and the
conciliar repudiation of Arianism, represent radical departures from both
the style and the content of the earlier portions of John's chronicle. Up to
this point, John, faithful to his genre, had resisted the temptation to
comment on the events that he reported. Outside of the occasional
insertion of a positive or negative adjective, he described events briefly,
without attempting to draw conclusions or moral lessons from their
outcomes. But in these two cases, John did not simply recount; he
interpreted. More specifically, he interpreted the battle against the Franks
and the renunciation of Arianism as if they were the actions of a

---

[27]Biclaro 91.
[28]Biclaro 92.

'Christian emperor'. Reccared had become a new Constantine at the hands of a Spanish 'Eusebius'.[29]

It is only when we recognize John's intention of transferring the symbolism traditionally associated with the Christian Roman emperors to the newly Catholic Gothic king of Spain, that his positive depiction of Leovigild makes sense. For if it was Reccared's conversion that first suggested the parallels between the Gothic kingdom and the empire, it was his father's military success that made it seem like God, who had once overseen the extension of an originally pagan Roman empire, was now looking favourably upon the Goths. To the extent, then, that John subscribed to the symbolic identification of Reccared and Constantine, he was obliged to emphasize Leovigild's military contributions—without which there would have been no 'empire'—and down play his anti-Catholic religious policies. Historiographically speaking, then, Leovigild was the beneficiary of the perspective adopted by John of Biclaro in his attempt to make sense out of the Visigothic conquest of Spain. Had John written his continuation of the universal chronicle during his exile, Leovigild would probably have emerged from the text as a tyrant and persecutor; another Geiseric. But from the vantage point of the year 590, the Arian king seemed instead to have provided the first of two key ingredients for the reproduction of a new Christian empire in the west: military dominance. His son Reccared supplied the second.

---

[29]John was the first *historian* in Spain to make this connection, but he did not invent it. The proceedings of Toledo III, which predated John's *Chronicle* by a year, are full of Christian imperial allusions. Reccared's address to the council enunciates the duty of the king to oversee those peoples that have been entrusted to him by God. Elsewhere, Reccared is depicted as a lover of God and a conqueror of new peoples for the church. Vives, pp. 108-9, 116-17. But John's specific comparison of Reccared to Constantine and Marcian may have been original. It is more risky attributing such imperial 'modeling' to Leovigild, since there is a tendency to interpret his reign in light of Reccared's. For this reason, it is hard to know what to make of Isidore's claim (in the short version) that Leovigild was the 'first among (the Gothic kings) to sit on a throne, dressed in royal vestments'. Rodríguez Alonso, p. 258. For more on this application of imperial political imagery to the Goths, see: J. N. Hillgarth, 'Historiography in Visigothic Spain', *La storiografia altomedievale*. Settimane di studio del centro italiano di studi sull'alto medioevo, 17 (Spoleto, 1970), pp. 264-70; Jacques Fontaine, *Isidore de Seville et la culture classique dans l'Espagne wisigothique*, 2 vol. (Paris, 1959), p. 872; Teillet, pp. 443-9.

ISIDORE OF SEVILLE AND THE GOTHS

Like John of Biclaro, Isidore of Seville contributed to the universal chronicle that Eusebius had begun. In Isidore's case, however, this meant not only bringing the account up to 615, but summarizing the previous components so as to produce a single, concise chronicle of world history from Adam to King Sisebut of Spain.[1] The latter portion of Isidore's *Chronicle* is organized by imperial reigns (rather than by the individual *years* of imperial reigns) each of which receives no more than a short paragraph that strains to accommodate events on opposite shores of the Mediterranean. Even the deeds of the Gothic monarchs, which receive preferential treatment, are relegated to one or two final sentences in each entry. Needless to say, Isidore's reputation as a historian rests more on his *History of the Kings of the Goths*[2] than on his contribution to the universal chronicle. Though still disconcertingly lean,[3] it has the distinction of being the very first chronicle devoted specifically to the Visigoths; the first attempt to give them a past commensurate with their political accomplishments in the late sixth and early seventh centuries.

Isidore probably began writing the *History of the Kings of the Goths* shortly after he completed his *Chronicle*, that is, during the last years of Sisebut's reign (612-21). At this time, the Gothic army, under the command of the general Suinthila, was beginning its final push against the imperial outpost of Cartagena. The timing is significant. Two centuries earlier, the Goths had been the interlopers in the empire, defeating Valens at Adrianople, sacking Rome, and appropriating Aquitaine and Spain. Now they enjoyed their own independent kingdom and it was the empire that seemed to be acting out the role of foreign intruder. The conquest of Cartagena represented, therefore, more than just the last step toward Gothic hegemony in Spain. It constituted a fitting, final chapter to what Isidore conceived of as a history of the rise of the

---

[1] For a closer look at Isidore's *Chronicle*, see: Paul M. Bassett, 'The use of History in the "Chronicon" of Isidore of Seville', *History and Theory* 15 (1976), pp. 278-92.

[2] I will be treating the *History of the Kings of the Goths* alone, without the appended histories of the Vandals and the Suevi.

[3] E. A. Thompson sarcastically observed that Isidore 'could hardly have told us less, except by not writing at all'. *The Goths in Spain* (Oxford, 1969), p. 7.

Goths at the expense of Rome, a history he would complete shortly after Cartagena fell.

Isidore had personal ties to Cartagena that may have contributed to his decision to write the chronicle when he did. In the chapter of his *De viris illustribus* dedicated to his older brother, Leander, Isidore identified his father as one Severianus, 'of the province of Cartagena'.[4] A letter from Leander to his sister Florentina suggests that the family may, in fact, have moved from Cartagena to Seville under duress, perhaps as a result of the occupation of the city by imperial troops sometime between 552 and 555.[5] If this was the case, Isidore—who may even have been born in Cartagena—would have had all the more reason to savour Sisebut's and Suinthila's successful campaign.

Other family circumstances may have encouraged Isidore to write a history dedicated to the Goths. Leander's letter hints, in an equally allusive manner, that his and Isidore's mother had been an Arian who converted to Catholic Christianity only after moving to Seville.[6] It is conceivable, then, that her children, as the products of a mixed marriage, grew up to be particularly sensitive to the religious divisions that had separated the Arian Goths from the Catholic Romans. This may help explain why Leander, who became the metropolitan of Seville in 584, devoted so much energy to the conversion of King Leovigild's sons, Hermenegild and Reccared. It may also explain why Isidore, who reaped the benefits of his brother's efforts and succeeded him as bishop around the year 600, chose to celebrate Gothic dominion over Spain in writing.

Yet presumably the most important influence on Isidore was his close working relationship with the monarchy at the time that he wrote. As Leander's successor he inherited his brother's close ties to Reccared. But it was during the nine-year reign of Sisebut, a former student of Isidore's, that he would have experienced the strongest personal attachments to Toledo. He may, in fact, have begun writing the *History* at the suggestion of Sisebut who, of all the Gothic kings, was the most likely to appreciate

---

[4]Isidore, *De viris illustribus* 41.

[5]Leander, *De institutione virginum* 31.3, 31.5. For a detailed look at the chronology of imperial conquest in Spain, see: Thompson, pp. 323-9.

[6]Leander, *De institutione virginum* 31.3. Ursicino Domínguez del Val, *Leandro de Sevilla y la lucha contra el arrianismo* (Madrid, 1981), p. 21. Justo Pérez de Urbel, *San Isidoro de Sevilla: su vida, su obra y su tiempo* (Barcelona, 1940), pp. 21-3.

a literary monument to the Gothic achievement.[7] The fact that Isidore modified the chronicle in 625, not only by incorporating Suinthila's final triumph at Cartagena but by transferring much of the praise originally bestowed on Sisebut to the new king, adds weight to the idea that Isidore's project was sponsored by the monarchy.[8] The words of encouragement at the end of the *History*, directed to Suinthila's son and designated heir, Riccimir, are also significant in this context. As it turned out, however, disaffected nobles forced Suinthila's abdication in 631 and Sisenand assumed the throne. Two years later, when the Fourth Council of Toledo met, the assembled dignitaries, under the leadership of Isidore himself, banished Suinthila and his family and called for the confiscation of his property.[9] Isidore, who died three years later (636), apparently never got around to amending his *History* in light of Suinthila's fall from grace. Some manuscripts of the work, however, contain a dedicatory preface to Sisenand which may represent a final attempt to keep the work *au courant* and preserve its official status.

In preparing the *History*, Isidore relied heavily on past historians, specifically the continuators of Eusebius' universal chronicle, for details about early Gothic rulers. For reasons discussed in the previous chapter, these chronicle references to the Goths lacked the rancour reserved for the Vandals, simplifying Isidore's task of extracting and 'cleaning up' the bits and pieces of information. Two of the continuators, however, provided Isidore with more than historical data. He seems to have borrowed the 'era' system of dating,[10] which allowed him to establish a chronological framework independent of the reigns of Roman emperors, from Hydatius, a fifth-century Galician chronicler who, like Prosper of

---

[7]For more information about efforts on the part of Visigothic kings to promote political unity through buildings, ceremony, coins, and histories, see: Hillgarth, 'Historiography,' pp. 271-8, 285-7, and Hillgarth, 'Coins and Chronicles', 483-508.

[8]Two versions of the *History* have survived. The short version, represented by only a few manuscripts, ends with the death of Sisebut in 621. The long version ends in the middle of Suinthila's reign (625). There has been much discussion about which came first. Most regard the long version as an expansion of the original, short version. But some have argued that the short version represents an expurgation of the original, longer chronicle, from which all of the positive references to Suinthila were removed. For a detailed look at the debate and evidence, see: Rodríguez Alonso, pp. 26-49.

[9]Vives, p. 221.

[10]The year zero of the 'era' system corresponds to the year 38 B.C.E.

Aquitaine, had written a continuation of Jerome. More significant for our purposes was the contribution of John of Biclaro, whose account of the reigns of Leovigild and Reccared provided Isidore with the elements of a particularly serviceable storyline for his history of the Goths. If John's opinion of Leovigild's reign shows signs of having been influenced by Reccared's conversion, Isidore's history represents a much more systematic effort to project recent Gothic military and religious achievements back onto the entire span of Gothic history.

Equally helpful to Isidore in his search for a way to present Gothic history in a positive light was the apologetic *History against the Pagans* of Paul Orosius. Enlisted by Augustine, Orosius had written his history (in 417) specifically to exculpate Christianity after Alaric's sack of Rome in 410. To this end he argued, first of all, that Rome had suffered from at least as much violence prior to its adoption of Christianity as after, and secondly, that, as sacks went, Alaric's was a remarkably mild one. Though Orosius did not share Isidore's personal stake in promoting a positive image of the Goths, his 'softening' of Alaric's sack served Isidore's needs well. A comparison of the texts reveals that the portion of Isidore's history that chronologically overlaps *the History against the Pagans* is little more that a paraphrase of everything that Orosius had to say about the Goths. The ill-fated invasion of Radagaisus, Alaric's merciful sack of Rome, the anecdote about the Goth and the nun, and the brief references to the reigns of Alaric's successors are all present in Isidore's chronicle with very little modification.

Textual comparison alone does not, however, allow for a full appreciation of Isidore's debt to Orosius. One passage that Isidore did not quote captures the spirit of the *History of the Kings of the Goths* more than any of those that he actually borrowed:

> If—God forbid!—the Goths achieve mastery over those whom they are now disrupting, and strive to govern them in accordance with their own laws, they will be regarded by posterity as great kings, though they are now judged by us to be fierce enemies.[11]

---

[11]Orosius 3.20.12.

Orosius wrote this passage as a historian who appreciated the perspective-bound nature of his craft. But to Isidore, with the benefit of some two hundred years of hindsight, it must have seemed prophetic. The Goths *had* succeeded in mastering imperial Spain. They *had* attempted to govern it by their own code. Now Isidore would set out precisely to transform those whom past Roman historians regarded as 'fierce enemies' into 'great kings'.

Giving the Goths this type of history meant more than simply tracing the succession of their rulers. It meant reshaping the 'fierce enemy' phase of their past into something worthy of their eventual domination of Roman Spain. First the Goths needed a respectable genealogy. Here Isidore relied primarily on the authority of Ambrose and Jerome. Noting the similarity between the words 'Goth' and 'Gog', Ambrose had suggested that the Goths, who were rebelling in the Balkans at the time he was writing, constituted a scourge that, according to his reading of Ezechiel,[12] would soon pass away.[13] That was on the eve of the Battle of Adrianople, where the Goths, far from 'passing away', actually annihilated the imperial army and mortally wounded the emperor Valens. Learning from Ambrose's mistake, Jerome substituted 'Getae', a people from the north identified by Herodotus and Pliny, for 'Gog' as a safer etymological basis for 'Goth'.[14]

Isidore is ambiguous. In his introduction, he repeated Jerome's caution, observing that 'in the past, learned men were in the habit of calling them "Getae" rather than "Gog" or "Magog"'.[15] Yet in the *recapitulatio* appended to his *History*, Isidore described the Goths as having 'originated from Magog, the son of Japheth'.[16] Isidore apparently decided that the genealogical connection to the line of Japheth was useful even if Ezechiel's prophecy, which cast the Goths as a scourge, was not. He went on to supplement the Goths' biblical heritage with the Getic one,

---

[12]Ezechiel 38-9.

[13]Ambrose, *De Fide ad Gratianum Augustum* 2.16.

[14]Jerome, *Liber hebraicarum quaestionum in Genesim* 10.2. Herwig Wolfram. *History of the Goths*, tr. Thomas J. Dunlap (Berkeley, 1988), p. 28.

[15]*HistGoth* 1.

[16]*HistGoth* 66.

going so far as to identify etymologically 'Getae' and 'Scythae',[17] which 'are not much different...with one letter changed and one removed'.[18]

Beyond the search for ennobling origins, Isidore sought to translate the 'barbaric ferocity' of the Goths into laudable military prowess. In the art of war they were unsurpassed, Isidore observed, being not only excellent horsemen, but physically well suited for fighting. They were agile, tall, strong, and 'impervious to wounds'.[19] In fact, Isidore concluded from his dubious etymological investigations, the very word, 'Goth', meant 'strength'.[20]

In contrast to John of Biclaro, who never bothered to mention that Leovigild's southern campaigns were conducted at the expense of imperial territory, Isidore felt no compunction about depicting the Goths and Romans as antagonists. Isidore reinterpreted the destruction inflicted on the empire by the Goths as evidence of their exceptional valour and strength. He borrowed from Orosius the references to the terror that the Goths inspired in Caesar.[21] Isidore even managed to glorify Gothic defeats by making much of the honours bestowed on Claudius and Constantine for their hard won victories against the Goths. The latter may have 'shone with the glory of his valour against many peoples, but he was most renowned for his victory over the Goths'.[22]

Isidore's rendering of the few occasions on which the Goths and Romans actually worked together is ambiguous. He seemed to have been positively disposed toward the agreement between Athanaric and Theodosius following the Battle of Adrianople, yet one detects a note of pride when he described Alaric's support as coming from those Goths who judged it 'demeaning to be subject to Roman power and to follow those whose laws and dominion they had previously spurned and from

---

[17]That is, Scythian, an inhabitant of Scythia, in the lower Don and Dnieper river region.
[18]*HistGoth* 66.
[19]*HistGoth* 67.
[20]Jerome interpreted 'Gog' as *tectum*, or 'covered', regarding it as a reference to Gog being a concealer or dissembler of the truth. Isidore, following Ambrose, identified 'Gog' and 'Goth' and translated 'Goth' as *tectum*, but he rejected Jerome's translation, opting for the more positive (and more strained), 'strength'. *HistGoth* 2. Wolfram (p. 29 and n. 91, p. 390) attributes this to Isidore's conflation of Jerome's consecutive etymologies of 'Gog' and 'Gaza', meaning, 'strength'.
[21]*HistGoth* 2-3.
[22]*HistGoth* 5; cf. *HistGoth* 4.

whose alliance they had removed themselves after being victorious in battle'.[23] On the other hand, Isidore reported that Wallia, though 'made king by the Goths for the sake of war...was directed by divine providence toward peace'.[24] He promised to 'fulfil every military obligation on behalf of the Roman state', and for his efforts received Aquitaine from the emperor.[25] Wallia's successor, Theoderid, resumed the tradition of hostility toward Rome, but, unlike Alaric, received little in the way of praise from Isidore, who, in this case, seemed to side with the Roman forces defending Arles and Narbonne.[26] Only when Theoderid came to terms with the Romans and allied with them against the Huns did Isidore seem to be positively disposed toward him.[27] Likewise, Isidore complimented Theodoric the Great, an interim king of the Visigoths, describing his foreign policy as well as his architectural restoration of Rome in glowing, pseudo-imperial terms.[28]

Isidore did not try very hard to balance the image of the Goths as a tenaciously independent people whose 'liberties' were won from the Romans in battle rather than negotiated in peace,[29] with that of the Goths as viable imperial allies. He did not really need to because neither stance vis-à-vis the empire was uncomplimentary to the Goths. But ultimately the future, which Isidore's hindsight allowed him to appreciate, lay along the path of Gothic independence from, and dominion over, Rome. Isidore's treatment of the marriage of the Gothic king Athaulf and Galla Placidia, the emperor's sister, is perhaps symbolic of the ultimate failure of Gothic-imperial cooperation as a narrative theme: the only child born from the union died within a few years of its birth.[30] Isidore made the marriage seem even more futile by invoking the prophecy of Daniel about the union of a northern king and the daughter of a southern king that would produce no lasting heir.[31]

---

[23] *HistGoth* 12.
[24] *HistGoth* 21.
[25] *HistGoth* 21-2.
[26] *HistGoth* 23-4.
[27] *HistGoth* 25.
[28] *HistGoth* 39.
[29] *HistGoth* 69.
[30] *HistGoth* 19, 21.
[31] Daniel 11:6. Isidore borrowed this from Hydatius (57). Interestingly enough, Jordanes, the editor of Cassiodorus' sixth-century history of the Ostrogoths, ended his account with a

Isidore's emphasis on the military power of the Goths is nowhere more apparent than in his depiction of the takeover of Spain, which he justified simply on the Roman legal grounds of 'right by conquest'.

They waged such great wars and had such a reputation for glorious victory, that Rome itself, the conqueror of all peoples, submitted to the yoke of captivity and yielded to the Gothic triumphs: the mistress of all nations served them like a handmaid.[32]

This 'might makes right' approach helps explain why Isidore began his chronicle with the famous *omnium terrarum* eulogy of Spain and its resources. His purpose was to present Spain as an incomparably rich trophy of victory, the very acquisition of which served to ennoble those who had won it. The reference to *mater Spania* evokes more than an image of fertility. It allowed Isidore to treat Spain as if it were the passive victim of virile aggression, the beautiful queen of an aging king with no choice but to submit to anyone who succeeded in deposing her husband.

Rightly did golden Rome, the head of the nations, desire you long ago. And although this same Romulean power, initially victorious, betrothed you to itself, now it is the most flourishing people of the Goths, who in their turn, after many victories all over the world, have eagerly seized you and loved you: they enjoy you up to the present time amidst royal emblems and great wealth, secure in the good fortune of empire.[33]

Spain wound up as the 'consort' of the Goths, bestowing upon them all of the benefits that she had reserved for her previous 'lover', Rome.

Aside from emphasizing their military prowess, Isidore elevated the Goths from their barbarism in other ways. For one thing, he was careful to note any Gothic victories over other invaders of the empire, victories that would make the Goths appear to be a cut above the rest:

Gothic-Roman marriage and the birth of a child as if to signal some future union between the rivals for Italy. Walter Goffart, *The Narrators of Barbarian History (A.D. 550-800): Jordanes, Gregory of Tours, Bede, and Paul the Deacon* (Princeton, 1988), pp. 72-3.

[32] *HistGoth* 67; cf. *HistGoth* 15.

[33] *HistGoth* prologue.

> All of the peoples of Europe feared them. The barriers of the Alps gave way before them. The Vandals, widely known for their own barbarity, were not so much terrified by the presence of the Goths as put to flight by their renown. The Alans were extinguished by the strength of the Goths. The Suevi, too, forced into inaccessible corners of Spain, have now experienced the threat of extermination at the hands of the Goths.[34]

Isidore's decision to append short histories of the Vandals and the Suevi to his history of the Goths should be understood in this context. By showing how the Goths forced the Vandals out of Spain and dominated the kingdom of the Suevi, he made their acquisition of Spain look all the more impressive and predetermined.

Isidore made even more out of the Gothic role in the defeat of the Huns. 'This people...was so savage that when they felt hungry during a battle, they would pierce a horse's vein and assuage their appetite by drinking its blood', noted Isidore in an effort to underscore the barbarism of the Huns and thus to impress upon his audience the cultural distance that separated them from the Goths.[35] The fact that the *Christian* Goths had allied with the *Christian* empire against the *pagan* Huns, allowed him to do with the Huns what Ambrose and others had done with the Goths: make them a scourge, 'raised up for the discipline of the faithful'.

> For they were the rod of the wrath of God. As often as his indignation went forth against the faithful, he punished them with the Huns, so that, chastened by their suffering, the faithful would force themselves away from the greed of this world and from sin and claim the inheritance of the celestial kingdom.[36]

It would have been easier for Isidore to treat the Goths and the Romans as co-sufferers of this scourge were it not for the fact that, at the time of the alliance against the Huns, the Goths were Arians. Compared to their barbarian origins, the heterodoxy of the Goths posed a far greater challenge for Isidore in his efforts to revamp Gothic history. He did his

---

[34] *HistGoth 68*; cf. *HistGoth* 21.
[35] *HistGoth* 29.
[36] Ibid.

best to account for their Arianism in a manner that would least compromise their claim to be the rightful heirs to Spain.

Isidore accomplished this in part by following Orosius' lead and placing the blame for Gothic heresy squarely on the shoulders of the emperor Valens.[37] As Isidore described it, the emperor had intervened successfully on the side of Athanaric during a crisis in leadership among the Goths. In gratitude, the pagan Athanaric asked Valens to send missionaries to his people. The emperor complied with his request by sending Arian priests who succeeded in injecting their 'deadly poison into this excellent people'.[38] Far from blaming the Goths for their religious deviance, then, Isidore made them the innocent victims of an evil emperor who was ultimately burned alive, a fitting end for one who had 'surrendered such beautiful souls to the eternal flames'.[39]

Isidore was also careful to show that prior to this 'infection', at least *some* Goths had converted to Catholic Christianity and, like their Roman counterparts, had suffered for it.[40] In fact, Isidore connected the invasion of the Huns to the pagan Athanaric's persecution of Gothic Christians: 'The Goths, who had previously expelled the Christians from their homeland, were themselves, along with their king Athanaric, expelled by the Huns'.[41] Isidore's point was not only to place Gothic history within a providential context, but to show that there was nothing inherently heretical about the Goths. They were simply the victims of unfortunate circumstances.

Though Isidore diverted the blame for Athanaric's choice of Arianism to the emperor, he still had to account for the fact that the Goths achieved their most impressive military and political gains before they converted to Catholic Christianity in 589. To this end he immediately assured his readers that the Goths would only maintain 'this evil blasphemy...for 213 years', ultimately renouncing 'this rank perfidy' and coming 'through Christ's grace to the unity of the Catholic faith'.[42] The Goths thus conquered Spain not as Arians but as future Catholics. Another technique

---

[37] Orosius 7.33.19.
[38] *HistGoth* 7.
[39] *HistGoth* 9.
[40] *HistGoth* 6, 9, 10.
[41] *HistGoth* 9.
[42] *HistGoth* 8.

that Isidore employed to vindicate the Arian kings was to emphasize their positive qualities as Christians over their poor choice of doctrine. Thus, as we saw above, Isidore, following Orosius, attributed Christian mercy to Alaric, contrasting it to the savagery of his pagan rival Radagaisus.[43] He explained the defeat of the Roman general Litorius in terms of his paganism, implying that God found this even more offensive than the Arianism of his opponent, Theoderid.[44] Isidore also provided examples of Gothic reverence for the saints, as in the case of the Goth who hesitated before stealing vases from the sanctuary of St Peter and that of Theoderic, who reconsidered his plans to plunder Mérida when 'terrified by the signs of the holy martyr Eulalia'.[45] Moreover, he had praise for Theudis who, despite his Arianism, gave permission to the Catholic bishops of Spain to hold councils and regulate their own ecclesiastical affairs.[46] It was also under Theudis that the Goths lost their foothold in Morocco because they would not fight on a Sunday.[47]

But for the most part, Isidore dealt with the problem of Gothic heresy by drawing as little attention to it as possible. Only when the conversion of the Goths was on the horizon did Isidore vent his frustration with regard to their deviance. After crediting Leovigild with impressive territorial gains, Isidore suddenly changed his tone, claiming that the 'error of his impiety tarnished the glory of his great success'.[48] He went on to report at some length how Leovigild, 'filled with the madness of Arian perfidy, ...launched a persecution against the Catholics', exiling bishops, confiscating church revenues, and forcing conversions to Arianism.[49]

I suggested above that John of Biclaro did not feel comfortable criticizing Leovigild in this way because, though a heretic, Leovigild was responsible for establishing the Gothic hegemony in Spain that his Catholic successor enjoyed. Isidore, however, seems to have found a way of crediting Leovigild with his success on the battlefield without having

---

[43] *HistGoth* 14.
[44] *HistGoth* 24.
[45] *HistGoth* 16, 32. He also showed how foolish any attempt to desecrate such a shrine could be: *HistGoth* 45.
[46] *HistGoth* 41.
[47] *HistGoth* 42.
[48] *HistGoth* 49.
[49] *HistGoth* 50.

to 'pull punches' as far as his Arianism was concerned. He did this by attributing Leovigild's conquests to his bellicosity and tying this bellicosity to his religious deviance. He was 'irreligious and had a very warlike disposition..., increasing the dominion of the Gothic people through the arts of war'.[50] For Isidore, Leovigild's taste for war was a symptom of the pervasive moral corruption that he suffered as an Arian king; a corruption that also manifested itself in his 'destructive' behaviour toward his nobles and his 'robbery of the citizens'.[51] But even though Leovigild's conquests were inspired by base motives, they nevertheless provided a firm territorial foundation for a future Catholic kingdom.

With the accession of Reccared, Isidore's interpretative difficulties were over: the Goths finally enjoyed not only military 'might' but religious 'right'. Isidore's praise for the Catholic king was unrestrained. Reccared was placid, mild, graceful, generous, clement, and peaceful.[52] If Leovigild extended the dominion of the Goths in war, Reccared elevated them 'by the victory of the faith'.[53] Like John of Biclaro, Isidore bestowed upon Reccared all of the trappings traditionally associated with the ideal Christian emperor.[54] But Isidore did not go as far as John had in the direction of ascribing 'chosen people' status to the Goths. When treating Claudius' unexpected victory over the Franks, Isidore deleted the comparisons to Gideon that he found in John's chronicle.[55] He simply reported the battle and claimed that 'no victory of the Goths in Spain was greater', presumably to help make up for the fact that the most significant territorial gains had been orchestrated by the king's Arian father. The idea of a Gothic 'chosen people' was apparently not one that Isidore wanted to develop. The victories that his Goths won were to be, like those enjoyed by the early Romans, a simple function of their valour and strength.

Isidore's hesitation to apply this metaphor may have had something to do with the fact that he, unlike John, had to deal with Reccared's immediate successors, who failed to live up to his standard of Christian

---

[50] *HistGoth* 52.
[51] *HistGoth* 51.
[52] *HistGoth* 55.
[53] *HistGoth* 52.
[54] Marc Reydellet, 'La conception du souverain chez Isidore de Seville', *Isidoriana*, ed. M. Díaz y Díaz (León, 1961), pp. 457-66.
[55] Biclaro 91. *HistGoth* 54.

leadership. Witteric tortured and executed Reccared's illegitimate son, Liuva, only to be assassinated himself.[56] The brevity of the notice of Gundemar's reign hints that he was not much better in Isidore's eyes. The situation improved dramatically with the accession of Sisebut, a former student of Isidore's, who, in his master's estimation, was not only just, pious, and militarily gifted, but 'eloquent in speech, informed in his opinions, and imbued with no little knowledge of letters'.[57] Isidore attributed the king's infamous attempt to convert the Jews to excessive zeal. Not surprisingly, Suinthila, who was king when Isidore finished the *History* in 625 and who brought Sisebut's campaign against the Byzantines to a successful conclusion, received even more effusive praise.[58] The fact that 'he was the first to obtain the monarchy of the entire kingdom of Spain north of the the straits, which had not been achieved by any previous ruler', made his reign the fulfillment of the Gothic destiny and the proper culmination of Isidore's history.

Isidore's attempt to compose a history of the Goths that would place their recent accomplishments within an appropriately positive historical context involved considerable manipulation of the information to which he had access. But his decision to approach his subject reign by reign meant that it was difficult for him to smooth over the frequent setbacks that the Goths experienced in their 'inevitable rise' to peninsular domination. Sometimes he attributed the problem to the moral failings of an individual ruler, as in the case of Theudis, who murdered a general; Gesalic, who was a bastard; and Theudigisel, who had adulterous relations with the wives of his magnates.[59] Other times he overlooked shortcomings on the part of a ruler who had proved more fortunate. Such was the case with Euric, who killed his brother in order to seize the kingdom for himself, yet was spared Isidore's criticism, presumably because he was the last king before Leovigild to have extended the realm of the Goths.[60] The best that Isidore could do with the ignominious defeat of the Gothic army at the hands of the Franks at Vouillé in 507 was to

---

[56] *HistGoth* 57, 58.
[57] *HistGoth* 60.
[58] *HistGoth* 62.
[59] *HistGoth* 43, 37, 44.
[60] *HistGoth* 34-5.

report it and get on with his account.[61] Similarly, the two storms that prevented the Goths from crossing to Sicily in Alaric's time and to Africa in Wallia's were simply presented as unfortunate accidents.

The principal reason for this inconsistency is that Isidore relied heavily on previous histories and chronicles with widely varying levels of narrativization. Though conveniently consistent with Isidore's needs, the *History against the Pagans* extended only as far as 417 and John of Biclaro's *Chronicle* did not reach back any further than Leovigild. The result was that in the beginning and ending portions of Isidore's *History*, that is, those parts based on Orosius and John, the virtues of the Goths and the steps they were taking in the direction of fulfilling their destiny were presented more clearly and consistently. In the middle portion, covering the period between the reigns of Wallia and Leovigild, where Isidore had only the undigested chronicles from which to work, this narrative pattern suffered. Hence the curious hybrid nature of the *History of the Kings of the Goths*, an ungainly cross between the fully narrativized history of Orosius and the practically narrative-free segments of the universal chronicle from which Isidore drew.

---

[61] *HistGoth* 36.

AN ANDALUSIAN CHRONICLER AND THE MUSLIMS

Isidore had been dead for seventy-five years when Tariq ibn Ziyad landed on the southern tip of Spain with his Arab and Berber forces. Their presence posed an immediate military threat that the Gothic army, under Roderic, proved unable to withstand. But the invasion also presented a significant historiographical challenge. Isidore had written his history of the Goths to provide a suitably positive historical context for the achievements of Sisebut and Suinthila. The result was a chronicle that made the monarchy of Toledo look like it was both meant to be and there to last. This put Iberian historians writing after 711 in an interesting position. They read Isidore's work exalting the Goths, yet they knew that his protagonists had proved incapable of defending their kingdom against the Muslims. Like Isidore, then, they were faced with the task of explaining how it was that a long standing peninsular power should have yielded to foreign domination. Yet unlike Isidore they did not enjoy the luxury of identifying religiously with the victors.

The earliest Latin chronicle written in Spain after the invasion was the so-called *Arabic-Byzantine Chronicle of 741*[1]. We know nothing about its author. The first entry, which records the death of Reccared, suggests that the author regarded his work as a continuation of John of Biclaro's chronicle. But the dissimilarities between the two works stand out more than the similarities. For one thing, the chronicler of 741 was not nearly as interested in Gothic history as was John of Biclaro. Having begun with notices about Reccared's death and the subsequent accessions of Liuva and Witteric, the author promptly turned his attention to the east: to Heraclius' rebellion against the emperor Phocas in 610 and his campaigns against the Persians and Arabs. From that point on, only three more Gothic kings are even mentioned, the last of them being Suinthila. Instead the chronicle provides a caliph-by-caliph report on the extension of the Muslim empire, with Spain re-entering the picture only as one of the

---

[1]The most detailed study of the *Chronicle of 741 (Chr741)*: César E. Dubler, 'Sobre la crónica arábigo-bizantina en la península ibérica', *Al-Andalus* 11 (1946), pp. 283-349.

many territories conquered during the reign of Walid.[2] The eastern focus of the chronicle is very consistent with the universal chronicle genre, into which the author, by continuing John of Biclaro, was tapping. But the paucity of references to the Goths and Spain is not at all consistent with John's own Iberian sympathies. It is possible that the chronicle represents a Latin summary of contemporary Greek chronicles, perhaps from other branches of the very same Eusebian tradition, modified, with an Iberian audience in mind, as a continuation of John of Biclaro.[3]

The other surviving Latin chronicle from Muslim-occupied Spain, the so-called *Mozarabic Chronicle of 754*, is far more Iberian in focus.[4] Its author is also somewhat easier to pin down. The fact that he eulogized so many Iberian churchmen indicates that he was probably an ecclesiastic himself. We can also infer from his intimate knowledge of events in Muslim Spain[5] that he benefited from close ties to the Cordoban court or at least from direct access to informed sources.[6] At times he expressed himself in ways that sound very Arabic, in particular when he described Spain as a 'pomegranate', or referred to the Frankish troops at Tours as immobile, 'holding together like a glacier in the cold regions'.[7] Likewise,

---

[2]*Chr741* 36.

[3]Dubler (p. 329) has traced many of these Greek sources.

[4]The most useful study of the *Chronicle of 754 (Chr754)*: José Eduardo López Pereira, *Estudio crítico sobre la crónica mozárabe de 754* (Zaragoza, 1980). Roger Collins is the first historian of the conquest of Spain to give this chronicle the credit it deserves as an historical source. *The Arab Conquest of Spain, 710-797* (Oxford, 1989), pp. 26-8.

[5]As evidenced not only by this chronicle, but by the other that he claimed to have dedicated specifically to the civil wars of the 740s. *Chr754* 86, 88, 94.

[6]There is no agreement about precisely where in al-Andalus the author lived. Córdoba and Toledo are the most popular choices, though López Pereira (*Estudio*, pp. 13-16) has made a case for the Murcia region. The chronicler's grasp of Andalusian politics suggests to me that he must have observed the governors' activities from close range. One piece of evidence that has not been addressed is the record of an unusual astronomical phenomenon that occurred in 750, 'with all the citizens of Córdoba watching' (*Chr754* 92). The fact that the chronicler specifically mentioned Cordoban witnesses for something that we would expect to have been visible over a wide area suggests to me that he was in Córdoba at the time.

[7]*Chr754* 81, 80.

his derogatory description of Berber physiognomy reflects the contemporary Arab disdain for the indigenous peoples of Morocco.[8] Such references, taken together with the fact that he supplemented his Christian-imperial dating schemes with Islamic chronologies,[9] strongly suggest that the chronicler had access to Arabic sources, whether written or oral.

It is quite possible that the author served the Arab government in some sort of ministerial capacity. We know that the Muslims, for lack of numbers, relied heavily on pre-existing administrative structures throughout their sprawling empire. The earliest evidence that we have for this kind of arrangement in Spain is the pact between Abd al-Aziz and Count Theodemir of Murcia, in which the former recognized the continued authority of the latter over the province.[10] Mid-ninth-century sources attest to the use of Christians as ministers to, and tax collectors for, the emir of Córdoba. Even bishops seem, on the whole, to have cooperated with the Muslim rulers despite religious differences, much as their sixth-century counterparts had worked with the Arian court of Toledo.[11] It is tempting in light of his detailed knowledge of Andalusian politics to speculate that the chronicler of 754 was a churchman with similarly close ties to the Muslim governor of Córdoba.

The *Chronicle of 754* begins with the accession of Heraclius and treats Byzantine and Arab history up to the conquests of the caliph Umar, before backtracking to cover Sisebut and his successors in Spain. Isidore had ended both his *Chronicle* and the first draft of the *History of the Kings of the Goths* with the reign of Sisebut, which would suggest that the chronicler of 754 regarded his work as a continuation of Isidore's. His dating system supports this. Following Isidore's *History*, he supplemented the year of the emperor with the corresponding 'era', and following Isidore's *Chronicle*, he referred to the *annus mundi* upon the

---

[8] *Chr754* 84.

[9] He made use of both the regnal years of the caliphs and years since the Hegira (Muhammad's flight from Mecca to Yathrib-Medina in 622).

[10] *Chr754* 87.1. Collins, *Arab Conquest*, p. 39.

[11] Kenneth Baxter Wolf, *Christian Martyrs in Muslim Spain* (Cambridge, 1988), pp. 5-20.

accession of each new emperor. But the content of the *Chronicle of 754*, covering events in the east as well as in Spain, is not consistent with the *History of the Kings of the Goths*. And the individual entries are far too detailed to have been modelled on Isidore's *Chronicle*.[12] In these respects, it more closely resembles the work of John of Biclaro. Both have a Mediterranean-wide scope, though with an Iberian focus. Both intersperse their accounts of military campaigns with information about church councils and heresy. And both pause to acknowledge the contributions of outstanding ecclesiastics. In short, the *Chronicle of 754* seems to have been conceived as an attempt to bring the universal chronicle up to date. Its author began where Isidore left off, but patterned his own continuation on the fuller treatments of John of Biclaro and his predecessors.[13]

Once we consider the *Chronicle of 754* within the universal chronicle genre, certain points at which the text diverges from the paradigm stand out. The most important of these are, first of all, the abortive attempt to narrativize the rise of the Arabs, and secondly, the exclusive focus on Muslim political, as opposed to religious, history. Both of these deviations, as we shall see, would seem to stem from the inherent difficulty of recording the rise of a non-Christian power within a Christian chronicle tradition.

Faithful to the traditional imperial focus of the genre, the *Chronicle of 754* opens in the east, with Heraclius' successful coup d'état and his subsequent campaigns against the Persians. But from the outset it is apparent that the chronicler intended to do more than simply record these events. Setting the stage for the decisive battle between Heraclius and the Persians, he had the two sides agree to select champions to determine the outcome of the war in man-to-man combat. The Persian ruler, 'Chosroes, puffed up in the manner of the Philistines, escorted a certain bastard, like

---

[12]Though we know that he read it. *Chr754* 74.1, 95.

[13]The work of Manuel C. Díaz y Díaz on the manuscript tradition of John of Biclaro supports this. *De Isidoro al siglo XI* (Barcelona, 1976), pp. 135-40.

another Goliath, out to the fight. Terrified, all of Heraclius' soldiers stepped back. But Heraclius, trusting in the assistance of the Lord, fell on the enemy and killed him with a single throw of his javelin'.[14] The Davidic imagery was no accident. The chronicler wanted to portray Heraclius as the ruler of a chosen people, and a ruler who, like David, had his share of human frailties.

When Chosroes' kingdom was finally destroyed and handed over to imperial dominion, the people did honour, not to God, but to Heraclius, and he, accepting this with pride, returned to Constantinople. Finally, after appropriately rewarding his army, he gloriously ascended his throne in triumph.[15]

Having committed such a sin,[16] Heraclius could not expect his good fortune to last.

They say that afterward many things pertaining to this event began to come to Heraclius in his dreams as a warning that he would be ravaged mercilessly by rats from the desert. He was also forewarned by astrological readings of the course of the stars.[17]

The chronicle then proceeds to describe the Arab incursions into imperial territory, implicitly identifying them with the rats of Heraclius' dream.

The Saracens rebelled...and appropriated for themselves Syria, Arabia, and Mesopotamia, more through the trickery than through the power of their leader Muhammad. They devastated the neighbouring provinces, proceeding not so much by means of open attacks as by secret incursions. Thus by means of cunning and fraud

---

[14]*Chr754* 3.

[15]*Chr754* 4.

[16]The author probably had in mind similar transgressions on the part of Moses (Numbers 20:11-13) or Herod (Acts 12:21-3).

[17]*Chr754* 5.

rather than power, they incited all of the frontier cities of the empire, which finally rebelled openly, shaking the yoke from their necks.[18]

This choice of narrative pattern in and of itself is not surprising. Faced with the task of explaining an unexpected victory over the Persians followed immediately by an equally unanticipated defeat at the hands of the Arabs, the historical books of the Old Testament provided a readily adaptable paradigm.[19] The Arabs were to be more than simply conquerors of imperial territory; they were to constitute a scourge sent by an angry God. What *is* surprising is that the author, consciously working within a genre that was known for reporting past events without taking the liberty of interpreting them, should have decided to apply any kind of narrative pattern at all.

But even more remarkable is that, having thus 'broken the rules' and depicted the Arab victory as a scourge, the author immediately disgarded this narrative pattern and reverted to a more traditional, unnarrativized record of past events for the remainder of his chronicle. This was patently not for lack of opportunity to apply the scourge narrative anew, in particular after the chronicler had turned his attention westward from the empire to Gothic Spain. Here, too, we find military challenges to the empire, that is, to the remnants of the empire in the west that had been reassembled under Justinian in the middle of the previous century. Indeed, Sisebut 'conquered the Roman cities throughout Spain',[20] and later, Suinthila, 'with a rapid victory, ...brought to an end the war that had been begun with the Romans and obtained the monarchy of Spain in its entirety'.[21] Yet despite the parallels between the imperial retreat east and west, there is no attempt to treat the Goths as a scourge or to describe

---

[18] *Chr754* 8.

[19] There are plenty of early examples of Byzantine interpretations of the Arab invasion in the east as a scourge, including those of Sophronios of Jerusalem and Pseudo-Methodius. See: D. J. Constantelos, 'The Moslem Conquest of the Near East as Revealed in the Greek Sources of the Seventh and Eighth Centuries', *Byzantion* 42 (1972), pp. 325-57.

[20] *Chr754* 13.

[21] *Chr754* 16.

their victories as a function of craftiness rather than might. Why? Because the author was too steeped in Visigothic historiography to regard the Catholic kings of Toledo as anything but the legitimate authority in Spain. In fact, the portion of the chronicle dedicated to Gothic Spain is dominated by detailed accounts of the 'wonderful' church councils that they convened.[22] No doubt with John of Biclaro's description of Toledo III in mind, the chronicler of 754 devoted disproportionately large entries to another seven councils of Toledo and one council of Seville, recording their dates, their settings, their attendance figures, and often their agenda.[23] He also highlighted the theological contributions of a number of Iberian bishops and deacons.[24]

A second missed opportunity for extending the scourge narrative is more difficult to explain. For despite the typological parallels that John of Biclaro and Isidore of Seville had cultivated between the Christian empire in the east and the Catholic monarchy in Spain, and despite the comparable speed with which both of these powers collapsed in the face of the Muslim armies, the chronicler of 754 chose not to portray the conquest of Spain as a scourge. He opted instead for a more mundane, political scenario: Roderic advanced to meet the invading Muslims 'and in that battle, the entire army of the Goths, which had come with him fraudulantly and in rivalry out of ambition for the kingship, fled and he was killed', along with his rivals.[25] The dreams and astrological readings that heralded the defeat of Heraclius are nowhere to be found on the eve of Tariq's crossing, an absence made all the more conspicuous by the fact that the chronicler had already linked an eclipse to a Basque attack during

---

[22]This was, no doubt, partly a reflection of the sources at his disposal. He clearly had access to the proceedings of the Visigothic church councils (*Chr754* 18 and note), but for information about more secular matters he may have had little more than a chronology of the Visigothic kings.

[23]*Chr754* 14, 17, 18, 23, 26, 36, 38, 41.

[24]*Chr754* 14, 17, 18, 23, 26, 36, 38, 41, 45, 48, 53, 70, 88.1, 93. In fact, the single longest entry in the entire chronicle (23) is dedicated to Bishop Taio of Zaragoza's voyage to Rome to secure a copy of Gregory's commentary on Job.

[25]*Chr754* 52.

the reign of Reccesuinth.[26] In fact, only a short time before the invasion, 'everyone in Spain, confident in their great joy, eagerly rejoiced' under the benevolent rule of Witiza.[27] Moreover, the only reference in the entire chronicle to a miracle-working bishop of Toledo occurs on the very eve of the conquest.[28] The closest the author came to interpreting the events of 711 in light of some divine plan was to attribute the fall of the once-mighty Zaragoza to a 'judgement of God'.[29] But instead of building on this image and explicitly depicting the Muslim forces as an instrument of divine will, the author flatly contradicted it, observing that the caliph Walid enjoyed remarkable success in extending the boundaries of the Arab empire, given that he was 'lacking in divine favour.'[30]

The chronicler had ample material to work with had he wished to interpret the conquest of Spain as a scourge. He had, first and foremost, an invasion that he seems to have regarded as a particularly violent one. The chronicler wrote that Musa ibn Nusayr, who came to Spain a year after Tariq and assumed control of the conquest, 'ruined beautiful cities, burning them with fire; condemned lords and powerful men to the cross; and butchered youths and infants with swords'.[31] Waxing eloquent, the

---

[26]*Chr754* 27. Cf. *Chr754* 92.

[27]*Chr754* 47, 44.

[28]*Chr754* 48.

[29]*Chr754* 54. Musa was himself the victim of a similar expression of divine will upon his return to Damascus. *Chr754* 56.

[30]*Chr754* 51. Cf. *Chr741* 36. The chronicler of 754 apparently relied on the same source as the chronicler of 741. López Pereira, *Estudio*, pp. 96-9. The chronicler's decision not to describe the conquest of Spain as a scourge is even more interesting when we realise that the missionary Boniface—who died the very year that the chronicle was finished— described the fall of the Visigothic monarchy as a scourge in his letter to King Aethelbald of Mercia. Boniface wrote the letter in the 740s, warning the king that if the Angles did not turn their backs on immorality, they would 'come to be neither strong in battle, nor stable in the faith, nor honourable to men, nor loved by God, as in the case of the peoples of Spain, Provence, and Burgundy, who were fornicators, turning their backs on God. The omnipotent judge permitted vengeance for such crimes to rage at the hands of the Saracens'. Boniface, *Epistola* 73. Collins discusses the durability of the 'Gothic decadence' thesis in *Arab Conquest*, pp. 6-8.

[31]*Chr754* 54.

author asked rhetorically, 'Who can relate such perils? Who can enumerate such grievous disasters? Even if every limb were transformed into a tongue, it would be beyond human capability to express the ruin of Spain and its many and great evils'.[32] Recalling the disasters suffered in the past by Troy, Jerusalem, and Rome, the chronicler concluded that Spain endured 'all this and more' at the hands of the invaders in 711.

The chronicler also had his share of potential 'sinners' who, like Heraclius, could have been portrayed as the targets of divine wrath. Had he chosen to, he could have moralized Roderic's rebellious assumption of power.[33] Or he could have transformed the cowardly flight of Bishop Sindered of Toledo or the complicity of Egica's son, Oppa, into a sign of Gothic decadence.[34] His decision to record for posterity the inscriptions from King Wamba's renovation of Toledo in the 670—'You, holy saints, whose presence shines here, protect this city and people with your accustomed favour'—would, in fact, have made more sense if he were preparing the reader for some future transgression on the part of the Goths.[35] But despite all of this raw material at his disposal, the chronicler made no attempt to balance his scourge in the east with one in the west.

Far from it. As the chronicler moved on from the invasion itself to recount the reigns and deeds of the subsequent governors of al-Andalus, he did so with remarkable even-handedness. Rather than decry the Muslim governors of Spain *en masse* as usurpers of the Visigothic kingdom, he judged them individually according to their effectiveness at promoting peace and justice on the peninsula. The two worst Muslim leaders from his perspective were those who had engineered invasions of Spain: Musa, whom we have already encountered, and the Syrian Balj ibn Bishr who overthrew the Cordoban government in 741. The first mention of the name Balj elicited a 'proh dolor!' from the chronicler and another admission of his inability to express such disasters in words.[36]

---

[32]*Chr754* 55. Cf. Jerome, *Epistola* 108.1.
[33]*Chr754* 52.
[34]*Chr754* 53, 54.
[35]*Chr754* 35.
[36]*Chr754* 84, 86.

Outside of Musa and Balj, only Abd al-Malik received anything comparable to this level of empassioned criticism, in his case, for his unbridled 'cupidity' and the financial ruin that it brought to Spain.[37] At the other extreme, the chronicler complimented the governor Uqbah for restoring Spain after the destructive policies of Abd al-Malik. Uqbah not only bound his predecessor in chains and condemned the evil judges appointed by him, but he deported 'Spanish malefactors' and enriched the fisc, all the while living austerely.[38] Furthermore, the chronicler described the governor Abd ar-Rahman as 'preeminent in courage and fame'.[39] He also praised Yusuf, the governor in power at the time he was writing, for crushing various rebellions in the wake of his accession. In the same breath, he abruptly condemned the rebels to hell.[40]

The author was also willing to give credit to those caliphs in Damascus whose reigns contributed to peace in the provinces. Yazid I 'was very well liked by all of the peoples subject to his rule. He never, as is the habit of men, sought glory just because he was king, but lived like a private citizen together with everyone else'.[41] Umar II, 'was so benign and patient in his rule that even today great honour and praise is bestowed upon him, so that he is extolled more than any of his predecessors not only by his own people but by foreigners. He was regarded as more conscientious in his government of the kingdom than anyone else from the people of the Arabs'.[42] Typically, the rulers that the author complimented were either the predecessors or successors of caliphs whose reigns suffered from large-scale rebellion.

Far less concerned was the author about the government's policies toward the subject Christian population. He did deplore the death of the

---

[37]*Chr754* 81. Barkai regards these references to cruelty as typical of the chronicler's attitude toward the Muslims. He considers the references to benevolent rulers as exceptions that show that the Christian 'image' of the Muslims was still not 'closed'. pp. 23, 26.
[38]*Chr754* 82.
[39]*Chr754* 79.
[40]*Chr754* 91.
[41]*Chr754* 31. Cf. *Chr741* 28.
[42]*Chr754* 67. Cf. *Chr741* 40.

bishop of Cerdanya at the hands of the rebel Munnuza, but his point seems to have been to illustrate not so much the mistreatment of Christians as the general disruption that follows from rebellion.[43] Elsewhere, the author branded the governor Yahya as a 'cruel and terrible despot' for having restored to the Christians of Spain property that had been taken from them at the time of the conquest. Though we would assume that the Christian beneficiaries of this change of policy did not complain, our chronicler denounced the action in no uncertain terms as deceitful, serving only to upset the Muslims and threaten peninsular peace.[44]

In short, the chronicler's depiction of individual Muslim rulers is much like his depiction of their Gothic predecessors. There is no evidence that he took into account religious affiliation when he was evaluating them. The real difference between the chronicler's reporting of events before and after the invasion is the amount of attention given to religious matters. Descriptions of councils and the contributions of churchmen dominate the space that the chronicler devoted to the reigns of the Gothic kings. But after the invasion, there are only three passing references to outstanding churchmen and no mention of any synods. We might have expected this, given the change in religious climate after 711. There were far fewer councils, and presumably the Andalusian bishops assumed a lower profile. But would we have anticipated the complete absence of information about the religious identity and activity of the conquerors?[45]

Here a comparison with the *Chronicle of 741*—the author of which apparently utilized the same source for Arab events in the east as the chronicler of 754—is instructive. The earlier chronicle is quite explicit, though brief, about the religious identity of the invaders. It describes

---

[43]*Chr754* 78.

[44]*Chr754* 75.

[45]Both Barkai (p. 22) and Collins (*Arab Conquest*, pp. 62-3) noted the lack of religious information in the chronicle, but neither really offered an explanation for it. Collins suggested fear, but if this was a factor—which is doubtful because the Muslim authorities seem to have given Christian authors substantial latitude for authoring polemical works (in Latin)—it does not explain the absence of neutral descriptions of Islam.

Muhammad as a 'prescient man, a foreseer of some future events',[46] and goes on to explain that 'today the Saracens worship Muhammad with great honour and reverence as they affirm him to be an apostle of God and a prophet in all of their sacraments and scriptures'.[47] The *Chronicle of 754*, in contrast, contains none of this information about Islam.[48] Muhammad, as depicted by the author, was, first and foremost, the leader (*ducator*) of a successful rebellion.[49] Only once in the seven times that his name appears is it linked to the word *propheta*, and then without any explanation. Furthermore, there are no references in the chronicle to the religion that Muhammad fostered, neither to its doctrine nor to its rituals. According to the chronicler, the caliph Umar was assassinated 'while he was in prayer', but there is nothing to indicate that Umar's form of worship was distinct from that of the chronicler.[50] The closest the author came to suggesting that the Muslims had a distinctive religious tradition was a passing reference to Mecca, 'the home of Abraham, *as they assert*'.[51]

The very terms that the chronicler used to refer to the Muslims are religiously neutral. Like the author of the *Chronicle of 741*, he consistently opted for terms indicating ethnicity rather than religious affiliation: *sarraceni, arabes, mauri*, and, occasionally, *plebs smahelitarum*, as opposed to *infideles, heretici,* or *pagani*. Of these, 'Saracen', 'Arab', and even 'Ishmaelite' were commonly used in the Mediterranean world long before Muhammad's time to identify the inhabitants of Arabia.[52] *Mauri*, or 'Moors', also true to Roman usage,

---

[46] *Chr741* 13.

[47] This positive portrayal of Islam has led some historians to see the author as a recent Muslim convert. For instance, Dubler, p. 331. Barkai (p. 55, n. 2) points out the ambiguities that make this hypothesis a difficult one to sustain.

[48] There is some awareness of cultural differences, specifically linguistic ones. *Chr754* 57, 94.

[49] *Chr754* 8.

[50] *Chr754* 12.

[51] *Chr754* 34. Italics my own.

[52] For the Romans, *sarraceni* carried with it nomadic connotations that *arabes* did not. The chronicler of 754 treated the two as synonyms. 'Ishmaelites' entered the Latin vocabulary

referred specifically to the peoples of Mauretania—the Berbers[53]—who constituted the bulk of the invading forces in 711.[54] This exclusive use of ethnic terminology to identify the invaders is consistent with the author's preference for *gothi, franci* or *europenses*,[55] and *romani* or *bizantici*,[56] when referring to the Christian populations that bore the brunt of the Arab attacks. It is interesting to note that after the conquest of Spain, *gothi* disappeared from the chronicler's vocabulary altogether. Apparently he considered the 'Goth' category to be a political one that could not appropriately outlive the *regnum gothorum*. On the few occasions that he referred to the peoples subject to the Muslim governor of Córdoba, he did use religious labels: *christiani*[57] and *iudei*.[58] But while the chronicler conceived of the subjects of Arab rule in Spain in religious terms, he never identified the invaders in this way.

Since the chronicler never bothered to identify the Muslims as Muslims, it comes as no surprise that there are no instances in which he drew religious lines when describing Christian-Muslim military encounters. He referred, without a hint of reproach, to one Urban, 'that most noble man of the African region, reared under the doctrine of the Catholic faith, who had accompanied (Musa) throughout Spain'.[59] He came the closest to setting up the Christians and Muslims as religious adversaries when recounting a campaign led by Abd al-Malik in the early

---

under the influence of Roman Jews and Christians. My thanks to Glen Bowersock for providing me with useful information on these matters.

[53]Neville Barbour, 'The Significance of the Word *Maurus*, with its Derivatives *Moro* and *Moor*, and of other Terms used by Medieval Writers in Latin to Describe the Inhabitants of Muslim Spain', *Actas do IV Congresso de Estudos Arabes e Islâmicos*, Coimbra, 1968 (Leiden, 1971), pp. 253-66.

[54]John of Biclaro used *Sarraceni* to refer to the inhabitants of Arabia and *Mauri* for the peoples of Mauretania. There was, of course, no religious or political connection between the two at the time he wrote. Biclaro 37; 8, 11, 16, 48.

[55]*Chr754* 80.

[56]*Chr754* 1.

[57]*Chr754* 64, 74, 79, 81, 91.

[58]*Chr754* 13, 74.

[59]*Chr754* 57.

730s. Apparently attempting to overcome a pocket of resistance somewhere in the Pyrenees, he met with little success and finally left, 'convinced of the power of God, from whom the small band of Christians holding the pinnacles awaited mercy'.[60] This sounds suspiciously like a reference to one of the Christian enclaves that relied more on their inaccessibility than their strength to resist Cordoban rule. It is difficult to know what to make of the passage. The chronicler may have used *christiani* simply because he did not know how to describe this group in ethnic terms. If he was willing to involve God in this case, it is odd that he did not describe the Frankish victories over the Muslims using similar language. Though he carefully recorded every Muslim setback at the hands of the Franks and even berated Charles Martel for not following up on his victory at Poitiers, he never depicted the Franks as *christiani* coming to the rescue of the Christians in Spain.[61]

Nor does the political terminology used to describe the Muslim caliphate and its components give any hints as to the religious aspects of the Muslim state. The caliphate of Damascus and the province of al-Andalus become, in the vocabulary of the chronicle, simply *regna*, not clearly distinguished in type from the displaced *regnum* of the Visigoths or that of the Franks, which checked Muslim progress north of the Pyrenees.[62] Despite the size of the Muslim empire and the diversity of the people subject to it, the chronicler reserved the term *imperium* for the Roman (Byzantine) empire.[63] *Princeps* appears from time to time in reference to either the caliph in Damascus or the governor in Kairouan,[64] to whom the governor of al-Andalus was theoretically subordinated. Muslim governors and military commanders alike emerge from the text

---

[60]*Chr754* 81.

[61]*Chr754* 80.

[62]See, for instance, *Chr754* 9, 88. The distinction that Barkai makes between the use of *regnum* in reference to the caliphate by the chronicler of 741 and the absence of the term in the *Chronicle of 754* is not supported by the texts, where *regnum* appears with similar frequency. Refer to the concordance in López Pereira's *Crónica mozárabe de 754*, p. 159.

[63]John of Biclaro had referred to the Persian ruler as an *imperator* (Biclaro 3. 15. 35, etc.).

[64]The capital of the Arab province of Ifriqiya, located in modern Tunisia.

rather generically as *duces*, though in a wonderfully anachronistic passage, Yusuf—the last of the governors of Spain before the establishment of the Umayyad emirate—was 'acclaimed by all of the senate of the palace as king of the land'.[65] The occasional use of the epithet *amir almuminin* ('leader of the faithful') in conjunction with the names of the caliphs toward the end of the work would have signaled to the reader that there was something religious about the Muslim *regnum* if the author had translated it literally. Instead he rendered it, 'carrying out all things prosperously'.[66]

What accounts for this reticence on the part of our chronicler with regard to the religious dimension of the conquest of 711? We could simply say that his interests were more political than religious. But then we would be hard pressed to explain the careful attention that he, following the lead of John of Biclaro, devoted to ecclesiastical matters in Spain that predated the Muslim invasion. Aside from councils and outstanding churchmen, he recorded instances of Christian heterodoxy and heteropraxy within the Spanish church, some of which occurred after the conquest.[67] He even noted in passing a case of Islamic deviance: Uqbah's suppression of certain rebels and heretics 'whom they call *Arures*'.[68] And he was intrigued by the caliph Marwan's use of Persian troops 'who still worshipped the sun and black demons'.[69] In short, the author expressed no lack of interest in religious matters nor a shortage of categories with which to organize such information, yet he applied neither to Islam.

It is conceivable that the chronicler simply did not know enough about the religion of the conquerors. But it seems more likely that he knew too much. As we saw in the first chapter, John of Biclaro interpreted the

---

[65] *Chr754* 91.
[66] *Chr754* 57. Barkai did not take this into account when hypothesizing, on the basis of the accuracy of the transliterations, that the author of the *Chronicle of 754* knew Arabic. Barkai, p. 21.
[67] *Chr754* 14, 88.1, 93.
[68] *Chr754* 82 and note.
[69] A reference to Zoroastrianism. *Chr754* 94.

military success of the Goths under Reccared as evidence of divine intervention. By so doing, he was simply tapping into a Eusebian historiographical tradition that described the military and political success of the Christian empire in Old Testament terms: as an empirical sign of God's favour. This device worked well as long as the Christian empire— or at least its barbarized, but Christian, components—held their ground. But the reversals of the seventh and eighth centuries changed all of that. Not only did the Arabs take control of the eastern, southern, and western shores of *Mare Nostrum*, but they did so while acknowledging the same God that had 'overseen' the building of the Christian Roman empire, interpreting their own achievements in light of his favour. Given this potentially embarrassing 'turning of the tables', it might have seemed safer to the chronicler of 754 to downplay the religious dimension of the invasion and treat it as a simple conquest.

Concerns of this type may also explain why the chronicler did not choose to describe the conquest of Spain as a scourge. Scourges, according to the model provided by the historical books of the Old Testament, were temporary punishments inflicted to correct the sins of a chosen people. They were to be lifted when the price for the transgression had been paid. It is unlikely that the chronicler, living in the second generation after the invasion, would have seen anything to suggest that the Muslim occupation was about to end. The possibility that the Gothic kingdom might someday be restored must have seemed distant at best. Under these circumstances, to have raised the issue of divine involvement at all was to run the risk of having readers, present and future, interpret the endlessness of the Muslim 'scourge' as evidence that the conquest was not so much a punishment inflicted on the Christians as a reward bestowed upon the Muslims. The chronicler's decision to describe the initial defeat of the imperial army in the east as a scourge may have simply been an attempt to pin the blame for the Arab invasion on the empire. The sin of Heraclius opened the door to the Arabs who, unfortunately, did not confine their depredations to imperial territory. The Goths, though innocent, suffered just as much, if not more, than the guilty party. In other words, the chronicler may have deliberately applied only half of the scourge paradigm, emphasizing the sins and punishment of the empire while avoiding potentially compromising implications about the future redemption of either the empire or Spain.

The difficulties posed by the conquest of Christian Spain by a non-Christian power seem not only to have determined that the chronicler of 754 would downplay the religious identity of the invaders and avoid depicting the invasion as a scourge, but to have limited his choice of genre. To have written a continuation of Isidore's *History of the Kings of the Goths* would have forced the chronicler to confront the implications of Isidore's narrative. Why, if the Goths were destined to succeed Rome as the legitimate heirs of Spain, did they lose their prize to the Muslims? If Isidore's case for the Goths was based on their superior strength, could not the same logic be extended to the conquest of 711? Had not the Muslims 'seized' *mater Spania* from the Goths just as the Goths had taken her from the Romans? These questions would not have been so difficult to answer if the invaders had been Christian or had converted to Christianity in the wake of their conquest. But this was not the case.

The universal chronicle, on the other hand, provided a model of unnarrativized history that allowed the author to record the events of his day without having to address such sensitive interpretative issues. The genre gave him license simply to 'record what happened' without trying to fit it all into a single, overarching narrative scheme. Hence the many inconsistencies present in the *Chronicle of 754*. We find Christian rulers in the east losing battles because of their moral failings and Christian rulers in the west losing battles because of political rivalry. We find Muslim rulers who are reviled for unleashing war in Spain and Muslim rulers who are held up as paradigms of benevolent rule. We find detailed descriptions of Christian councils and complete silence about Islamic beliefs and practices.

While such inconsistencies inhibit any attempt to distill a clear 'view of the conquest', the simple fact that the chronicler was able to make room for the Muslims in Latin history represented a major step in the direction of accepting the political transformation of Spain. By describing the Muslim caliphs as *reges* and their generals as *duces*, he 'dressed' a foreign people in terms familiar to a reader versed in the language of Latin history. By glossing over the differences between the Gothic and Saracen regimes, he managed to impose historiographical continuity on political rupture. It is worth reminding ourselves at this point that the author of this chronicle was probably a deacon or a bishop living in al-Andalus a generation after the Muslim conquest of Spain. The problems that he faced as a historian trying to find a way to recount the invasion without challenging his Christian world-view are perhaps reflections of the problems that he faced as an elite Christian trying to find a way of participating in a society that was no longer dominated by Christians. The solutions to the historiographical problems that he found within the genre of the universal chronicle are, then, probably as good a reflection of the rationale that permitted Christians to involve themselves in Andalusian government and society as we are likely to find. By downplaying religious differences, and treating al-Andalus as simply another Mediterranean *regnum*, the old Christian ruling class did not have to let ideological differences preclude positive interaction with their conquerors.

AN ASTURIAN CHRONICLER AND THE MUSLIMS

At first glance, the *Chronicle of Alfonso III* does not look much like a continuation of Isidore's *History of the Kings of the Goths*. Its Asturian author began with the accession of King Wamba, forty-seven years after Isidore's work concludes. He also used a different method of dating, for the most part recording only the 'era' in which one reign ended and another began. From a narrative standpoint, however, the two chronicles are closely linked. In fact, one can argue that the Asturian work was specifically designed as a sequel to the *History of the Kings of the Goths*. If Isidore traced the rise of the Goths from their humble beginnings in the east to the establishment of their kingdom in the west, his Asturian continuator described how, having won Spain, the Goths 'fell from grace', lost their kingdom, and had to start all over again.

The *Chronicle of Alfonso III* survives in two forms, traditionally referred to as the Roda and the Oviedo versions.[1] The prologue of the Oviedo text was written during the reign of Alfonso III's son and successor, García (910-14). That of the Roda version dates from the reign of Alfonso's other son, Ordoño II (914-24). But the chronicles themselves cover nothing later that the death of Ordoño I (866) and the accession of Alfonso III, suggesting that both versions originally date from some time during the reign of Alfonso (866-910). It is likely that were written in the early 880s, a period which saw not only a significant—though temporary—shift in the balance of power in favour

---

[1] Most historians today agree that the Roda version is the earlier of the two and that the Oviedo variant represents a revised, 'official' version. I have chosen to translate and study the Roda version because it contains the most interesting elements from a narrative standpoint. But I have included pertinent references to the Oviedo version as well as to the other Asturian chronicles produced in this period.

The most useful and concise studies of the historiography of this period are: Manuel C. Díaz y Díaz, 'La historiografía hispana desde la invasión árabe hasta el año 1000', *La storiografia altomedievale*, Settimane di studio del centro italiano di studi sull'alto medioevo (Spoleto, 1970), pp. 313-43; Abilio Barbero and Marcelo Vigil, *La formación del feudalismo en la península ibérica*, 3rd ed. (Barcelona, 1982), pp. 232-78; and Collins, *Arab Conquest*, pp. 141-51.

of the Asturians, but the production of two other chronicles whose dates we know. *The Chronicle of Albelda* ends in 881 with Alfonso's raid to Mt. Oxifer near Mérida, 'which no prince before him had ever tried to approach, but where he triumphed over his enemies with a glorious outcome'.[2] Two years later someone added to the chronicle, incorporating two consecutive Asturian victories over invading Andalusian armies.[3] The so-called *Prophetic Chronicle* dates from 883. This work, combining royal annals with apocalyptic exegesis, boldly predicted that Saracen rule in Spain would come to an end within eighteen months.[4] It is tempting, in light of the activity of these Asturian chroniclers, to treat the *Chronicle of Alfonso III* as a product of this same self-congratulatory period of Alfonso's reign.[5] Indeed, it is possible that the king was personally involved in its composition. A reference to the resettlement of Viseo states that the town was repopulated 'on our orders', as if the author and repopulator were one.[6] Whether it was Alfonso or, more likely, a member of his court, the author of the Asturian chronicle sought, as Isidore had in the early seventh century, to create an historical context appropriate for a successful monarchy. To this end he wrote a continuation of the *History of the Kings of the Goths* that depicted Asturian history as if it were a new chapter in Gothic history.[7] Alfonso III was not to be just another conqueror of Spain, but the heir to a past regime, fighting to restore his birthright.

The chroniclers of the 880s were probably not the first to make the connection between the Gothic and Asturian monarchies. Describing Alfonso II's (791-842) new capital in Oviedo, the *Chronicle of Albelda* states that the king 'established the entire order of the Goths, just as it had been in Toledo.'[8] Though the exact meaning of *ordo gothorum* remains a mystery, the use of Goths as a model is significant. What we know about

---

[2]*Crónicas Asturianas*, p. 177.

[3]*Crónicas Asturianas*, pp. 178-81.

[4]*Crónicas Asturianas*, p. 188.

[5]The author may have had access to the *Prophetic Chronicle* (meaning that he would have had to have written sometime after 883). Barbero and Vigil, pp. 265-70.

[6]*ChrAlf* 7.

[7]The connection to Isidore is made explicit in the prefatory letter from Alfonso to Sebastian that introduces the Oviedo version. *Crónicas Asturianas*, p. 115.

[8]*Crónicas Asturianas*, p. 174.

Alfonso II's ambitious architectural programme suggests that this passage may not have been anachronistic. Alfonso's reign seems also to have witnessed the production of annals or chronicles, which, while no longer extant, formed the basis of the early portions of the later chronicles that do survive.[9] Modern historians have speculated that ninth-century Christian immigrants from al-Andalus—the so-called Mozarabs—may have been responsible for introducing the idea that the kings of Oviedo were the natural heirs to the kings of Toledo.[10]

The author of the *Chronicle of Alfonso III* elaborated this connection between Gothic and Asturian history by depicting the Muslim invasion as a scourge designed to punish the Goths for transgressing divine law. By so doing, the chronicler could account for the fact that the Goths had lost Spain, while still maintaining that they were its legitimate rulers. God had raised up the Muslims to punish the sinful Goths and would restore their kingdom once they had paid the price for their sins. It also allowed him to interpret the success of Alfonso's raids against the Muslims as more than a simple function of Asturian strength or Andalusian weakness. Alfonso was leading the chastened remnant of the Gothic 'chosen people' toward the recovery of their 'promised land'.

The Asturian chronicler did not find an explicitly developed 'chosen people' narrative in the *History of the Kings of the Goths*. As we have seen, Isidore placed more emphasis on the Roman concept of 'right by conquest' than on the Hebrew notion of a people with a special relationship to God. But it was easy enough to treat Isidore's account of the Gothic invasion of Spain and the displacement of the Romans as if it *were* the story of a divinely orchestrated occupation of a promised land. Spain, as described in Isidore's prologue, certainly looked like a land of milk and honey. What the Asturian chronicler had to do as he continued Isidore's account of the reigns of the Gothic kings, was to show how the Goths, after occupying Spain, had managed to offend the God who had originally bestowed Spain upon them. Isidore had emphasized the moral probity and justice of Reccared, Sisebut, and Suinthila. His continuator

---

[9]Claudio Sánchez Albornoz, '¿Una crónica asturiana perdida?' *Investigaciones sobre historiografía hispana medieval* (Buenos Aires, 1967), pp. 111-60. Bonnaz, pp. lxxvi-lxxxiii.

[10]Barbero and Vigil, pp. 262-75. Bonnaz, pp. liv-lv, lxxii-lxxiv.

had to show how their successors had fallen away from these high standards and kindled the anger of God.

The author began his chronicle with the death of Reccesuinth and the accession of Wamba in 672. His choice of Wamba rather than Sisebut or Suinthila as his point of departure was apparently a function both of his sources and of his choice of narrative. The prefatory letter appended to the Oviedo version of the chronicle refers to Isidore's *chronica gothorum* as if it covered the Gothic kings up through Wamba.[11] Either the Asturian historians had access to a continuation of Isidore,[12] or the author of the letter was conflating the work of Isidore and Julian of Toledo, who wrote a history specifically devoted to Wamba's reign. Be that as it may, the reign of Wamba, as idealized by Julian, provided the Asturian chronicler with the perfect foil against which the last four Visigothic kings could be unfavourably compared. The fact that Wamba was an anointed king, who, at least according to the Asturian chronicler, had turned back an attempted Saracen invasion in the 670s,[13] made him an even more attractive point of departure from a narrative standpoint.

The problems with the Toledan monarchy began, according to the chronicler, when Count Ervig secretly administered a potion to Wamba which temporarily deprived him of his senses. In anticipation of the king's death, the bishop of Toledo conscientiously administered the rite of penance. When Wamba recovered from the effects of the potion, he had no choice canonically but to relinquish the throne and live out his days in a monastery.[14] Ervig was then elected to succeed Wamba on the basis of his own blood ties to King Chindasuinth, giving his daughter Cixilo in marriage to Egica, a nephew of Wamba.[15] Ervig died without a son and was succeeded by his son-in-law, but Egica, at the bidding of his uncle, Wamba, who was still bitter about the circumstances of his abdication, repudiated Ervig's daughter. Cixilo had, however, already given Egica a son by the name of Witiza, who ultimately succeeded his father to the throne. In marked contrast to the Witiza of the *Chronicle of*

---

[11] *Crónicas Asturianas*, p. 115.
[12] Collins, *Arab Conquest*, p. 64.
[13] *ChrAlf 2*.
[14] *ChrAlf 2* and note.
[15] *ChrAlf 3*.

754, the Witiza of the *Chronicle of Alfonso III* 'was a reprobate and was disgraceful in his habits. He dissolved the councils. He sealed the canons. He took many wives and concubines.'[16] It was the latter of these novelties that was the most damaging, in the chronicler's estimation, because in order to forestall ecclesiastical censure, he ordered all of the bishops and priests of his realm to follow his example and marry.[17]

> This, then, was the cause of Spain's ruin. Thus says the scripture, 'Because iniquity abounded, charity grew cold'.[18] And another passage from scripture says, 'If the people sin, the priest prays, but if the priests sin, there will be a plague upon the people'.[19] They withdrew from the Lord and did not walk in the paths of his precepts nor did they attentively observe how the Lord prohibited priests from acting evilly when he said to Moses in Exodus, 'Let the priests who come to the Lord be sanctified lest the Lord forsake them'.[20] And again: 'When they approach to serve at the holy altar, let them not bring along any sin within them lest perchance they die'.[21] And because the kings and priests forsook the Lord, all of the armies of Spain perished.[22]

This is the earliest point at which the chronicler made clear his intention to interpret the invasion as a scourge. It is significant that Witiza's—or the chronicler's—choice of sin was one that clearly violated Mosaic law. It is also significant that the chronicler deviated from his account of the Gothic kings long enough to remind the reader that God had made the proscription, and the consequences of its violation, very clear to a previous 'chosen people'.

---

[16]*ChrAlf* 5.
[17]Collins is most likely correct in interpreting this passage in light of the decisions of the council held in Constantinople in 692 allowing for clerical marriage if the marriage had occurred prior to ordination. Witiza may simply have been attempting to implement this decision in Spain. *Arab Conquest*, pp. 15-19. Cf. *Chr754* 53.
[18]Matthew 24:12.
[19]Numbers 8:19, 16:46-8.
[20]Exodus 19:22.
[21]Leviticus 21:33.
[22]*ChrAlf* 5.

Once Witiza had violated this law, there was little that his successor Roderic could do. 'Spain grew even worse in its iniquity'. Aided by the 'treachery of the sons of Witiza', the Saracens entered Spain and advanced to meet the armies of Roderic.[23]

> But, weighed down by the quantity of their sins and exposed by the treachery of the sons of Witiza, the Goths were put to flight. The army, fleeing to its destruction, was almost annihilated. Because they forsook the Lord and did not serve him in justice and truth, they were forsaken by the Lord so that they could no longer inhabit the land that they desired.[24]

Appropriating almost verbatim Isidore's rhetorical epitaph for Rome after its sack at the hands of Alaric, the chronicler lamented, 'The city of Toledo, victor over all peoples, succumbed, vanquished by the victories of the Ishmaelites; subjected, it served them'.[25] But while for Isidore the fall of Rome was a necessary precondition for the rise of the Goths, the fall of Toledo was not, for Isidore's continuator, a signal that the Goths had come to the end of their road, but simply a punishment for transgressing divine law.

The Asturian chronicler, then, portrayed the last four kings of the Goths in such a way as to support his thesis that the later Gothic kings had invited disaster by failing to live up to the standards set by their predecessors. But his manipulation of the past to make it fit his choice of storyline did not end with the invasion. For if the Saracens were to appear as a scourge, then it was necessary to show how they began to lose ground as soon as the Goths recognized their error and made amends. But the Gothic monarchy had ended with the defeat of Roderic. Or had it?

No one knows how many—if any—Gothic refugees actually made their way north to the mountains of Asturias in the wake of Roderic's

---

[23] The Oviedo version blames Roderic not only for failing to correct Witiza's transgression, but for adding to it. It is also more explicit about the nature of the treachery of the sons of Witiza: they sent messengers to negotiate with the Muslims of Morocco for assistance. *Crónicas Asturianas*, p. 121.

[24] *ChrAlf* 7.

[25] *ChrAlf* 8.

defeat. The *Chronicle of 754* records that some fled 'to the mountains where they risked hunger and various forms of death',[26] when they could not come to terms with the invaders. But we have no way of knowing whether the author was in fact referring to the Cantabrian mountains or simply the Sierra Morena immediately to the north of Córdoba. Elsewhere the same chronicle recounts how the governor Abd al-Malik tried in vain to subdue a group of Christians somewhere in the Pyrenees, but the details that might have allowed us to identify these Christians are lacking.[27]

The *Chronicle of Alfonso III* is more precise, if less trustworthy. It recounts the exodus of one Pelayo, identified as the swordbearer of the last two Gothic monarchs, who, 'oppressed by the dominion of the Ishmaelites, had come to Asturias'.[28] The chronicler also described Pelayo's son-in-law, Alfonso, as the 'son of Peter, who was the leader of the Cantabrians and was from the royal line'.[29] The Oviedo version is more explicit. Peter is described as a descendant of Leovigild and Reccared, and Pelayo and his father are included among those 'of royal stock' (*ex semine regio*) who fled north to Asturias.[30]

The author of the *Chronicle of Alfonso III* relied more on narrative than on genealogical consistency to ease the transition from the Gothic to the Asturian monarchies.[31] Pelayo's lineage was less important than his fateful decision to resist the Muslim occupation, a decision based at least initially on his unwillingness to see his sister married to the local Muslim

---

[26]*Chr754* 54.

[27]*Chr754* 81. A few other sources refer to individual Goths in exile. See: *Crónicas Asturianas*, pp. 67-70.

[28]*ChrAlf* 8.

[29]*ChrAlf* 11.

[30]*Crónicas Asturianas*, pp. 123, 131. The Oviedo version also states that Pelayo was elected king not by the Asturians, but by the Gothic remnant that had fled to the north. Ibid., p. 123. *The Chronicle of Albelda* reports that Pelayo had originally been expelled from Toledo as the result of an altercation between his father and King Witiza. Ibid., p. 171.

[31]Gil has suggested that the author of the Roda version wanted to avoid calling attention to Pelayo's close ties to the family of Witiza, which he deduces on the basis of Oppa's reference to Pelayo as *confrater et fili*. *Crónicas Asturianas*, p. 65. But if indeed *confrater* was meant to suggest a family connection that the chronicler wanted to obscure, why did he include it in Oppa's salutation? I am of the opinion that *confrater*, like *filius*, should be interpreted rhetorically.

'prefect', but ultimately on his desire to effect the 'salvation of the church'. He would not have been able to withstand the scourge that had laid low the army of Roderic if he had not been hand-picked by God to begin the restoration of Gothic Spain.

The chronicler devoted the single largest portion of his entire history to the story of Pelayo's resistance at Covadonga. Within this episode, the verbal exchange between Oppa, 'on account of whose treachery the Goths had perished',[32] and Pelayo, whose destiny it was to begin the restoration of the Gothic kingdom, is the focal point. Oppa, the bishop of Toledo[33] and a collaborator with the Saracens, has come to talk some sense into the rebel Pelayo. Speaking first, he reminds Pelayo that, although Gothic Spain had 'outshone all other lands in learning and knowledge', the Gothic army had proved unable to withstand the Saracen assault. Does Pelayo expect his meagre forces to accomplish what the entire army of Roderic could not? Ironically Oppa, the bishop, could not see the hand of God at work in the recent debacle. But Pelayo could and promptly shared his insights with Oppa:

Have you not read in the divine scriptures how the church of God is compared to a mustard seed and that it will be raised up again through divine mercy?[34]...Christ is our hope that through this little mountain, which you see, the well-being of Spain and the army of the Gothic people will be restored. I have faith that the promise of the Lord which was spoken through David will be fulfilled in us: 'I will visit their iniquities with the rod and their sins with scourges; but I will not remove my mercy from them'.[35] Now, therefore, trusting in the mercy of Jesus Christ, I despise this multitude and am not afraid of it. As for the battle with which you threaten us, we have

---

[32]*Chr Alf* 7. The chronicler identified Oppa as the son of Witiza. Cf. *Chr 754* 54 and note. The ensuing dialogue was probably based on an oral legend that the chronicler chose to incorporate into his account. Collins, *Arab Conquest*, pp. 33-4. Bonnaz, pp. lxxxiii-lxxxvi.

[33]According to the Oviedo version, Oppa was the bishop of Seville. *Crónicas Asturianas*, p. 123.

[34]Matthew 17:19.

[35]Psalm 88:33-4.

for ourselves an advocate in the presence of the Father, that is, the Lord Jesus Christ, who is capable of liberating us from these few.[36]

This dialogue explicitly interprets the Gothic loss of Spain as a scourge, and prepares the reader to see God's hand in Pelayo's subsequent victory. 'On this occasion', in marked contrast to the previous encounter between Goths and Saracens, 'the power of the Lord was not absent'. Miraculously, the stones that the Saracens shot from their catapults turned in mid-flight and cut down the very men who had launched them. 'Because', concluded the author, 'the Lord does not count spears, but offers the palm of victory to whomsoever he will', most of the Saracens died in the ensuing battle. Those who escaped the sword were hurled to their deaths when an earthquake tore apart the mountain over which they were fleeing. 'He who once parted the waters of the Red Sea so that the children of Israel might cross, has now crushed, with an immense mass of mountain, the Arabs who were persecuting the church of God'.[37]

From the perspective of the Asturian chronicler, the victory of Pelayo's forces marked the beginning of the newly restored harmony between God and his people: 'the country was populated and the church was restored. Everyone together gave thanks to God, saying, "Blessed be the name of the Lord who strengthens those who believe in him and destroys wicked peoples"'. 'To the extent that the dignity of Christ's name grew, the derisive calamity of the Chaldeans wasted away'.[38] It should be noted that nothing had as yet been done about restoring the purity of the church by rescinding Witiza's order that the clergy marry. Pelayo's recognition of the hand of God in the loss of Spain and his own success against the

---

[36] *ChrAlf* 9.

[37] *ChrAlf* 10. There is some debate among historians of medieval Spain as to the significance of Pelayo's resistance. Was it simply a generic Asturian reaction against outside encroachment of any kind, or was it the self-conscious beginning of the *reconquista*? All agree, however, that the Asturian sources exaggerate the encounter. To appreciate this, consider the same event from the perspective of the eleventh-century Arabic *Akhbar Majmu'a*, pp. 38-9. The author describes how a Muslim army besieged a band of 300 Christians under a 'king called Balay' in the mountains of Galicia until its numbers had become so diminished by famine that the Muslims left: 'Thirty men! What could they matter?'

[38] *ChrAlf* 11.

'Chaldeans', show that the Asturians had already regained the divine confidence that their Gothic predecessors had forfeited.

After the climactic confrontation at Covadonga, the chronicler reverted to a simple recording of reigns and royal deeds more akin to Isidore's model. Whenever events permitted, he reminded the reader of the Gothic-Asturian connection and the victories of Pelayo's successors over the Saracens. Dispensing quickly with the inauspicious reign of Favila, the chronicler devoted his account of Alfonso I's rule to a litany of all the cities he conquered and the regions he repopulated. These successes, coupled with his church-building efforts, made him a good example of a Joshua-like leader reclaiming a promised land. Significantly enough, Alfonso is the first king since Wamba to have been graced by signs of divine favour.[39] Fruela, Alfonso's son and successor, killed his brother with his bare hands and was in turn killed by conspirators in his own court. But the choice of narrative dictated that these shortcomings would not detract from the credit he deserved for being the one who finally 'put an end to that crime whereby priests since the time of Witiza had become accustomed to taking wives. Applying whips to the many who remained in sin, he confined them to monasteries'. At long last the sin of Witiza that had evoked the ire of God had been extirpated and, 'observing canonical doctrine once again, the church grew great'.[40]

The Asturian chronicler passed quickly through the reigns of Aurelio, Silo, Mauregato and Vermudo presumably because they saw no notable expansion of the realm at the expense of the Saracens. Alfonso II enjoyed a much fuller treatment because he accomplished things that fit the narrative pattern. The chronicler recorded Alfonso's three victories over invading Saracen armies and described how the king withstood a rebellion led by a former Arab ally. The king's architectural achievements, by which he transformed Oviedo into the new capital of the Asturian realm, were as important as his military feats. The author credited him with the construction of four churches as well as a palace complex. These projects, combined with the fact that he never married,

---

[39]*ChrAlf* 15.
[40]*ChrAlf* 16.

made him appear to be a particularly saintly king who, after fifty-two years of rule, 'sent his most holy spirit to heaven'.[41]

King Ramiro added to the number of royal and ecclesiastical buildings in Oviedo and, 'with the help of God', emerged victorious in his two encounters with the Saracens. But the chronicler spent more time recounting how he withstood an unprecedented naval attack by the Northmen, a 'pagan and extremely cruel people previously unknown to us'. His victory over them seemed all the more impressive in light of what the chronicler knew of the Viking attacks further south in Seville, where 'they annihilated many bands of Chaldeans...partly by the sword and partly by fire'.[42] He probably regarded the success of the Northmen in southern Spain as one more indication that time was beginning to run out on the Saracens.

The last of the kings covered received the fullest treatment, outside of Pelayo's. Ordoño not only defeated the Saracen armies whenever he met them in battle, but he actively promoted the refortification and repopulation of key cities in the north. The chronicler devoted most of his attention to the victory that Ordoño won over the forces of the Banu Qasi, a powerful family of Christian converts to Islam that had wrested control of the province of Zaragoza from the emirate. The leader of the Banu Qasi posed enough of a challenge to the Andalusians and the Asturians that he, according to the chronicler, 'demanded that his men call him the third king of Spain'.[43] But Ordoño proved stronger. Coopting a line from the book of Judges, which recounted the divinely-orchestrated triumphs of the chosen people of Israel, the chronicler described how the Asturian king annihilated the forces of the Banu Qasi.[44]

'With Ordoño dead, his son Alfonso succeeded him as king'. If, as we suspect, the chronicler survived to see enough of Alfonso's reign to convince himself that the Asturians would enjoy a speedy conquest of

---

[41] *ChrAlf* 21-22.
[42] *ChrAlf* 23. See also: *ChrAlf* 27.
[43] *ChrAlf* 25.
[44] *ChrAlf* 26.

southern Spain, he left the task of recording the king's victories to someone else.[45]

The image of the Muslim invaders of Spain that emerges from the *Chronicle of Alfonso III* is, in many ways, similar to that of the *Chronicle of 754*. As in the Andalusian chronicle, the references to the religious identity of the invaders are few and far between. On a single occasion toward the end of the chronicle, the Asturian chronicler identified the leader of the Banu Qasi as a 'Goth by birth, but deceived by the Muhammadan rite (*ritu mamentiano*)'.[46] The fact that he used the category 'pagan' when describing Northmen but not the Saracens suggests that he knew that the latter group did not properly belong to that category. Beyond this, it is difficult to squeeze any other information about Islam, and therefore about the chronicler's understanding of it, from the text.

Moreover, like his Andalusian counterpart, the Asturian chronicler used ethnic rather than religious labels when referring to the Muslims. 'Saracen', 'Ishmaelite', and 'Arab' all appear. But the Asturian chronicler preferred, above all, 'Chaldean', a term that the earlier chronicler did not use, outside of a single geographical reference to the ancient city of Ur.[47] This is a significant choice for the Asturian chronicler because it allowed him to tap into the repeated references to the Chaldeans in Jeremiah and other prophetic books, where the term was used almost generically to refer to the scourges suffered by the people of Israel.[48] The reference to the caliph as the 'Babylonian king' should also be seen in this light.[49]

The Asturian chronicler did not regard the occasional cases of Christian-Muslim cooperation as unusual or aberrant. Alfonso II received the Meridan rebel Muhammad with honour and allowed him to settle in Galicia. When the two came to blows later it was a result of Muhammad's treachery, not a product of his religious affiliation.[50] And

---

[45]The prologues that were added to the two versions in the 910s suggest that the optimism lasted into the early tenth century.

[46]*ChrAlf* 25.

[47]*Chr754* 34.

[48]Barkai, p. 33, missed the point of this use of 'Chaldeans'. treating it as a pejorative reference to the Arabs as astrologers and diviners.

[49]*ChrAlf* 8. There is no such reference in the *Chronicle of 754*.

[50]*ChrAlf* 22.

after Ordoño defeated Musa ibn Musa, the leader of the Banu Qasi family of converts to Islam, he had no qualms about accepting the military service of his Muslim son, Lupe.[51]

Again the lack of references to the religious component of the Muslim threat seems curious at first glance. It is perhaps even more curious than in the case of the *Chronicle of 754* because the whole point of the Asturian chronicle is to present the invading forces as a scourge inflicted to punish the Gothic monarchy for its desecration of the church. It would seem to make sense to describe the invasion as the temporary conquest of Christian territory by non-Christian forces and, therefore, to elaborate on the religious distinctions between the two camps.

It is possible that the Asturian chronicler, like his Andalusian counterpart, felt uncomfortable with the fact that the Muslims claimed to worship the same God as the Christians. By not elaborating on Islamic doctrine, he could forestall any doubts that the Christians were, in fact, God's chosen people. This may explain why the only direct reference to Islam in the *Chronicle of Alfonso III* is to the Banu Qasi's practice of the 'Muhammadan rite'. This way of referring to the religion of the Banu Qasi, and of the Muslims as a whole, made it sound almost pagan.

But the choice of narrative pattern in and of itself could account for the chronicler's reticence about Islam. In the scourge stories of the Old Testament, the religious identities of the protagonist and especially the antagonist are subsumed into their identities as opposing nations: it is 'Israelites versus Chaldeans' more than 'Jews versus pagans'. The Goths, like the Israelites, are depicted as a people with a special relationship to God, a relationship that is expressed primarily in political terms. The Muslims, like the Chaldeans, are given no independent religious identity, except as a people that is *not* chosen, a people 'raised up' by God to chastise the errant Goths by temporarily depriving them of their homeland. Looked at this way, there was no more reason for the Asturian chronicler to be specific about the beliefs of the Muslims than for the author of the book of Jeremiah to expound on the religion of the Chaldeans. It was not the Muslims that he was describing, but a scourge,

---

[51]*ChrAlf* 26.

the characteristics of which were determined more by the author's understanding of the metaphor than his actual knowledge of Islam.

JOHN OF BICLARO, *CHRONICLE*

(Prologue)

Victor, bishop of the church of Tunnuna of the province of Africa,[1] has recorded the chronology of years past. We have carefully added to it those events that have followed since the time that he wrote.

Bishop Eusebius of the church of Caesarea,[2] the priest Jerome, known throughout the entire world,[3] Prosper, that most religious man,[4] and Bishop Victor of the church of Tunnuna in Africa, have woven together the history of practically all peoples with the greatest brevity and diligence, bringing the accumulation of years up to our own age, and passing on, for our understanding, those things which happened in the world. We, in turn, with the assistance of our Lord Jesus Christ and for the sake of informing those who will come after us, have taken pains to record, using a concise format, those events which have occurred in our own times. Some of those events we have witnessed faithfully with our own eyes, while others we have learned from the reports of trustworthy individuals.

1. In the fifteenth indiction, as it is reported,[5] Justinian[6] died and the younger Justin, his nephew, was made emperor of the Romans.

---

[1]Victor of Tunnuna (d. post-567). The precise location of Tunnuna (one of several orthographic variants of Victor's see to be found in the extant manuscripts of the chronicle as well as in Isidore's *De viris illustribus* 49) within the Roman province of Africa is unknown. The late fifth-century *Nomina episcoporum provinciae proconsularis*, which lists the sees under the jurisdiction of Carthage, includes "Temnonensis". Campos. p. 102.

[2]Eusebius of Caesarea (c. 260-c. 340).

[3]Jerome (c. 340-420).

[4]Prosper of Aquitaine (c. 390-c. 463).

[5]Here John is referring to the last entry in Victor's chronicle. The indiction is a chronological unit of fifteen years used by the Romans.

[6]Justinian I (527-65).

2. Justin the younger, the fifty-third emperor of the Romans, ruled for eleven years.[7] In the first year of his reign, Justin removed those points which had been approved in contradiction to the synod of Chalcedon and he introduced the creed of the 150 holy fathers who had gathered at Constantinople—which had been laudably approved by the synod of Chalcedon—to be recited by the people in every Catholic church prior to the Lord's Prayer.[8]

3. When the Armenians and the Iberians,[9] who had received the faith as a result of the preaching of the apostles of Christ, were compelled by Chosroes, the emperor of the Persians,[10] to worship idols,[11] they rejected such an impious command and handed themselves, along with their provinces, over to Rome. This broke the peace treaty between the Romans and the Persians.[12]

---

[7] Justin II (565-78).

[8] One of many episodes in the complicated history of Trinitarian struggles in the east. Justin's predecessor, Justinian, had attempted (in 553) to placate Monophysite bishops by condemning as Nestorian the so-called 'Three Chapters' of the Council of Chalcedon (451). In the process, he alienated others, including the bishop of Rome, who regarded the decisions of the ecumenical councils as firm and binding. Justin reconfirmed the Chalcedonian position. For more information on the controversy, see: Judith Herrin, *The Formation of Christendom* (Oxford, 1987), pp. 119-27. The First Council of Constantinople met in 381.

[9] A reference to the inhabitants of Iberia Caucasi (as opposed to Iberia Hispaniae), located in the Caucasus mountain region north of Armenia.

[10] Chosroes I, Sasanian emperor (531-79).

[11] Chosroes attempted to impose Zoroastrianism on these subject territories.

[12] Justinian's effort to reconstitute the Roman empire in the west required that he come to terms with Chosroes in the east. The last of these treaties, which included a large annual payment to Chosroes, was signed in 562. When Justin succeeded to the throne, he decided against continuing the payments. This, and the rivalry for control of Armenia, which was strategically located between the two empires, led to the termination of the treaty. George Ostrogorsky, *History of the Byzantine State*, tr., Joan Hussey, rev. ed. (New Brunswick, NJ, 1969), p. 79.

IN THE SECOND YEAR OF THE AFOREMENTIONED RULER (568)[13]

4. In the royal city,[14] the patricians Aetherius and Addaeus[15] sought to bring about the death of Justin, not with the sword, but by means of a poison administered by his doctors. They were detected and sentenced to death. The first was devoured by beasts. The second was burned to death.

5. Justin,[16] son of the patrician Germanus and cousin of the emperor Justin, was killed in Alexandria by a faction loyal to the empress Sophia.

6. At this time, Athanagild,[17] king of the Goths in Spain, came to the end of his life and Liuva[18] was elevated as king in his place.

IN THE THIRD YEAR OF THE EMPEROR JUSTIN (569)

7. The Garamantes,[19] desiring to be associated with the peace of the Roman state[20] and the Christian faith, requested as much through their envoys. Both requests were granted immediately.

8. Theodore, the prefect of Africa, was killed by the Moors.[21]

---

[13] The parenthetical dates are meant only to clarify John's references to the 'years of the emperors'. They do not necessarily correspond to the currently accepted dates for the events listed under each heading.

[14] *In regia urbe*, that is, in Constantinople. The chroniclers will refer to Toledo, the 'royal city' of the Visigothic monarchy of Spain, in the same way.

[15] J.B. Bury, *A History of the Later Roman Empire from Arcadius to Irene (395 A.D. to 800 A.D.)*, 2 vols. (London, 1889), 2:71.

[16] This Justin had been the emperor Justin's chief rival for the throne. Germanus was Justinian's cousin.

[17] Athanagild (551-68).

[18] Liuva I (568-73).

[19] A people living in the Garama region (southwestern Libya).

[20] John prefers to use *Romana rei publica* when referring to the Roman empire. I have translated this as the 'Roman state' throughout.

[21] The *Mauri* were the inhabitants of the Roman province of Mauretania (northwest Africa).

9. The Maccuritae[22] received the faith of Christ at this time.

10. In the third year of the emperor Justin, Leovigild,[23] the brother of King Liuva, was appointed king of Hispania Citerior[24] while his brother was still living. He received in marriage Gosuintha, the widow of Athanagild,[25] and wonderfully restored to its former boundaries the province of the Goths, which by that time had been diminished by the rebellions of various men.

IN THE FOURTH YEAR OF THE EMPEROR JUSTIN, WHICH WAS THE SECOND YEAR OF KING LEOVIGILD (570)

11. Theoctistus, *magister militum*[26] of the province of Africa, was overcome by the Moors in battle and killed.

12. King Leovigild laid waste the region of Bastetania[27] and the city of Málaga, defeating their soldiers, and returned victorious to his throne.

13. The emperor Justin waged war against the the Avars[28] in Thrace through Tiberius, the *comes excubitorum*.[29] Tiberius returned victorious to Constantinople.

---

[22]A people living in the Oursenis region (north-central Algeria). Charles Diehl, *L'Afrique Byzantine: Histoire de la domination Byzantine en Afrique (539-709)*, 2 vol. (Paris, 1896), 1:327-8.

[23]Leovigild (569-86).

[24]A Roman geographical unit corresponding roughly to the eastern half of the Iberian peninsula. The other half was referred to as Hispania Ulterior.

[25]This was Leovigild's second marriage. His first wife, whose name is unknown, was the mother of Hermenegild and Reccared. Thompson, p. 64.

[26]Literally, 'master of the soldiers'. The *magistri militum* were the regional commanders of the Roman legions. *Magister militiae* appears as a variant, though I have rendered all such references in the *magister militum* form.

[27]The region around the city of Baza (Basti) between Málaga and Cartagena, which had been occupied by imperial troops during the reign of Justinian.

[28]Asiatic nomads who succeeded the Gepids and Lombards as invaders of Pannonia (modern Hungary) in the 560s.

14. In the province of Galicia, Miro was made king of the Suevi after Theodemir.[30]

IN THE FIFTH YEAR OF THE EMPEROR JUSTIN, WHICH WAS THE THIRD YEAR OF KING LEOVIGILD (571)

15. The emperor Justin defeated the Persians, making Armenia and Iberia Caucasi Roman provinces. The emperor of the Persians prepared for war through his generals.

16. Amabilis, *magister militum* of Africa, was killed by the Moors.

17. King Leovigild seized Sidonia,[31] that strongest of cities, by night through the treachery of a certain Framidaneus. He executed its garrison and restored the city to the jurisdiction of the Goths.

18. Donatus, abbot of the monastery of Servitanum,[32] was held in high esteem as a worker of miracles.

IN THE SIXTH YEAR OF THE EMPEROR JUSTIN, WHICH WAS THE FOURTH YEAR OF KING LEOVIGILD (572)

19. The kingdom of the Gepids came to an end when they were defeated in battle by the Lombards.[33] King Cunimund died on the battlefield and his treasure in its entirety was taken to the emperor Justin

---

[29]Another military title. Literally, 'count of the guard'.

[30]Miro (570-83). The Suevi were a Germanic people that had crossed the Rhine with the Vandals in 406 and followed them into Spain. They formed a kingdom in the northwestern part of the peninsula until they were finally defeated by Leovigild.

[31]Medina Sidonia.

[32]According to Ildephonsus, Donatus came to Spain from Africa with a number of monks and a library and founded the monastery of Servitanum, the precise location of which is unknown. Ildephonsus, *De viris illustribus* 4.

[33]The Gepids were a Germanic people residing in the Balkans. They were defeated by combined Avar and Lombard forces in 567. A year later the Lombards, who had migrated south from the Baltic coast, began their conquest of Italy.

in Constantinople by Bishop Trasaric of the Arian sect and Reptila, the nephew of Cunimund.

20. King Leovigild seized by night the city of Córdoba, which had rebelled against the Goths a long time before.[34] He slaughtered the enemy troops and made the city his own. He restored many cities and fortresses to the dominion of the Goths, killing a multitude of common people.

21. Miro, king of the Suevi, waged war against the Ruccones.[35]

22. Domninus, bishop of the church of Helna,[36] was held in high esteem.

IN THE SEVENTH YEAR OF THE EMPEROR JUSTIN, WHICH WAS THE FIFTH YEAR OF KING LEOVIGILD (573)
23. King Alboin[37] of the Lombards was killed at night by a faction of his own men loyal to his wife. But his treasure, along with the queen herself, came under the dominion of the Roman state and the Lombards found themselves without king or treasure.

24. At this time King Liuva came to the end of his life and all of Spain and Gallia Narbonensis came together under the rule and power of Leovigild.

---

[34]Córdoba had been in revolt against the Gothic kings ever since the reign of Agila in 550. It is not entirely clear what role the imperial re-settlement of southeastern Spain played in the rebellion. The city may have allied itself to the empire. Thompson, 321-3.

[35]Identity unknown. Probably a Cantabrian people. Thompson, p. 161.

[36]The town of Elne, south of Narbonne, on the Mediterranean coast.

[37]Alboin (565-72). He was responsible for leading the Lombards into Italy in 568.

25. The emperor Justin was stricken with a serious illness.[38] Some thought his infirmity to be the result of a movement of the brain, others, a vexation by demons.

26. In the royal city, a deadly bubonic plague broke out, in the course of which we saw many thousands of people waste away.[39]

27. King Leovigild invaded Sabaria[40] and ravaged the Sappi, bringing the province under his dominion. He made Hermenegild and Reccared, his two sons by his repudiated wife, associates in his rule.

28. Envoys from the Maccuritae came to Constantinople. Offering elephant tusks and a giraffe as gifts to the emperor Justin, they placed themselves on friendly terms with the Romans.

29. After John, Benedict was ordained bishop of the church of Rome.[41] He presided for four years.

30. Masona, bishop of the church of Mérida, was held in high esteem as an exponent of our doctrine.[42]

IN THE EIGHTH YEAR OF JUSTIN, WHICH WAS THE SIXTH OF LEOVIGILD (574)

31. The Persians broke the peace treaties with the Romans. They launched an attack and overcame by force the strongly fortified city of

---

[38] Justin II went insane in early 574.

[39] John's use of the first person plural reminds the reader that he was in Constantinople at the time of the outbreak. He returned to Spain about 576.

[40] Precise location unknown.

[41] John III (561-74). Benedict I (575-9).

[42] *Vitas sanctorum patrum Emeretensium* 5. By 'our' doctrine, John means Catholic as opposed to Arian Christianity.

Dara.[43] After slaughtering a multitude of Roman soldiers, they entered the city and emptied it of people.

32. At this time King Leovigild entered Cantabria. He overcame and killed the invaders of the province, seized Amaya, and restored the province to his dominion.

33. The emperor Justin made Tiberius—whom we said above was the *comes excubitorum*—Caesar[44] and shortly after elevated him to the imperial dignity, with the title *princeps reipublicae*.

34. On Tiberius' first day as Casesar, the bubonic plague subsided in the royal city.

IN THE NINTH YEAR OF THE EMPEROR JUSTIN, WHICH WAS THE SEVENTH YEAR OF KING LEOVIGILD (575)

35. Chosroes, emperor of the Persians, advanced with a great army to devastate the territory of the Romans. Against him Tiberius sent Justinian,[45] a general of the Roman army and *magister militum* of the East. He prepared for battle and on the plains which are located between Dara and Nisibis,[46] he attacked with a fierce assault. He had with him some very powerful peoples, which are known as the Herinan[47] in their barbarian language, and he overcame the Persian emperor in battle. Turning in flight with his army, Chosroes made for his camp and the victorious Justinian laid waste the territory of the province of Persia, sending the spoils back to Constantinople in triumph.[48] The twenty-four elephants—among other things—provided a great spectacle to the

---

[43]In northern Mesopotamia.
[44]Tiberius was appointed Caesar in late 574 due to Justin's mental incapacity.
[45]The son of the Justin mentioned in Biclaro 5.
[46]In northern Mesopotamia.
[47]Precise identity unknown.
[48]*Cambridge Medieval History* 2 (1936), p. 274.

Romans in the royal city. The booty taken by the Romans was sold along with a multitude of Persians, resulting in no small profit to the public finances.

36. King Leovigild entered the Aregensian mountains[49] and led away Aspidius, the lord of the region, along with his wife, children, and treasure, bringing the region under his power.

37. Aramundarus, king of the Saracens,[50] came to Constantinople with his clan and hastened to the prince Tiberius with gifts from barbarian lands. He was received kindly by Tiberius and was permitted to return to his native land, laden with splendid gifts.

IN THE TENTH YEAR OF THE EMPEROR JUSTIN, WHICH WAS THE EIGHTH YEAR OF KING LEOVIGILD (576)
38. Baduarius, son-in-law of the emperor Justin, was defeated in battle by the Lombards in Italy. Not long after, he came to the end of his life there.

39. Romanus, son of the patrician Anagastus and *magister militum*, captured the king of the Suani.[51] He took him, along with his treasure, his wife, and his children, to Constantinople and brought his province under the dominion of the Romans.

40. King Leovigild harassed the territory of the Suevi in Galicia, but at King Miro's request, conveyed by envoys, Leovigild granted them peace for a short time.

---

[49] Near Orense in Galicia.
[50] In Arabia.
[51] In the Caucasus mountain region.

41. In Thrace the Sclaveni[52] overran many Roman cities, leaving them empty of people.

42. The Avars deceitfully set up blockades, making the coasts of Thrace very dangerous for sailors to navigate.

43. After Benedict, Pelagius the younger was ordained bishop of the Roman church.[53] He presided for eleven years.

44. In the eleventh year of Justin's reign, he ended his days and Tiberius obtained the empire for himself.

45. Tiberius, the fifty-fourth emperor of the Romans, ruled for six years.[54]

IN THE FIRST YEAR OF THE IMPERIAL RULE OF TIBERIUS, WHICH WAS THE NINTH YEAR OF THE REIGN OF LEOVIGILD (577)

46. The Avars devastated Thrace and besieged the royal city from the long wall.

47. King Leovigild entered Orespeda[55] and seized cities and fortresses in the same province, making it his own. Not long after, in the same place, the Goths suppressed a revolt of the common people and after that Orespeda was held in its entirety by the Goths.

---

[52] A Slavic people inhabiting the territory north of the Danube (modern Rumania).
[53] Pelagius II (579-90).
[54] Tiberius I Constantine (578-82).
[55] In southeastern Spain, west of Cartagena.

IN THE SECOND YEAR OF THE EMPEROR TIBERIUS, WHICH
WAS THE TENTH YEAR OF KING LEOVIGILD (578)

48. Gennadius, the *magister militum* in Africa, ravaged the Moors.[56]
He defeated in battle that most powerful king Garmul, who had already
killed the three previously named commanders of the Roman army, and
killed him with the sword.

49. Tiberius appointed Maurice, the *comes excubitorum*, to be the
magister militum of the East and sent him to resist the Persians.

50. The Romans waged a disastrous war against the Lombards in Italy.

51. With tyrants destroyed on all sides and the invaders of Spain
overcome, King Leovigild had peace to reside with his own people. He
founded a city in Celtiberia, which he named Recopolis after his son.[57]
He endowed it with splendid buildings, both within the walls and in the
suburbs, and he established privileges for the people of the new city.

52. The priest John of the church of Mérida was held in high esteem.

IN THE THIRD YEAR OF THE EMPEROR TIBERIUS, WHICH WAS
THE ELEVENTH YEAR OF KING LEOVIGILD (579)

53. The Avars were expelled from the territory of Thrace but they
seized parts of Greece and Pannonia.

54. King Leovigild gave the daughter of King Sigibert of the Franks to
his son Hermenegild in marriage and gave him part of the province to
rule.[58]

---

[56]Paul Goubert, *Byzance avant l'Islam*, 2 vol. (Paris, 1965), 2:182-4.

[57]That is, his son Reccared. It is believed to have been located northeast of Toledo.

[58]Sigibert I was king of the Austrasian Franks (561-75). His daughter was named Ingundis,
whose mother, Brunechildis, was the daughter of the Gothic king Athanagild. Ingundis'

55. With Leovigild thus ruling in peace and quiet, secure from external enemies, a domestic quarrel arose. For in that same year, his son Hermenegild, with a faction loyal to the queen Gosuintha,[59] seized power illegitimately and broke out in open revolt in the city of Seville. He made other cities and fortresses rebel with him against his father, causing greater destruction in the province of Spain—to Goths and Romans alike—than any attack by external enemies.

56. Novellus, bishop of Complutum,[60] was held in high esteem.

IN THE FOURTH YEAR OF TIBERIUS, WHICH WAS THE TWELFTH YEAR OF LEOVIGILD (580)

57. Maurice, the *magister militum* of the East, waged war against the Persians. He defeated a multitude of Persians and wintered in the east.

58. King Leovigild assembled a synod of bishops of the Arian sect in the city of Toledo and amended the ancient heresy with a new error, saying, 'Those coming from the Roman religion to our Catholic faith[61] ought not to be baptized, but ought to be cleansed only by means of the imposition of hands and the receiving of communion,[62] and be given the "Glory to the Father through the Son in the Holy Spirit"'.[63] By means of this seduction, many of our own inclined toward the Arian doctrine out of self-interest rather than a change of heart.

---

brother, Childebert II (575-96), was Sigibert's successor as the Austrasian king. Thompson, p. 65.

[59] The reasons for the queen's involvement are unclear. The role and timing of Hermenegild's conversion have been much discussed. See: Thompson, pp. 76-8 and Collins, *Early Medieval Spain*, pp. 45-9.

[60] Alcalá de Henares.

[61] A reference to Arianism from the perspective of an Arian.

[62] Rebaptism had posed a serious obstacle to Catholics who might otherwise have considered converting to Arianism.

[63] The Arian liturgical form of the 'Gloria'. Leovigild's pronouncements were also published in a book that was subsequently condemned at the Third Council of Toledo (589). Vives, p. 119.

IN THE FIFTH YEAR OF TIBERIUS, WHICH WAS THE THIRTEENTH YEAR OF LEOVIGILD (581)

59. The Lombards in Italy elected one of their own people, by the name of Authari,[64] to be king. At this time, the Roman soldiers were completely destroyed and the Lombards seized for themselves the territory of Italy.

60. The Sclaveni devastated Illyricum and Thrace.

61. King Leovigild seized part of Vasconia[65] and founded the city which is called Victoriacum.[66]

62. The emperor Tiberius gave his daughter in marriage to Maurice, *magister militum* of the East.

IN THE SIXTH YEAR OF TIBERIUS, WHICH WAS THE FOURTEENTH YEAR OF LEOVIGILD (582)

63. Tiberius came to the end of his life and Maurice was made emperor of the Romans in his place.

64. Maurice, the fifty-fifth emperor of the Romans, ruled for twenty years.[67]

65. King Leovigild raised an army to subdue his rebel son.

---

[64] Authari (584-90).
[65] The territory inhabited by the Basques, east of Cantabria.
[66] Probably modern Vitoria.
[67] Maurice (582-602).

IN THE FIRST YEAR OF THE EMPEROR MAURICE, WHICH WAS
THE FIFTEENTH YEAR OF KING LEOVIGILD (583)

66. After assembling his army, King Leovigild surrounded the city of
Seville and trapped his rebel son with a very tight siege. King Miro of the
Suevi came to relieve Seville in support of Hermenegild and there he
ended his days. His son Eboric[68] succeeded him as king of the province
of Galicia. Meanwhile King Leovigild afflicted the city first with hunger,
then with the sword, and finally with a blockade of the Baetis river.[69]

IN THE SECOND YEAR OF THE EMPEROR MAURICE, WHICH
WAS THE SIXTEENTH YEAR OF LEOVIGILD (584)

67. Leovigild restored the walls of the ancient city of Italica,[70] which
proved a great misfortune for the people of Seville.

68. At this time Audeca[71] illegitimately seized the kingship of the
Suevi in Galicia and received in marriage Siseguntia, the widow of King
Miro. He deprived Eboric of the kingship and made him a monk.

69. King Leovigild entered Seville by force after his son Hermenegild
had fled to imperial territory.[72] Leovigild captured the cities and
fortresses that his son had seized and not long after apprehended him in
the city of Córdoba. He exiled Hermenegild to Valencia, depriving him of
his rule.

70. The emperor Maurice paid the Franks to attack the Lombards and
thus inflicted no small damage on both peoples.

---

[68]Eboric (583-4).
[69]The Roman name for the Guadalquivir.
[70]Near Seville.
[71]Audeca (584-5).
[72]*Ad rem publicam.*

71. Abbot Eutropius of the monastery of Servitanum, a disciple of the holy Donatus, was held in high esteem.

IN THE THIRD YEAR OF MAURICE, WHICH WAS THE SEVENTEENTH YEAR OF LEOVIGILD (585)

72. Maurice waged war on the Persians through his generals.

73. King Leovigild devastated Galicia, deprived its captured King Audeca of his rule, and brought the people, treasure, and land of the Suevi under his own power. He made Galicia a province of the Goths.

74. Hermenegild was killed in the city of Tarragona by Sisbert.[73]

75. The Franks entered Gallia Narbonensis with their army, wanting to seize it. Leovigild sent his son Reccared to meet them. He drove back the army of the Franks and the province of Gallia Narbonensis was freed from their attacks. Reccared captured two fortresses, one peacefully, and one in battle, along with a great multitude of men. In a violent battle, King Reccared attacked and seized the fortress called Ugernum, which is located very securely on the edge of the Rhone river.[74] He returned victorious to his father and his country.

76. Deprived of his rule, Audeca was tonsured and dignified with the honour of the priesthood, after having held that of the kingship. He suffered no doubt because he had made himself king in place of Eboric, son of King Miro. He was exiled to the city of Beja.

---

[73]It is not clear what Hermenegild, apparently confined to Valencia, was doing in Tarragona. Gregory I treated the Catholic prince as a martyr of Arian persecution in his *Dialogues* (3.31).

[74] With the dealth of Hermenegild, Reccared became the undisputed heir. This may acount for this reference to 'King Reccared' a year before his accession.

77. Malaric illegitimately seized power in Galicia, in his attempt to be king. He was immediately defeated by King Leovigild's generals and was captured and presented in chains to Leovigild.

78. Bishop Leander of Seville was held in high esteem.[75]

IN THE FOURTH YEAR OF THE EMPEROR MAURICE, WHICH WAS THE EIGHTEENTH YEAR OF LEOVIGILD (586)

79. Authari, king of the Lombards, met the Romans in battle and overcame them. He seized the territory of Italy, destroying a multitude of Roman soldiers.

80. In this year King Leovigild ended his days and his son Reccared[76] took up the royal sceptre with tranquillity.

IN THE FIFTH YEAR OF MAURICE, RULER OF THE ROMANS, WHICH WAS AUSPICIOUSLY THE FIRST YEAR OF KING RECCARED (587)

81. Maurice made his son Theodosius—whose mother was the daughter of the emperor Tiberius—Caesar.

82. Pelagius the younger died and Gregory succeeded to the episcopate of the church of Rome.[77] He presided for fifteen years.

83. The Romans ravaged the Lombards with the help of the Franks and brought part of the province of Italy back under their power.

84. Sisbert, the murderer of Hermenegild, died a disgraceful death.

---

[75] Leander of Seville (c. 577-c. 600).
[76] Reccared I (586-601).
[77] Gregory I (590-604).

85. In the first year of his reign, in the tenth month, Reccared became a Catholic, with the help of God. He then approached the priests of the Arian sect with words of wisdom and converted them to the Catholic faith through reason rather than force. He thus restored all the people of the Goths and the Suevi to the unity and peace of the Christian church. The Arian sects came over, by means of divine grace, to Christian doctrine.

86. Desiderius, a general of the Franks, was attacked and defeated by the Gothic generals of King Reccared. He died on the battlefield, along with a multitude of Franks.

87. King Reccared generously restored the property that had been seized by his predecessors and incorporated into the fisc. He became a founder and patron of churches and monasteries.

IN THE SIXTH YEAR OF MAURICE, WHICH WAS THE SECOND OF RECCARED (588)
88. Some of the Arians, Segga, Bishop Sunna, and others, were detected trying to seize power illegitimately.[78] Of the guilty men, Sunna was forced into exile and Segga was sent to Galicia after having his hands cut off.

89. Maurice made his son Theodosius—whom we said above had been named Caesar—emperor of the Romans.

IN THE SEVENTH YEAR OF MAURICE, WHICH WAS THE THIRD OF KING RECCARED (589)
90. A conspiracy on the part of Bishop Uldida, who plotted with Queen Gosuintha, was revealed to Reccared and it became known that the two had rejected the communion of the Catholic faith which they had only

---

[78]Sunna was the Arian rival of Masona, the Catholic bishop of Mérida. See: Biclaro 30, and *Vitas sanctorum Emeretensium* 5.

pretended to assume. When this evil deed was uncovered, Uldida was condemned to exile, and Gosuintha, who had always been hostile to Catholics, came to the end of her life at that time.

91. The army of the Franks, sent by King Gunthchramn[79] under the general Boso, came to Gallia Narbonensis and set up their camp next to the city of Carcasonne. Claudius, the commander of Lusitania,[80] was ordered by King Reccared to intercept him and hastened to that place. When the battle began, the Franks were put to flight, their camp was seized, and the army was slaughtered by the Goths. In this battle divine grace and the Catholic faith—which King Reccared along with the Goths had faithfully taken up—were at work, since it is not a difficult thing for our God to give victory to a few over the many. For the general Claudius, with scarcely three hundred men, is known to have put to flight almost 60,000 Franks and to have cut down the greater part of them with the sword. Not unworthily is God praised in our own times for having intervened in this battle. In a like manner, many years ago, God is known to have destroyed, at the hand of the general Gideon with only three hundred men, many thousands of Midianites who were attacking the people of God.[81]

IN THE EIGHTH YEAR OF THE EMPEROR MAURICE, WHICH WAS THE FOURTH YEAR OF KING RECCARED (590)

92. A holy synod of seventy-two bishops from all of Spain, Gallia Narbonensis, and Galicia, was assembled in the city of Toledo by order of King Reccared.[82] That most Christian Reccared was present at the synod, offering to the bishops the account of his own conversion and the confession of faith of all the priests and the Gothic people, written in a

---

[79]Gunthchramn, Frankish king of Burgundy (561-93).
[80]The southwestern-most of the Roman provinces in Spain, the greater part of which falls within the borders of modern Portugal.
[81]Judges 7.
[82]The Third Council of Toledo (589). Vives, pp. 107-45.

book with his own hand, and making known all things pertaining to the profession of the orthodox faith. The holy synod of bishops decreed that this account was to be added to the canonical records. The most important part of the synodal business was in the hands of holy Leander, bishop of the church of Seville, and Eutropius, most blessed abbot of the monastery of Servitanum. Reccared was, as we have said, present at the holy council, reviving in our own times the image of the ruler Constantine the Great,[83] whose presence illumined the holy synod of Nicaea, or that of the most Christian emperor Marcian,[84] in whose presence the decrees of the Council of Chalcedon were established. The Arian heresy first appeared and was rightly condemned in the city of Nicaea, but its roots were not cut. In Chalcedon, Nestor and Eutyches,[85] as well as their patron Dioscorus, were condemned along with their particular heresies. In the present holy synod of Toledo, at the command of King Reccared, finally the perfidy of Arius—after so much killing of Catholics and slaughtering of innocents—has been cut at its very roots so that it will not sprout up again, a Catholic peace having been bestowed upon churches everywhere. This accursed heresy—about which it is written: 'May temptation depart from the house of the Lord'—grew out of the Alexandrian church through the priest Arius[86] and was uncovered by the holy bishop Alexander[87] of the same city. By the judgement of the 218 bishops present at the Council of Nicaea, in Constantine's twentieth year as emperor, Arius and his error received synodal condemnation. Yet, after that, the heresy stained not only the eastern and western regions, but ensnared in its perfidy the south as well as the north and even the islands.

---

[83]Constantine (306-37), who presided over the Council of Nicaea (325).

[84]Marcian (450-7), who presided over the Council of Chalcedon (451).

[85]Nestor (d. c. 451) and Eutyches (d. 454) were condemned as heretics for their extreme (and opposite) views about the relationship between the human and divine natures of Christ.

[86]Arius (d. c. 336) was condemned as a heretic for his Trinitarian views that subordinated the Son to the Father.

[87]Alexander of Alexandria (d. 328). He was succeeded by Athanasius.

So from Constantine's twentieth year as emperor, when the Arian heresy first emerged, to the eighth year of Maurice, emperor of the Romans, which is the fourth year of the reign of Reccared, 280 years passed, during which time the Catholic church struggled against the attack of this heresy. But by the grace of God the church finally emerged the victor because it is built upon a rock.[88]

93. At this same time, while Omnipotent God was restoring the peace of his church and rendering the poison of this foul, old heresy completely harmless, the emperor of the Persians received the faith of Christ and established peace with the emperor Maurice.[89]

94. While Reccared ruled in orthodox peace and quiet, domestic conspiracies spread. For a member of his own private household, indeed a provincial general by the name of Argimund, wanted to seize power illegitimately from King Reccared and, if successful, deprive him of his kingdom and his life. But the machinations of his wicked counsel were detected and he was seized and bound in iron chains. His accomplices, having confessed their impious conspiracy, were tried and executed in an appropriate manner. But Argimund, who had desired to take possession of the kingdom, was first interrogated while being whipped, then his head was shaved in disgrace and his right hand was cut off. He was paraded, sitting on an ass, through the city of Toledo, as an example to all, teaching servants not to be presumptuous to their lords.

(Epilogue)

Adding up all of the years:

---

[88]Matthew 16:18; 7:24.
[89]Maurice supported Chosroes (II) in his bid to rule Persia in exchange for the ceding of key parts of Armenia and Mesopotamia to the empire. The rumor of Chosroes' conversion seems to be based on this treaty and his reported marriage to a Christian. Ostrogorsky, p. 80. Campos, p. 149.

From Adam to the flood: 2,242.

From the flood to Abraham: 942.

From Abraham to the nativity of our Lord Jesus Christ: 2,015.

There are altogether: 5,199.

From the nativity of our Lord Jesus Christ to the eighth year of Maurice, emperor of the Romans: 592.

Altogether, from Adam to the eighth year of Maurice, emperor of the Romans, which is the fourth year of Reccared, king of the Goths, that is, era 630 (592), there are 5,791 years.

ISIDORE OF SEVILLE, *HISTORY OF THE KINGS OF THE GOTHS*

(Prologue:) In Praise of Spain

Of all the lands from the west to the Indies, you, Spain, O sacred and always fortunate mother of princes and peoples, are the most beautiful. Rightly are you now the queen of all provinces, from which not only the west but also the east borrows its shining lights. You are the pride and the ornament of the world, the most illustrious part of the earth, in which the Getic people are gloriously prolific, rejoicing much and flourishing greatly.

Indulgent nature has deservedly enriched you with an abundance of everything fruitful. You are rich with olives, overflowing with grapes, fertile with harvests. You are dressed in corn, shaded with olive trees, covered with the vine. Your fields are full of flowers, your mountains full of trees, and your shores full of fish. You are located in the most favourable region in the world; neither are you parched by the summer heat of the sun, nor do you languish under icy cold, but girded by a temperate band of sky, you are nourished by fertile west winds. You bring forth the fruits of the fields and the wealth of the mines, as well as beautiful and useful plants and animals. Nor are you to be held inferior in rivers, which the brilliant fame of your fair flocks ennobles.

Alpheus yields to you in horses and Clitumnus in cattle, although Alpheus, regarded as sacred for his Olympic victories, exercised fleet chariots on the track of Pisa, and Clitumnus once sacrificed great oxen as victims on the Capitol.[1] You do not need the fields of Etruria,[2] for you

---

[1] The Alpheus is a river in the Peloponnese. According to tradition, it flowed through an underwater channel to Sicily. There, as Isidore observed in his *Etymologies* (14.6.33), it watered a pasture renowned for the quality of its horses. These horses were famous for their success at the Olympic games held near Pisa and Elis in the Peloponnese. The Clitumnus is a small river in the Umbria region of Italy. Isidore referred to it in his *Etymologies* (13.13.6)

have more abundant pasturage, nor do you marvel at the groves of Molorchus,[3] for you have palm trees in plenty, nor do your horses run less swiftly than the Elian chariots.[4] You are fertile with overflowing rivers, you are tawny with gold-flowing torrents, you have a spring that fathered a horse. You have fleeces, dyed with native purples, that glow with Tyrian crimson.[5] You have rock, shining in the shadowy depths of the mountains, that is aflame with radiance like the sun.

You are as rich in purple-clad rulers[6] as you are in native gems, and, rich in imperial gifts, you are as wealthy in adorning your princes as you are blessed in producing them. Rightly did golden Rome, the head of the nations, desire you long ago. And although this same Romulean[7] power, initially victorious, betrothed you to itself, now it is the most flourishing people of the Goths, who in their turn, after many victories all over the world, have eagerly seized you and loved you: they enjoy you up to the present time amidst royal emblems and great wealth, secure in the good fortune of empire.[8]

On the Origin of the Goths

1. The people of the Goths is a very ancient one. Some suspect that they originated from Magog, son of Japheth, on the basis of the similarity

---

as a lake known for the size of the cattle that grazed nearby. These cattle were the preferred victims of sacrifices to the gods. Isidore's intention throughout his famous prologue (known as the *Laus Spaniae*) was to compare Spain favourably to the Italy and Greece of the Roman poets, using their own points of classical reference.

[2] In west-central Italy.

[3] Molorchus was a poor farmer who, according to tradition, entertained Heracles.

[4] 'Elian chariots' is a poetic way of referring to the chariots of the Olympic games, held near Elis.

[5] A reference to the famous Tyrian dyes that were extracted from a particular kind of mollusk.

[6] A reference to the Roman emperors who were born in Spain.

[7] Referring to Romulus, the traditional founder of Rome.

[8] For a detailed look at the way in which Isidore crafted the *Laus Spaniae* from classical and patristic sources, see Rodríguez Alonso, pp. 113-9. Pacatus' *Panegyric to the Emperor Theodosius* (4) seems to have been Isidore's principal model.

of the last syllable, or they conclude the same from the prophet Ezechiel.[9]
But in the past, learned men were in the habit of calling them 'Getae'
rather than 'Gog' or 'Magog'.[10]

2. However, the meaning of their name in our language is *tectum*, by
which is meant strength, and rightly so, for there was never a people on
earth that succeeding in exhausting the Roman empire to such an extent.
These were the ones that Alexander himself declared should be avoided,
the ones that Pyrrhus feared, the ones that made Caesar shudder.[11] In the
past, many centuries ago, they employed military leaders and later kings,
whose reigns it is fitting to review quickly and in succession, weaving
together the information extracted from the histories about their identities
and deeds.

3. In the twelfth year before the beginning of the era,[12] when the consul
Pompey and Gaius Caesar were engaged in civil war in their efforts to
seize control of the republic, the Goths came to offer help to Pompey,
ready to fight against Caesar in Thessaly. When the Ethiopians, Indians,
Persians, Medes, Greeks, Scythians, and the rest of the eastern peoples
were summoned to fight against Julius, the Goths resisted him more
powerfully than the rest. It is said that Caesar, shaken by the number and
valour of the Goths, considered fleeing, but nightfall put an end to the
battle.

---

[9]Ezechiel 38-9.

[10]See pp. 16-17 above.

[11]Orosius 1.16.2. I have noted throughout the principal sources, in so far as they can be
known, from which Isidore culled his information. For a more complete treatment, see:
Rodríguez Alonso, pp. 75-92.

[12]The 'era' system of chronology, which Isidore borrowed from Hydatius, begins with the
year 38 B.C.E. The civil war that Isidore is describing took place in 49-8 B.C.E.

4. In the era 294 (256), in the first year of the emperors Valerian and Gallienus,[13] the Goths came down from the Alps,[14] where they lived, and devastated Greece, Macedonia, Pontus, Asia Minor, and Illyricum.[15] Of these they held Illyricum and Macedonia for almost fifteen years. They were then defeated by the emperor Claudius and they returned to their homeland.[16] The Romans placed a gold statue in the Capitol and a gold medallion portrait in the forum in honour of Claudius Augustus, for having removed such a powerful people from within the boundaries of the empire.[17]

5. In the era 369 (331), in the twenty-sixth year of the emperor Constantine,[18] the Goths invaded the land of the Sarmatians[19] and overran the Romans with a very large army. With their overwhelming strength, they slaughtered the people and plundered the land. Constantine himself organized the battle line against them, and, after an enormous struggle, he managed to defeat the Goths, driving them over the Danube.[20] Constantine shone with the glory of his valour against many peoples, but he was most renowned for his victory over the Goths. The Romans, with the acclamation of the senate, honoured him with public praise because he had beaten such a people and because he had restored the territory of the empire.

---

[13]Valerian (253-9). His son, Gallienus, served as co-emperor and then succeeded Valerian (259-68).

[14]More precisely, from the area west and north of the Black Sea.

[15]In 257, the Goths attacked the southern shore of the Black Sea and Asia Minor by land and sea. In 268 they launched another attack into the Aegean. Wolfram. pp. 51-3.

[16]Claudius II (268-70) defeated the Goths at the battle of Naissus (in the Balkans) in 269. He was the first of the emperors to assume the honorary title, 'Gothicus'.

[17]Eusebius-Jerome, pp. 303-4.

[18]Constantine (306-37).

[19]A rival barbarian confederation in the Balkans.

[20]After this confrontation in 332, Constantine negotiated the earliest documented *foedus* (treaty) with the Goths, whereby the Goths received an annual payment in exchange for supplying soldiers to the empire. Wolfram, p. 62.

6. In the era 407 (369), in the fifth year of the emperor Valens,[21] Athanaric became the first to accept the governance of the people of the Goths, ruling for thirteen years.[22] He launched a very cruel persecution against the faith, wanting to exert himself against those Goths among his people who were found to be Christians. He made many of them martyrs because they would not agree to sacrifice to idols. Athanaric was afraid to kill the rest because they were so numerous, so, after afflicting them with great persecution, he gave them permission, or rather forced them, to leave his kingdom and move into Roman territory.[23]

7. In the era 415 (377), in the thirteenth year of the emperor Valens, the Goths in Istria[24] were divided against themselves under Athanaric and Fritigern,[25] afflicting each other with mutual slaughter. But Athanaric overcame Fritigern with the support of the emperor Valens. In recognition of this assistance, Athanaric sent envoys with gifts to this same emperor and requested teachers so that they might receive instruction in the Christian faith.[26] Valens, however, had deviated from the truth of the Catholic faith and was caught up in the perversity of the Arian heresy.[27] So he sent heretical priests and, with evil persuasion, added the Goths to the error of his doctrine.[28] With this pernicious seed,

---

[21]Valens (364-78).

[22]Athanaric (d. 381).

[23]Orosius 7.32.9.

[24]The hinterland of the northernmost coast of the Adriatic.

[25]A rival of Athanaric.

[26]It was actually Fritigern, not Athanaric, who negotiated with Valens, offering to convert to Christianity in exchange for imperial support against his rival. This began a struggle between the two Gothic leaders that was never really resolved. The advance of the Huns in the mid-370s encouraged most of the Goths to follow Fritigern, who had the best chance of convincing Valens to let them cross the Danube into the empire. Athanaric and his followers weathered the storm somewhere in the Balkans. Wolfram, pp. 70-3.

[27]Between the initial condemnation of Arianism at the Council of Nicaea (325) and the final one at the Council of Constantinople (381), a number of emperors, including Valens, supported the Arian cause.

[28]Orosius 7.33.19.

he infused a deadly poison into this excellent people, who held and maintained for a long time the error which they had trustingly accepted.

8. Then their bishop Ulfilas fashioned Gothic letters and rendered the scriptures of the New and Old Testaments into this language.[29] As soon as they had letters and the law, the Goths constructed for themselves churches of their doctrine, holding, in accordance with Arius, the following doctrine with regard to divinity. They believed the Son was inferior in majesty to the Father and subsequent to Him in eternity. They held that the Holy Spirit was not God and that it did not proceed from the substance of the Father, but was created through the Son, and dedicated to the service of both and subject in obedience to both. They asserted that there was one person and one nature of the Father, another of the Son, and finally another of the Holy Spirit, so that they did not worship the one God and Lord in accordance with the tradition of holy scripture, but rather three gods in accordance with the superstition of idolatry. They maintained this evil blasphemy over the passage of time and the succession of kings for 213 years. Finally, mindful of their salvation, they renounced this rank perfidy and came through Christ's grace to the unity of the Catholic faith.

9. In the era 416 (378), in the fourteenth year of the emperor Valens, the Goths, who had previously expelled the Christians from their homeland, were themselves, along with their king Athanaric, expelled by the Huns. Crossing the Danube, they surrendered—though without laying down their arms—because they were unable to withstand the power of

---

[29] Ulfilas (c. 311-c. 383) was a Gothic Christian who was consecrated as 'bishop of the Christians in the Gothic lands' by Eusebius around 341. He worked as a missionary throughout his life, periodically threatened on the one hand by the pagan Athanaric and on the other by changing definitions of Trinitarian orthodoxy. He attended the Council of Constantinople in 381 as an Arian and probably died two years later. Wolfram, pp. 76-8, 84.

the emperor Valens, and received Thrace to inhabit.[30] But when they found themselves oppressed by the Romans against the tradition of their own liberty, they were forced to rebel. They ravaged Thrace with sword and fire, and destroyed the army of the Romans, burning to death Valens himself, who, after having been wounded by a spear, had fled to a certain villa. He who had surrendered such beautiful souls to the eternal flames deserved to be burned alive by the Goths.[31]

10. In that battle, the Goths came upon the earlier Gothic confessors whom they had expelled from their own land a short time before on account of their faith, and wanted to join them as partners for the distribution of booty. When the Gothic confessors did not acquiesce, some were killed. Others, dwelling in mountainous places and constructing various types of refuges for themselves, not only persevered as Catholic Christians, but remained on good terms with the Romans, who had welcomed them some time before.

11. In the era 419 (381), in the third year of the emperor Theodosius the Spaniard,[32] Athanaric arranged a treaty of friendship with Theodosius and headed for Constantinople. There, fifteen days after he had been honourably received by Theodosius, he died.[33] With their king dead, the Goths, considering the friendliness of the emperor Theodosius, negotiated a treaty and placed themselves under Roman dominion.[34]

---

[30] The agreement was worked out between Valens and Fritigern in 376.

[31] The Battle of Adrianople (378). Ammianus Marcellinus was the first to record that Valens was burned. Later Christian historians regarded it as poetic justice. Wolfram, pp. 120-8. Isidore's source: Orosius 7.33.19.

[32] Theodosius (379-95).

[33] Theodosius received Athanaric, who had lost virtually all of his authority over the Goths, in 381. A short time later, Athanaric died. The Goths under Fritigern were still 'at large.' Wolfram, pp. 73-4.

[34] Orosius 7.34.6-7. The *foedus* signed in 382 gave the Goths tax-free land along the Danube in the Balkans in exchange for military service to the empire. Wolfram. pp. 73-4, 132-3.

12. In the era 420 (382), in the fourth year of the emperor Theodosius, the Goths rejected the protection of the Roman treaty and established Alaric as their king. They regarded it as demeaning to be subject to Roman power and to follow those whose laws and dominion they had previously spurned and from whose alliance they had removed themselves after being victorious in battle.[35]

13. In the era 437 (399), in the fourth year of the emperors Honorius and Arcadius,[36] though the Goths had violently divided their kingdom into two parts, split between Alaric and Radagaisus,[37] they nevertheless came to an agreement regarding the destruction of the Romans and, with this common purpose, decided on a plan to divide the various regions of Italy between themselves for plundering.

14. In the era 443 (405), in the tenth year of the emperors Arcadius and Honorius, Radagaisus, king of the Goths, of Scythian stock, dedicated to the cult of idolatry and wild with fierce barbaric savagery, destructively invaded parts of Italy with 200,000 soldiers, vowing, in contempt of Christ, to offer the blood of the Romans to his gods if he should be victorious.[38] His army was surrounded by the Roman general Stilicho in a mountainous part of Tuscany and was overcome by hunger rather than by the sword. Afterwards the king himself was captured and killed.

15. In the era 447 (409), in the fifteenth year of the emperor Arcadius, with Radagaisus dead, Alaric, his partner in the kingship—who was a Christian in name, though a heretic by profession—grieved that so many Goths had been killed by the Romans. So he did battle against Rome to

---

[35] Alaric I (395-410) led the Goths out of their settlement in the Balkans in 395 and headed south toward Constantinople.

[36] Arcadius (395-408) and Honorius (395-423).

[37] Radagaisus' identity is not clear. He appears to have been the leader of a separate, perhaps Ostrogothic, contingent of Goths. Wolfram, pp. 168-70.

[38] Orosius 7.37.4-5.

avenge his people's blood. Laying siege to Rome, he burst in with a highly destructive attack.[39] Thus the City, victor over all peoples, succumbed, vanquished by the victories of the Goths; subjected and captive, it served them. But the Goths were conspicuous for the mercy they showed in Rome. They had previously sworn an oath that if they managed to enter the city, they would not send any Romans found in churches[40] back out into the devastation of the city. Indeed after this vow, when they stormed the city, everyone who fled to the dwellings of the saints was spared death or captivity.[41] Even those who were outside of the churches of the martyrs, who simply uttered the names of Christ and the saints, were spared by the Goths with similar mercy.

16. Although the plundering of the rest of the population by the enemy forces was undeniable, the frightfulness of their savagery was nonetheless restrained. As the Goths were rushing through the city amidst that devastation, a certain powerful man came upon a consecrated virgin of advanced years. He advised her, in a decent manner, that if she had with her anything of gold or silver, she should hand it over. In good faith she brought out what she had. While he was marvelling at the form and beauty of the vases, a product of that ancient opulence of the Romans, the virgin said, 'These vases were entrusted to me from the sanctuary of the Apostle Peter: take them, if you dare. I dare not give such sacred things to the enemy'. Terrified at the mention of the Apostle's name, the Goth reported the incident to his king through a messenger. The king immediately ordered everything to be returned with the greatest reverence to the sanctuary of St Peter, saying that he was waging war against the Romans, not against the Apostles.[42]

---

[39] Alaric's famous sack of Rome (410).
[40] *In locis Christi.*
[41] Orosius 7.39.1.
[42] Orosius 7.39.3-6.

17. And so the virgin returned, honoured with the most reverent ceremonies, and with her came all who had associated themselves to her, carrying those gold and silver vases on their heads while singing hymns and songs, with armed guards placed everywhere by order of the king for their protection. Bands of Christians ran out of their hiding places everywhere at the sound of the singing voices. Even pagans ran and mingled with them, pretending to be Christians so that they too might escape destruction in this disaster.[43]

18. At that time the Goths in Rome captured Galla Placidia, daughter of the ruler Theodosius, and sister of the emperors Arcadius and Honorius,[44] along with an immense amount of gold. Obtaining great riches from the Romans, they left on the third day, having burned and demolished various parts of the city.[45] From there, boarding ships, they decided to cross over to Sicily, which is separated from Italy by a narrow strait. Risking a hostile sea, they lost much of their army. But so great was the glory of having captured Rome, that by comparison they figured that they had suffered no damage in that storm; thus they compensated the losses from the shipwreck with the victory. The death of Alaric followed shortly after. He died in Italy in the twenty-eighth year of his reign.

19. In the era 448 (410), the sixteenth year of the emperors Honorius and Arcadius, with Alaric dead after the sack of the City, Athaulf was placed over the Goths in Italy as king and ruled for six years.[46] In the fifth year of his reign, he left Italy and went to Gaul. He took as his wife Galla Placidia, the daughter of the emperor Theodosius, whom the Goths had captured in Rome. Some believed that this fulfilled Daniel's prophecy, which says that the daughter of a king of the south would marry a king of

---

[43] Orosius 7.39.7-10.

[44] Orosius 7.40.2.

[45] Orosius 7.39.15.

[46] Athaulf (410-16). According to Orosius (7.43.5), Athaulf toyed with the idea of replacing 'Romania' with 'Gothia'. Isidore left this out of his account.

the north, but that no children from his line would survive.[47] The same prophet added more in the following passage, saying, 'Nor shall his line continue'.[48] Indeed no son was born from that womb who might have succeeded to his father's kingdom.[49] After Athaulf left Gaul and went to Spain, his throat was cut by one of his own men in Barcelona in the midst of a friendly conversation.[50]

20. In the era 454 (416), in the twenty-second year of the emperors Arcadius and Honorius, Sigeric was elected after Athaulf as king over the Goths.[51] Most eager to make peace with the Romans, he was soon killed by his own men.[52]

21. In the above era and year, Wallia succeeded Sigeric and ruled for three years.[53] He was made king by the Goths for the sake of war, but he was directed by divine providence toward peace. As soon as he began to rule, he entered into a treaty with the emperor Honorius. He honourably restored to him his sister, Galla Placidia, who had been captured by the Goths at Rome. He also promised the emperor to fulfil every military obligation on behalf of the Roman state.[54] Then he was summoned to Spain by the patrician Constantius.[55]

22. Wallia inflicted great slaughter on the barbarians in the name of Rome. He annihilated in battle all of the Silingian Vandals in Baetica. He

---

[47]Hydatius 57.

[48]Daniel 11:6.

[49]Their only child, a son, died shortly after birth. Wolfram, p. 163.

[50]Hydatius 60.

[51]Sigeric (416).

[52]Orosius 7.43.9.

[53]Wallia (416-19).

[54]Orosius 7.43.10, 12. The treaty, signed in 416, specified that the Goths were to receive much-needed food supplies in exchange for returning Galla Placidia to Constantinople and ridding Spain of other barbarian groups. Wolfram, p. 171.

[55]Constantius was, at that time, the *magister militum* of the West.

destroyed the Alans, who used to rule the Vandals and the Suevi, to such an extent that, once their king Atax was killed, the few who survived forgot the name of their kingdom and subjected themselves to the rule of King Gunderic of the Vandals who lived in Galicia.[56] Ending the war in Spain, Wallia planned to cross over to Africa with the naval forces he had equipped. But battered by a serious storm in the straits of the sea of Cádiz[57] and mindful of the shipwreck that occurred under Alaric, he decided to avoid the dangers of navigation and return to Gaul.[58] In recognition of his victory, the emperor gave to him Lower Aquitaine,[59] along with certain cities of the neighbouring provinces, all the way to the ocean.[60]

23. In the era 457 (419), the twenty-fifth year of the emperors Honorius and Arcadius, King Wallia died and Theoderid succeeded him as king, ruling for thirty-three years.[61] Not content with the Aquitainian kingdom, he rejected the peace treaty with Rome and seized many Roman cities adjacent to his territory. He attacked Arles, that most noble city of Gaul, and besieged it with great force. But he ultimately withdrew from the siege, not unpunished by the forces of Aëtius, commander of the Roman army.[62]

---

[56]Hydatius 63, 67, 68. The Vandals, Alans, and Suevi crossed the Rhine frontier in 406 and subsequently made their way through Gaul to Spain.

[57]The Straits of Gibraltar.

[58]Orosius 7.43.11, 12. Wallia's attempt to cross over to Africa was. like Alaric's abortive expedition to Sicily, motivated by the search for sufficient grain supplies. It actually predated, and precipitated, the agreement with Constantinople. Wolfram, p. 170.

[59]The Roman administrative unit of Aquitania II, which corresponds roughly to the western half of modern France.

[60]Prosper 1271. Constantius settled the Goths there in 418 after the Spanish campaigns. This was the beginning of the so-called Visigothic kingdom of Toulouse. Wolfram, p. 172-3.

[61]Theoderid, also known as Theodoric I (419-51).

[62]Prosper 1290. Aëtius was the *magister militum* of the West. The Goths, beginning in 425, regularly pressured Arles but never succeeded in conquering it. Wolfram, p. 175.

24. After Aëtius had been removed from his military command by order of the emperor Valentinian,[63] Theoderid subjected the city of Narbonne to a long siege and famine. Again he was put to flight, this time by Litorius, commander of the Roman army,[64] with the assistance of the Huns. But although Litorius initially won victories against the Goths, later, deceived by the signs of demons and the words of soothsayers, he recklessly entered into war with the Goths. As a result the Roman army was lost and Litorius died miserably in defeat. It was clear from this that the multitude that perished with him would have accomplished a great deal if it had chosen to rely on faith rather than the deceptive portents of demons.[65]

25. Theoderid negotiated peace again with the Romans and, with the help of the Roman commander Aëtius, engaged in battle in the Catalaunian fields against the Huns, who were devastating the Gallic provinces, savagely killing the inhabitants and destroying many cities. There Theoderid died in battle, but, as it turned out, he died victorious. The Goths, fighting under Thorismund, the son of Theoderid, attacked so violently that between the first and last battles close to 300,000 men were killed.[66]

26. Many signs in the heavens and on earth preceded these events, prodigies signifying a particularly cruel war. Earthquakes occurred constantly, the moon was obscured in the east, and from the west an

---

[63]Valentinian III (425-54).

[64]Prosper 1324. Litorius was actually one of Aëtius' lieutenants. The siege of Narbonne occurred in 437. Wolfram, p. 176.

[65]Litorius was a pagan, prompting Isidore to moralize his defeat at the hands of a Christian (albeit Arian) Goth. Prosper (1335), Isidore's source, wrote: 'It was clear from this that the army that perished with him would have accomplished a great deal it had chosen to rely on better advice rather than his foolhardiness'. Isidore's rendering made the religious issue more explicit.

[66]Hydatius 150. The famous battle of the Catalaunian Fields (451), near Troyes, marked the beginning of the end of the threat to Europe posed by the Huns.

enormous comet appeared and shone for some time. In the north the sky reddened, having the appearance of blood or fire, permeated with bright lines shaped like golden spears.[67] It is not surprising that the slaughter of so many men in battle should have been divinely heralded by such a display of signs.

27. The Huns, slaughtered almost to the point of extermination, left Gaul with their king Attila and fled into Italy, attacking certain cities. There they suffered, afflicted partly by hunger and partly by punishments sent from heaven. Moreover, the emperor Marcian[68] sent an army and cut down the Huns with a violent attack. Greatly weakened, the Huns returned to their own homeland, where Attila, their king, died shortly after.[69]

28. Immediately there arose among Attila's sons a great struggle to secure the kingship.[70] And so the Huns, who had already been diminished due to such great destruction, began to annihilate each other with their own swords. It should be noted that, while every battle is damaging to the peoples involved, the Huns actually served a purpose by perishing. This is because they had been raised up for the discipline of the faithful, just like the nation of the Persians.[71]

29. For they were the rod of the wrath of God. As often as his indignation went forth against the faithful, he punished them with the Huns, so that, chastened by their suffering, the faithful would force themselves away from the greed of this world and from sin and claim the inheritance of the celestial kingdom. This people of the Huns was so

---

[67]Hydatius 149.
[68]Marcian (450-7).
[69]Hydatius 154. Attila died in 453.
[70]Prosper 1370.
[71]A reference to the Persian conquest (or 'scourge') of Judah in the sixth century B.C.E.

savage that when they felt hungry during a battle, they would pierce a horse's vein and assuage their appetite by drinking its blood.

30. In the era 490 (452), in the first year of the emperor Marcian, Thorismund, the son of Theoderid, was elevated to the kingship for one year.[72] Fierce and injurious from the very outset of his reign, he inspired enmity and did many things in an arrogant manner. He was killed by his brothers Theodoric and Frideric.[73]

31. In the era 491 (453), in the second year of the emperor Marcian, Theodoric succeeded his dead brother as king and ruled for thirteen years.[74] Because Theodoric had, along with the Gauls, offered aid to the emperor Avitus in his rise to the imperial dignity,[75] he had Avitus' support when he entered Spain from Aquitaine with a huge army.[76] Rechiarius, king of the Suevi,[77] hastened to meet him with a great number of soldiers, twelve miles from the city of Astorga, at the river which is called Orbigo. As soon as the battle had begun, Rechiarius was defeated: some of his soldiers were killed, others were captured, and many more were put to flight. Ultimately Rechiarius himself fled. Wounded by a spear, and lacking the protection of his army, he was captured at Oporto and handed over alive to King Theodoric.[78]

32. Once Rechiarius had been killed and those who had survived from the first battle had surrendered—of whom some were killed anyway—the

---

[72]Thorismund (451-3).

[73]Hydatius 156.

[74]Theodoric II (453-66).

[75]Avitus was one of many who held the imperial post in the west in quick succession after the death of Valentinian III (455).

[76]This was the beginning of the Visigothic acquisition of Spain, which would make the kingdom of Toulouse the single largest territorial unit in the west, until the defeat of the Visigoths at the hands of the Franks in 507.

[77]Rechiarius (448-56).

[78]In 457. Hydatius 173, 175.

kingdom of the Suevi was almost destroyed and it almost came to an end. But the Suevi who had remained in the most remote part of Galicia installed Maldras, the son of Massila, as their king and proceeded to restore the kingdom of the Suevi.[79] After Rechiarius was killed, the victor Theodoric moved from Galicia into Lusitania. When he attempted to plunder the city of Mérida, he was terrified by the signs of the holy martyr Eulalia. He hastily retreated along with his entire army and returned to Gaul.[80]

33. A short time later, Theodoric sent one part of his army, under the general Ceurila, to the province of Baetica, and sent the other, under the generals Sumeric and Nepotianus, to Galicia where they plundered and laid waste the land of the Suevi at Lugo. In Gaul, the count and citizen Agrippinus, a rival of the Roman count Aegidius,[81] surrendered Narbonne to Theodoric so as to win the assistance of the Goths.[82] Later, several envoys sent by Remismund, son of King Maldras of the Suevi, came to Theodoric asking for peace and friendship. Theodoric in turn sent back to Remismund arms, gifts, and a woman to have for a wife. Theodoric also sent Salla as an envoy to Remismund. When Salla returned to Gaul, he found that Theodoric had been killed by his brother, Euric.[83]

34. In the era 504 (466), in the eighth year of the emperor Leo,[84] Euric, by means of a crime equal to the one committed by his brother,

---

[79]Maldras (456-60).

[80]Hydatius 181-2. Theodoric II's withdrawal perhaps had more to do with the death of Avitus in 457 and his concern for the security of the kingdom of Toulouse. Wolfram, p. 179.

[81]Aegidius was the *magister militum* appointed by the new emperor in Rome, Majorian (457-61).

[82]In 462.

[83]Hydatius 192, 201, 217, 226, 237.

[84]Leo I (457-74).

succeeded him as king and ruled for seventeen years.[85] As soon as his crime had brought him to power, he sent envoys to the emperor Leo and without delay launched a massive and devastating attack on Lusitania.[86] From there he sent an army which took Pamplona and Zaragoza and subjected northern Spain to his power. He also overthrew, as the result of an invasion by his army, the nobility of the province of Tarraconensis which had fought against him. Returning to Gaul, he seized the cities of Arles and Marseilles in battle and added both to his own kingdom.[87]

35. One day, when the Goths had gathered in assembly, Euric noticed that the weapons which they all held in their hands temporarily changed: the natural appearance of the blade's iron changed colour. Some turned green, some pink, some yellow, and some black.[88] Under King Euric, the Goths began to record their legal statutes in writing whereas previously they had been bound only by tradition and custom.[89] Euric died a natural death in Arles.

36. In era 521 (483), in the tenth year of the emperor Zeno,[90] upon the death of Euric, Alaric, his son, was made king of the Goths in the city of Toulouse, ruling for twenty-three years.[91] Clovis, king of the Franks,[92] coveted the kingdom of Gaul and moved in war against Alaric with the assistance of the Burgundians. He put the army of the Goths to flight and

---

[85] Euric (466-84).

[86] In 468. Hydatius 238.

[87] These campaigns took place in 472-3.

[88] A portent of the Battle of Vouillé described in the next paragraph. Hydatius 243.

[89] For a concise treatment of the Visigothic law codes, see: Collins, *Early Medieval Spain*, pp. 25-9, and Wolfram, pp. 194-7.

[90] Zeno (474-91).

[91] Alaric II (484-507). The *Chronicle of Zaragoza*, which survives only as a fragment, may have provided Isidore with some of the factual basis for *HistGoth* 36-47. but the textual ties between the two are tenuous at best.

[92] Clovis (481-511).

finally overcame the defeated king Alaric at Poitiers and killed him.[93] But when Theodoric, king of Italy,[94] learned of his son-in-law's death,[95] he left Italy at once and routed the Franks. He took the portion of the kingdom that the enemy forces had occupied and restored it to the jurisdiction of the Goths.

37. In the era 544 (506), the seventeenth year of the emperor Anastasius,[96] Gesalic, the son of the previous king, born to a concubine, was made ruler in Narbonne and ruled for four years.[97] Of worthless stock, he excelled only in ill fortune and cowardice. In the end, when Narbonne was seized by Gundobad, king of the Burgundians,[98] Gesalic fled to Barcelona bringing great disgrace upon himself and great destruction upon his men. There he remained until, as a result of his shameful retreat, he was deprived of his authority over the kingdom by Theodoric.

38. From there Gesalic made for Africa, asking for the assistance of the Vandals, hoping to be restored to the kingship. When he was unable to obtain help, he soon returned from Africa and, fearful of Theodoric, headed for Aquitaine. After taking refuge there for one year, he returned to Spain. He engaged in battle with Ebba, a general of King Theodoric, twelve miles from the city of Barcelona but finally turned in flight. Gesalic was captured on the other side of the river Durance in Gaul and was killed. Thus he lost first his honour and then his life.[99]

---

[93] The Battle of Vouillé (507) marked the end of the Visigothic kingdom of Toulouse. But the Goths retained their territory in Spain as well as in Gallia Narbonensis.

[94] Theodoric the Great, king of the Ostrogoths (489-526).

[95] One of Theodoric's daughters had married Alaric II.

[96] Anastasius I (491-518).

[97] Gesalic (507-11).

[98] Gundobad (d. 516).

[99] c. 514.

39. In the era 549 (511), in the twenty-first year of the emperor Anastasius, Theodoric the younger had ruled in Italy for eighteen years. He had been made consul and king of Italy long before by the emperor Zeno in Rome after Odoacer, king of the Ostrogoths,[100] had been killed and his defeated brother Honoulf had fled across the Danube frontier. When King Gesalic of the Goths was killed, Theodoric assumed the kingship of the Goths in Spain for fifteen years, relinquishing it in his lifetime to his grandson Amalric.[101] Returning from there to Italy, he ruled very prosperously for a long time. The dignity of the city of Rome was restored to no small degree by him. He rebuilt its walls, in recognition of which the senate deemed him worthy of a golden statue.

40. In the era 564 (526), in the first year of the emperor Justinian,[102] after Theodoric had returned to Italy, his grandson Amalric ruled for five years.[103] Defeated by Childebert, king of the Franks, at a battle in Narbonne, Amalric fled in fear to Barcelona.[104] Having become contemptible to everyone, his throat was cut by one of his own men and he died.

41. In the era 569 (531), in the sixth year of the emperor Justinian, Theudis was made king in Spain, after Amalric, and ruled seventeen

---

[100]Odoacer was the barbarian commander responsible for deposing Romulus Augustulus, the last of the Roman emperors in the west, in 476. He does not appear to have been an Ostrogoth. In 488, Theodoric the Great, the Ostrogothic king, invaded Italy as an agent of the emperor Zeno. In 493 he captured Odoacer, executed him, and assumed control of Italy.

[101]Theodoric technically ruled the Visigothic kingdom (511-26) as a regent on behalf of his grandson, Amalric, the son of Alaric II and Theodoric's daughter.

[102]Justinian (527-65).

[103]Amalric (511-31).

[104]Childebert I (511-58). Other sources explain that Childebert was upset at the treatment of his sister Chlotild at the hands of her husband Amalric, who was intent on forcing her to abandon her Catholicism for Arianism. Thompson, pp. 11-12.

years.[105] Though he was a heretic, he granted peace to the church, insofar as he gave permission to the Catholic bishops to gather together in the city of Toledo and to legislate openly and freely whatever seemed necessary for the discipline of the church.[106] During the reign of Theudis, the kings of the Franks came to Spain with innumerable forces and ravaged the province of Tarraconensis. The Goths, under the general Theudigisel, closed off the passes into Spain and laid low the army of the Franks, greatly amazed at their own victory. In response to their entreaties and to the offer of a large sum of money, the general provided the remaining enemy troops a path of escape for the period of one day and one night. The miserable crowd of Franks who were unable to pass through within the allotted time were massacred by the swords of the Goths.[107]

42. After this fortunate victory, the Goths undertook an ill-advised campaign across the straits of Cádiz. They crossed over to do battle with the soldiers who had assaulted the city of Ceuta and had expelled the Goths.[108] The Goths initially attacked the fortress with great power. But on the following Sunday they put down their arms so as not to defile the sacred day with fighting. Seizing this opportunity, the opposing forces made a surprise attack and laid low the invading army, trapped as it was between land and sea, so that not a single man escaped death in the ensuing massacre.

---

[105] Theudis, also known as Theodoric III (531-48), was an Ostrogoth who had originally served Theodoric the Great as a general in Spain.

[106] The Second Council of Toledo was actually convened during the reign of Theudis' predecessor, Amalric, in 527. Vives, p. 42.

[107] This was the first recorded Visigothic victory over the Franks (541).

[108] Isidore is referring to imperial soldiers. It is not clear precisely when the Goths had originally taken Ceuta from the Vandals before losing it (534) in Justinian's bid to reconquer the western empire. Theudis' attempt to recapture the city took place in 547. Thompson, p. 15.

43. A short time later, King Theudis met the death that he deserved. He was wounded by a man in the palace who for a long time had been pretending to be insane so as to deceive the king. Artfully feigning madness, he stabbed the ruler. Felled by the wound, Theudis breathed out his angry soul. As his blood gushed forth, he is reported to have extracted an oath from his supporters that no one kill his assailant, saying that he had been justly recompensed for having once provoked and killed his own commander.

44. In the era 586 (548), in the twenty-third year of the emperor Justinian, after Theudis had been killed, Theudigisel was placed over the Goths, ruling for one year.[109] He publicly defiled the marriages of a great many magnates and because of this decided to kill many of them. He was prevented by a band of conspirators in Seville. His throat was cut in the midst of a feast and he died of the fatal wound.

45. In the era 587 (549), in the twenty-fourth year of the emperor Justinian, after Theudigisel had been killed, Agila was made king and ruled for five years.[110] Moving against the city of Córdoba in battle,[111] Agila, in contempt of the Catholic religion, inflicted injury on the church of the most blessed martyr, Acisclus. At the outset of his struggle against the citizens of Córdoba, this profane man polluted the sacred site of Acisclus' tomb with the remains of his enemies and their horses.[112] He thus deserved the punishments unleashed by the saints. Struck in vengeance in the middle of the same campaign, he lost both his son, who was killed there along with a large part of the army, and his remarkably rich treasure.

---

[109]Theudigisel, also known as Theodisclus (548-9).

[110]Agila (549-54).

[111]It is possible that this rebellion in 550 was connected in some way to the recent occupation of North Africa by Justinian's troops.

[112]*Hostiumque ac iumentorum horrore.*

46. Vanquished, Agila fled in wretchedness and fear, reaching Mérida. After a period of time, Athanagild launched a rebellion against him in his desire to assume power. With his military might, Athanagild laid low the army that Agila sent to meet him at Seville. The Goths, seeing that they were destroying themselves and fearing that the imperial army might invade Spain on the pretext of providing assistance,[113] killed Agila in Mérida and handed themselves over to the rule of Athanagild.

47. In the era 592 (554), in the twenty-ninth year of the emperor Justinian, after Agila had been killed, Athanagild held the kingship which he had seized for fourteen years.[114] When he launched the rebellion in his attempt to deprive Agila of power, he requested military assistance from the emperor Justinian. Afterwards, he was unable, despite his efforts, to remove these soldiers from the boundaries of his kingdom. Up until the present day the Goths have struggled against them.[115] But worn down by frequent fighting, they have now been broken and defeated, suffering many losses. Athanagild died a natural death in Toledo and the kingship remained vacant for five months.

48. In the era 605 (567), in the second year of the emperor Justin the younger,[116] Liuva was, after Athanagild, made king of the Goths in Narbonne and ruled for three years.[117] In the second year after he had secured his rule, he established his brother Leovigild not only as his successor, but as his partner in the kingship, appointing him to rule Spain, while he contented himself with the rule of Gallia Narbonensis. Thus the

---

[113]In response to Athanagild's request, imperial troops landed in Spain in 552, followed by a three-year war that ended with Agila's death. In the meantime, the imperial forces occupied Baetica. Thompson, p. 17.

[114]Athanagild (554-68).

[115]Isidore was writing in 625, just after the imperial holdouts in Cartagena had finally been overcome.

[116]Justin II (565-78).

[117]Liuva I (568-73).

kingdom had two rulers, despite the fact that no power willingly accepts a consort. In the succession of reigns, only one year is counted to that of Liuva, the rest are counted to his brother Leovigild.

49. In the era 606 (568), in the third year of the emperor Justin the younger, after Leovigild had obtained the position of king of Spain as well as Gallia Narbonensis, he set about to enlarge the kingdom through warfare and to increase his riches.[118] With the zeal of his army and the concomitant success of his victories, he brilliantly achieved a great deal. He obtained Cantabria and took Aregia. Sabaria was completely conquered by him. Many rebellious cities of Spain yielded to his forces. He put soldiers to flight in various battles and captured certain fortresses which they had seized. Then he laid siege to his son Hermenegild, who was in revolt against his father's rule, and defeated him. Finally, Leovigild waged war against the Suevi and, with marvellous speed, brought their kingdom under the jurisdiction of his people. He extended his power over the greater part of Spain, for previously the people of the Goths had been confined to a small area.[119] But the error of his impiety tarnished the glory his great success.

50. Filled with the madness of Arian perfidy, Leovigild ultimately launched a persecution against the Catholics, sent bishops into exile, and took away many of the revenues and privileges of the churches.[120] By means of these terrible acts, he forced many into the Arian disease. Others he deceived without persecution, enticing them with gold and property. Among the other infections of his heresy, he even dared to rebaptize Catholics, not only laymen but also members of the priestly

---

[118]Leovigild (569-86). For explanatory notes, see the corresponding portions of the *Chronicle* of John of Biclaro.

[119]Isidore culled this information about Leovigild's territorial expansion from Biclaro 27, 32, 36, 55, 66.

[120]Both Thompson (pp. 78-87) and Collins (*Early Medieval Spain*, pp. 50-3) minimize the extent of this persecution.

order, such as Vincent of Zaragoza, who went from being a bishop to an apostate and was thus cast down from heaven into hell.[121]

51. Leovigild was also very destructive to some of his own men, for those whom he saw excelling in nobility and power, he either beheaded or sent into exile. He was the first to enrich the fisc and the first to enlarge the treasury, robbing the citizens and despoiling the enemy. He also founded a city in Celtiberia which he named Recopolis after his son.[122] With regard to the laws, he corrected those which seemed to have been irregularly promulgated by Euric, adding many that had been left out and removing a number of superfluous ones. He ruled for eighteen years and died a natural death in Toledo.

52. In the era 624 (586), in the third year of the emperor Maurice,[123] after Leovigild had died, his son Reccared was crowned king.[124] He was a devout man, very different from his father in his way of life. For while the one was irreligious and had a very warlike disposition, the other was pious and outstanding in peace; while the one was increasing the dominion of the Gothic people through the arts of war, the other was gloriously elevating the same people by the victory of the faith. For in the very beginning of his reign, Reccared adopted the Catholic faith, recalling all the peoples of the entire Gothic nation to the observance of the correct faith and removing the ingrained stain of their error.[125]

53. Reccared then convoked a synod of bishops from various provinces of Spain and Gallia Narbonensis to condemn the Arian heresy.

---

[121]In his *De viris illustribus* (43), Isidore referred to a book written by Bishop Severus of Málaga, criticizing Vincent for his conversion to Arianism.

[122]Biclaro 51.

[123]Maurice (582-602).

[124]Reccared (586-601). For explanatory notes, see the corresponding portions of the *Chronicle* of John of Biclaro.

[125]Biclaro 85.

This most religious ruler attended the council himself and confirmed its deeds with his presence and signature. He abjured, along with all of his subjects, the false teaching of Arius, which the people of the Goths had held up to that time. He then proclaimed the unity of the three persons in God, the Son born consubstantially from the Father, and the Holy Spirit proceeding inseparably from the Father and Son and being the one Spirit of them both, making them all one.[126]

54. With the help of his newly received faith, Reccared gloriously waged war against hostile peoples. With the Franks invading Gallia Narbonensis with almost 60,000 soldiers, Reccared sent his general Claudius against them and won a glorious victory. No victory of the Goths in Spain was greater than or even comparable to this one. Many thousands of the enemy were laid low or captured, and the remaining part of the army desperately turned in flight with the Goths following after them, until they were cut down within the boundaries of their own kingdom.[127] Reccared often pitted his strength against the excesses of the Romans[128] and the attacks of the Basques. In these cases, he seemed not so much to be waging wars as to be exercising his people to keep them fit as one would do in the sport of wrestling.

55. The provinces which his father conquered in war, Reccared preserved in peace, administered with equity, and ruled with moderation. He was kind and mild, of remarkable goodness, and he had such a graceful demeanour and so benevolent a heart, that, influencing the minds of everyone, he led even bad men to desire his love. He was so generous that he restored by his own authority the wealth of private citizens and the treasure of the churches which his father had shamefully appropriated to

---

[126]Biclaro 92.
[127]Biclaro 91.
[128]That is, the imperial troops in Spain.

the fisc. He was so merciful that he often reduced the required tribute of his people by a grant of indulgence.

56. Reccared enriched many with gifts and elevated even more with honours. He deposited his wealth among the wretched and his treasures among the impoverished, knowing that the kingship had been conferred on him for this reason, so that he might enjoy it in a salutary manner, attaining a good end from these good beginnings. He crowned the glory of his true faith, which he had held from the beginning of his reign, with a final public confession of penance. He passed away peacefully in Toledo, having ruled for fifteen years.

57. In the era 639 (601), in the seventeenth year of the emperor Maurice, after the death of King Reccared, his son Liuva ruled for two years.[129] Though born of a humble mother, he was famous for the innate quality of his virtue. But Witteric seized power illegitimately and removed this innocent one from the kingship while he was still in the first flower of his manhood. Cutting off Liuva's right hand, Witteric killed him in his twentieth year, the second of his reign.

58. In the era 641 (603), in the twentieth year of the emperor Maurice, after Liuva had been killed, Witteric assumed for seven years the kingship that he had seized during Liuva's lifetime.[130] Though active in the art of war, he never won a victory. For though he often exerted himself in battle against the army of the Romans, he accomplished nothing of particular glory except that he captured through his generals some soldiers at Saguntum.[131] In his life he did much that was unlawful and because he had lived by the sword, he died by the sword. The death of the innocent Liuva did not go unavenged. For Witteric was killed in

---

[129]Liuva II (601-3).
[130]Witteric (603-10). He had been instrumental in suppressing the Mérida-based rebellion of Sunna and Segga. Biclaro 88. Thompson, p. 102.
[131]North of Valencia.

the midst of a meal as the result of a conspiracy. His corpse was removed without ceremony and buried.

59. In the era 648 (610), in the sixth year of the emperor Phocas,[132] Gundemar ruled for two years after Witteric.[133] He devastated the Basques during one expedition and besieged the army of the Romans on another. He died a natural death in Toledo.

60. In the era 650 (612), in the second year of the emperor of Heraclius,[134] Sisebut was called to the royal dignity after Gundemar, and ruled for eight years and six months.[135] At the beginning of his reign he forced the Jews into the Christian faith, indeed acting with zeal, 'but not according to knowledge',[136] for he compelled by force those who should have been called to the faith through reason.[137] But, as it is written, 'whether through chance or truth, Christ is to be proclaimed'.[138] Sisebut was nonetheless eloquent in speech, informed in his opinions, and imbued with no little knowledge of letters.[139]

61. Sisebut was famous for his military example and his victories. Dispatching an army, he brought the rebellious Asturians under his dominion. Through his generals, he overcame the Ruccones,[140] who were protected by steep mountains on all sides. He had the good fortune to

---

[132]Phocas (602-10).

[133]Gundemar (610-12).

[134]Heraclius (610-41).

[135]Sisebut (612-21).

[136]Romans 10:2.

[137]The forced conversions were later criticized by the ecclesiastics, including Isidore, who gathered at the Fourth Council of Toledo in 633. For an overview of Visigothic policies vis-à-vis the Jews, see: Collins, *Early Medieval Spain*, pp. 129-45.

[138]Philippians 1:18.

[139]Some letters, poems, and a saint's life have survived. Sisebut also patronized Isidore, who in turn dedicated some of his works to the king. Thompson, p. 163.

[140]See: Biclaro 21.

triumph twice over the Romans in person and to subject certain of their cities in battle. He was so merciful in the wake of victory that he ransomed many of the enemy, who had been reduced to slavery and distributed as booty by his army, using his own treasure for their redemption. Some claim that he died a natural death, others, that he died as the result of an overdose of some medication. He left a small son, Reccared,[141] who was recognized as king for a few days after the death of his father until his own death intervened.

62. In the era 659 (621), in the tenth year of the emperor Heraclius, the most glorious Suinthila received the royal sceptre by divine grace.[142] Having risen to the position of general under King Sisebut, he captured Roman fortresses and overcame the Ruccones. After he had ascended to the summit of royal dignity, he waged war and obtained all the remaining cities which the Roman army held in Spain. With amazing fortune, he triumphed even more gloriously than had the other kings. He was the first to obtain the monarchy of the entire kingdom of Spain north of the straits, which had not been achieved by any previous ruler. He increased his claim to fame in that struggle by capturing two patricians, one by cunning, the other by force.

63. At the beginning of his reign, Suinthila also launched an expedition against the Basques who had invaded the province of Tarraconensis. There the mountain peoples were struck with such terror at his coming that they immediately threw down their weapons and freed their hands for prayer, submitting their necks to him as suppliants and giving him hostages, as if aware of his rightful jurisdiction. They built the city of Ologicus[143] for the Goths with their own taxes and labour, promising to

---

[141] Reccared II (621).

[142] Suinthila (621-31).

[143] Precise location unknown.

be obedient to Suinthila's rule and dominion and to carry out whatever they were ordered to do.

64. Beyond this reputation for military glory, there were in Suinthila many virtues of royal majesty: faith, prudence, industry, keen scrutiny in judicial matters, and a vigorous concern for government. He was generous to all in his munificence, and quite prompt in his mercy toward the poor and needy. He was thus not only the ruler of the people, but was also worthy to be called the father of the poor.

65. His son, Riccimir, made a partner in his rule, presently shares the throne with his father. Even in childhood the splendour of his royal nature shines, so that in him the image of his father's virtues may be seen both in his merits and in his physical appearance. Let us implore the ruler of heaven and humankind on his behalf, that, just as Riccimir is now, by his father's consent, co-ruler, so, after his father's long reign, may he prove worthy to succeed him as king. Computing the years of the kings of the Goths from the accession of King Athanaric to the fifth year of the most glorious ruler Suinthila, the kingdom of the Goths is found to have lasted, with divine favor, for 256 years.[144]

Recapitulation

66. The Goths originated from Magog, the son of Japheth, and have been proved to have a common origin with the Scythians. That is why they are not much different in name: with one letter changed and one removed, 'Getae' becomes 'Scythae'. They were inhabitants of the icy peaks of the west and they lived on the mountain slopes with other peoples. Driven from their territory by the attack of the Huns, they

---

[144]According to Isidore (*HistGoth* 6), Athanaric began his rule in era 407, that is, 369 C.E. Adding 256 years to 369 brings us to 625, the fifth year of Suinthila's reign (621-31) and the date of Isidore's authorship of (at least this part of) the *History of the Kings of the Goths*.

crossed the Danube and surrendered themselves to the Romans. But when they could no longer tolerate their unjust treatment, they took up arms in their wrath, invaded Thrace, devastated Italy, besieged and captured Rome, entered Gaul and, bursting through the Pyrenees, reached Spain, where they established their homeland and dominion.

67. The Goths are agile by nature and quick to understand. They have a strong sense of duty. Robust in bodily strength and lofty in stature, they are impressive in their carriage and demeanour. Skilful with their hands, they are also impervious to wounds, just as the poet says about them, 'The Getae despise death while praising the wound'.[145] They waged such great wars and had such a reputation for glorious victory, that Rome itself, the conqueror of all peoples, submitted to the yoke of captivity and yielded to the Gothic triumphs: the mistress of all nations served them like a handmaid.

68. All of the peoples of Europe feared them. The barriers of the Alps gave way before them. The Vandals, widely known for their own barbarity, were not so much terrified by the presence of the Goths as put to flight by their renown. The Alans were extinguished by the strength of the Goths. The Suevi, too, forced into inaccessible corners of Spain, have now experienced the threat of extermination at the hands of the Goths: the kingdom which they had held in idle lethargy, they have now lost at a shameful cost. It seems quite amazing how they managed to retain up to the present day that which they have now given up without any show of resistance.

69. But who could express the great strength of the Getic people? Since the right to rule is rarely granted to peoples who choose to rely on entreaties and gifts, the Goths opted to secure their liberty in battle rather than through negotiations. For whenever the need to fight presents itself,

---

[145]Unknown reference.

the Goths always prefer to go to battle than to resort to treaties. In the arts of war they are quite spectacular, fighting on horseback not only with spears but with javelins. Though they enter battle on horseback as well as on foot, they trust more in the swift running of their horses. As the poet says, 'where the Getan goes, he goes with his horse'.[146]

70. They love to exercise themselves with weapons and compete in battle. They hold contests in sport every day. Until recently they lacked experience in only one aspect of fighting: they had no desire to wage naval battles. But ever since King Sisebut took up the royal sceptre, they have made such great and successful progress that they now go forth with their forces on sea as well as on land. Subjected, the Roman soldier now serves the Goths, whom he sees being served by many peoples and by Spain itself.

---

[146]Unknown reference.

THE CHRONICLE OF 754

1. In the era 649 (611), Heraclius became the fifty-seventh to be crowned emperor of the Romans.[1] He ruled for thirty years, 5,838 years having elapsed since the beginning of the world. For love of the noble virgin, Flavia[2]—to whom he was betrothed in Africa before assuming power, but who had been deported from Libya to Constantinople by order of the emperor Phocas—Heraclius, along with Nicetas, the *magister militum*, stirred up a rebellion against Phocas. After devising a plan against the government, Heraclius assembled a fleet and Nicetas an army and they made the following pact with one another: that whichever of the two reached Constantinople first would be crowned emperor there.[3] Coming up from Africa with his fleet, Heraclius arrived at the royal city more swiftly by sea. The Byzantines surrendered the captive Phocas, who had resisted for a short time in battle, to the shining sword. As soon as Heraclius saw Phocas' throat cut, he was immediately elevated as emperor.

2. Nicetas, penetrating the desert wilderness, attacked Egypt, Syria, Arabia, Judaea, and Mesopotamia, fiercely pursuing the Persians and restoring imperial dominion over these provinces. But the Persians, hastening forth from their homeland, confident in their power and numbers, incited the neighbouring provinces to rejoin them.[4] The son of

---

[1]Heraclius (610-41).

[2]Known in Greek sources as Fabia or Eudokia. The emperor Phocas (602-10) held Fabia and Epiphania (Heraclius' mother) hostage in expectation of trouble from the exarchate of Africa. The exarch, Heraclius senior (Epiphania's husband), delegated the task of executing the rebellion to his son, Heraclius, and Nicetas, the son of his general, Gregory. Bury, 2:203-5.

[3]The plan was presumably for Heraclius to attack Constantinople by sea while Nicetas neutralized Alexandria.

[4]Damascus fell to the Persians in 613, Jerusalem in 614 (with the Holy Cross taken as booty to Ctesiphon), and Alexandria in 619.

Chosroes,[5] king of the Persians, rebelliously fled his father and offered his services to the Roman ruler, vigorously promising to surrender all of Persia to the emperor.[6]

3. Heraclius assembled an army consisting of all of his armed forces and set out to attack Persia.[7] Informed of this turn of events by messenger, Chosroes went forth to meet Heraclius and to resist him with the entire Persian army. When Heraclius and Chosroes, thus threatening one another, came into close contact on the same field, they agreed that two warriors, one selected from each army, would engage in man-to-man combat, and that the two armies, separated from each other, would regard as preordained whatever outcome they witnessed. This they agreed under God, establishing, as we said, by their own reason and counsel, that with regard to these two champions, whatever the result of their efforts might be, as revealed through the exercise of their swords, it would be binding on their fellows, who would by all means respect the sign and without delay grant to the victor the right to rule, submitting their necks to his yoke. Chosroes, puffed up in the manner of the Philistines, escorted a certain bastard, like another Goliath, out to the fight. Terrified, all of Heraclius' soldiers stepped back. But Heraclius, trusting in the assistance of the Lord, fell on the enemy and killed him with a single throw of his javelin.[8]

4. With the Persians erupting in flight, Heraclius pursued them with the sword as far as the city of Susa, which is their capital and the centre of their power. When Chosroes' kingdom was finally destroyed and handed over to imperial dominion, the people did honour, not to God, but to

---

[5]Chosroes II (589-628).
[6]This seems to be a reference to a later event. In 628, when Chosroes died. his son Siroes sued for peace. Ostrogorsky, p. 103.
[7]There were two Persian campaigns: 623-5 and 627-8.
[8]Compare this with the account of the duel in the continuation of the *Chronicle of Fredegar*, pp. 52-3.

Heraclius, and he, accepting this with pride, returned to Constantinople.[9] Finally, after appropriately rewarding his army, he gloriously ascended his throne in triumph.[10]

5. They say that afterward many things pertaining to this event began to come to Heraclius in his dreams as a warning that he would be ravaged mercilessly by rats from the desert. He was also forewarned by astrological readings of the course of the stars.[11]

6. Heraclius, as we have said, subdued the rebellious Persians and fought to restore the imperial territories. But seduced, it is said, by the praise of his people who heaped the honour of victory not on God but on Heraclius himself, he was terrified by the rebuke which was being foretold in his recurring visions.

7. In the time of Heraclius, in the era 653 (615), in his fourth year as emperor, the Slavs seized Greece.

8. The Saracens rebelled in the era 656 (618), the seventh year of the emperor Heraclius, and appropriated for themselves Syria, Arabia and Mesopotamia, more through the trickery than through the power of their leader Muhammad. They devastated the neighbouring provinces, proceeding not so much by means of open attacks as by secret incursions.[12] Thus by means of cunning and fraud rather than power, they

---

[9]The chronicler here refers to Constantinople as *Roma*, that is, the 'New Rome', built under Constantine.

[10]Shortly after his return, Heraclius went to Jerusalem to preside over the restoration of the Holy Cross. Ostrogorsky, pp. 103-4.

[11]Compare the *Chronicle of Fredegar* (p. 54), in which Heraclius is depicted as a devotee of astrology, though there is no mention of rats. See Kedar (p. 28) for references to (later) Byzantine sources that elaborate similar themes.

[12]Muhammad occupied Mecca in 630. Before his death in 632, many tribes throughout Arabia had accepted his rule. Abu Bakr (632-4) consolidated Muslim power in Arabia and began moving into Persian territory. Umar (634-44) presided over the extension of Islamic

incited all of the frontier cities of the empire which finally rebelled openly, shaking the yoke from their necks. In the era 656 (618), the seventh year of the emperor Heraclius, the warriors invaded the kingdom, which they forcefully appropriated with many and various consequences.

9. After fighting many battles against the Saracens, Theodore, the brother of the emperor Heraclius, withdrew from combat to increase and consolidate his forces, at the admonition of his brother, who was mindful of the prophecy of the rats. But with the lumps in their throats swelling more each day, such fear spread amongst the Roman legions that when they engaged in battle at the town of Gabata, their army was totally destroyed. Theodore himself was slain and departed this world.[13] Then the Saracens, firmly confident and free from fear after such a slaughter of noble men, established their rule in Damascus, the most splendid city in Syria.

10. When Muhammad had completed his tenth year, Abu Bakr, from his own tribe, succeeded to the throne. He too launched major attacks against the power of the Romans and the Persians.[14]

11. So, as we have acknowledged, in the era 653 (615), the fourth year of the emperor Heraclius, the Arabs rebelled and in the era 656 (618) they attacked Theodore, the emperor's brother, wearied by almost ten years of war and ultimately overextended in battle, and killed him as he bitterly resisted them. They openly established their kingdom in Damascus,

---

rule in Syria and Egypt, as well as Persia. Marshall G. S. Hodgson, *The Venture of Islam: Conscience and History in a World Civilization*, 3 vol. (Chicago, 1974), 1:189, 200, 205.

[13]The sources do not agree about the role of Heraclius' brother in the defence of imperial Syria. Some Arabic sources have him leading the Greek forces that were decisively beaten at Yarmuk in 636. Some Greek sources, on the other hand, depict him as the commander of the earlier battle at Gabata (Gabitha or al-Jabiya) and identify the leader of the Greeks at Yarmuk as a different Theodore, the imperial treasurer. Fred McGraw Donner, *The Early Islamic Conquests* (Princeton, 1981), pp. 134-5, 145.

[14]Abu Bakr (632-4).

supported by their prophet Muhammad and free now from fear of the Roman name. After the tenth year of Muhammad's rule had expired in the era 666 (628), in the seventeenth year of the emperor Heraclius, the Arabs chose the aforementioned Abu Bakr, of Muhammad's own tribe, in his place, and wielded their swords against Persia,[15] which had been abandoned by the Roman empire. Abu Bakr ruled for almost three years, all the while powerfully waging war.

12. In the time of Heraclius, in the era 669 (631), in his twentieth year as emperor, and in the beginning of the fourteenth year of the Arabs,[16] Abu Bakr came to the end of his life, after ruling for three years, and left Umar on the throne.[17] Taking over the entire government from his predecessor, Umar rigidly maintained his rule over the people for ten years. He subjected Alexandria, that most ancient and prosperous metropolitan city of Egypt, to the yoke of tribute.[18] When he had carried the triumph of victory away from all parts east as well as west, waging war on both land and sea, he was struck by the sword of one of his own slaves while he was in prayer. He ended his life, having completed, as we have said, his tenth year of rule.

13. In the time of Heraclius, in the era 650 (612), in his second year as emperor, when the Saracens were still under tribute to the Romans, Sisebut, a wise man of profound learning, became king of Spain and ruled for eight years.[19] He conquered the Roman cities throughout Spain. He compelled the Jews to enter the Christian faith.

---

[15]The battle of Qadisiyyah, south of the Euphrates (637). Shortly afterwards, the Persian capital of Ctesiphon fell to the Arabs.

[16]From this point on, the chronicler supplemented his imperial dating with the Muslim method, which counts the years since the Hegira (Muhammad's flight from Mecca to Yathrib-Medina) in 622.

[17]Umar (634-44).

[18]In 642. Alexandria was reconquered by imperial forces in 645 only to fall again to the Muslims a year later.

[19]Sisebut (612-21).

14. The church proclaimed the venerable Helladius,[20] resplendent in the fame of his sanctity, as metropolitan bishop of the see of the royal city of Toledo. Spain also celebrated the illustrious teacher Isidore, metropolitan bishop of Seville.[21] In the seventh year of the ruler Sisebut, Isidore organized a council with great authority in the sacristy of the church of Holy Jerusalem in Seville, against the heresy of the Acephali.[22] Arguing on the basis of the true testimony of the doctors, he overcame a certain Syrian Acephalian bishop who was defending the heresy. Confirming the truths asserted by the council, Isidore condemned the bishop's propositions and, attacking him at length, finally freed him from his error.

15. Reccared eventually succeeded Sisebut to the throne, ruling for only three months.[23] His life was so brief that there is nothing worthy to report.

16. In the time of Heraclius, in the era 659 (621), in his tenth year as emperor and the fourth year of the Arabs, with Muhammad ruling over them, Suinthila worthily received the sceptre of government of the kingdom of the Goths, ruling for ten years.[24] With a rapid victory, he brought to an end the war that had been begun with the Romans and obtained the monarchy of Spain in its entirety.

17. In the time of Heraclius, in the era 669 (631), in his twentieth year as emperor, and the fourteenth year of the Arabs, Umar having ruled over them for almost a year, Sisenand was placed on the royal throne for five

---

[20]Helladius of Toledo (615-33).

[21]Isidore of Seville (c. 600-36).

[22]The Second Council of Seville (619). Vives, pp. 163-85 (especially pp. 171-2). The Acephali were an extreme branch of Monophysites that had rejected the church leadership of the time and were thus 'without heads'. Thompson, p. 164.

[23]Reccared II (621).

[24]Suinthila (621-31).

years, after having seized the kingship of the Goths by means of a revolt.[25] In the third year of his reign, he, like Reccared, the former king of the Goths,[26] celebrated a council, in the church of the holy virgin and martyr of Christ, Leocadia, to consider various issues.[27] Sixty-six bishops from Gallia Narbonensis and Spain congregated there in Toledo, along with the vicars of those who were absent and the lords of the palace, with the support of Bishop Isidore of Seville, renowned for his many books. At this holy synod, Braulio, the bishop of Zaragoza—whose eloquence Rome, mother and queen of cities, was to marvel at in the form of an epistolary exhortation—shone above the rest.[28]

18. In the time of Heraclius, in the era 674 (636), in his twenty-fifth year as emperor and the eighteenth year of the Arabs, Umar having ruled over them for five years and having just begun his sixth, Chinthila was placed over the Goths, ruling for six years.[29] He organized a Toledan council attended by twenty-four bishops, which enlightened the minds of the ignorant on many things, both sacred and profane.[30] *The Book of Canons*[31] indicates how great was the congregation of holy men, along with the episcopal vicars and the lords of the palace who were considered worthy to be among them, gathered in council in the church of the virgin and martyr of Christ, Leocadia. At this synod, Braulio, the bishop of Zaragoza—whose works the church still reads today—excelled the others in dignity and properly infused godly doctrine into the Christian minds.

---

[25] Sisenand (631-6).

[26] That is, Reccared I, who presided over Toledo III in 589.

[27] Toledo IV (633). Vives, pp. 186-225.

[28] Braulio of Zaragoza (631-51).

[29] Chinthila (636-9).

[30] Toledo V (636). Vives, pp. 226-32.

[31] The collected canons from the Spanish councils (a.k.a. the *Hispana*) that the chronicler consulted for most of his information about church matters in Visigothic Spain.

19. In the time of Heraclius, in the era 678 (640), his twenty-ninth year as emperor, and the twenty-third year of the Arabs, Umar having ruled over them for ten years, Tulga, of good character and ancestry, received the kingship of the Goths and ruled for two years.[32]

20. In the era 678 (640), Constantine, the son of Heraclius, became the fifty-eighth to be crowned emperor of the Romans, ruling for six years, 5,844 years having elapsed since the beginning of the world.[33]

21. In the time of Constantine, in the era 680 (642), in his first year as emperor, and the twenty-fifth of the Arabs, Uthman assumed the administration of this people for twelve years.[34] As he extended his rule into its second year, he brought under the control of the Saracens and subjected to their dominion Libya, Marmorica, and Pentapolis[35] as well as Gazania and Ethiopia—territories which lie in the desert regions upriver from Egypt—and made tributaries out of many Persian cities. He was ultimately killed during an uprising of his own men, after having ruled for twelve years.

22. In the time of Constantine, in the era 680 (642), in his first year as emperor, and the twenty-fifth of the Arabs, with Uthman ruling over them in his second year, Chindasuinth triumphantly ruled the kingdom of the Goths in Iberia, which he seized by means of a revolt. He devastated the Goths,[36] whom he ruled for six years alone without his son as co-ruler.[37]

---

[32]Tulga (639-42).

[33]Constantine III (641).

[34]Uthman (644-56).

[35]All within the boundaries of modern Libya.

[36]Apparently a reference to the king's brutal treatment of suspected conspirators. Thompson, pp. 190-1.

[37]Chindasuinth (642-53; from 649 with his son).

23. In the fifth year of his reign, Chindasuinth wonderfully ordered a synod to be celebrated in the city of Toledo, with thirty bishops and all the clerics and vicars of those bishops whose lack of strength or means prevented them from being present, along with the assembly of palace officials[38] who deserved, by selection of the council, to be included, and with notaries scurrying about, whose services were required for reciting and recording.[39] The king also sent Taio, bishop of Zaragoza—a man of solid learning and a friend of the scriptures—to Rome by sea with a request for the remaining books of the *Moralia*.[40] There Taio was put off by the pope of Rome[41] each day for a long time on the grounds that, due to the multitude of books in the archives of the Roman church, the desired volumes could by no means be located with ease. After Taio had spent the night begging the Lord's mercy at the shrine of blessed Peter, prince of the Apostles, the Lord revealed to him, through an angel, the chest in which the books were located. When the pope realized that he might be reprimanded, he most respectfully gave Taio assistance in transcribing the books and sent them with him to Spain as a gift. For up to that time, only part of the commentary of the book of blessed Job had been brought to Spain, honourably transported by the blessed Leander, bishop of Seville. Bishop Taio was asked by the pope, who placed him under oath, to reveal how the location of the books had been revealed to him so precisely. After fervent prayer, he joyfully confessed to the pope that on a certain night he had asked the guards of the church of blessed Peter the Apostle to keep watch with him. Suddenly in the middle of the night, while he lay prostrate before the tomb of blessed Peter the Apostle, praying and weeping, a heavenly light shone forth so that the whole

---

[38]*Palatinum collegium*. Its precise composition remains unclear.

[39]Toledo VII (646). Vives, pp. 249-59.

[40]Taio of Zaragoza (651-post-656). Gregory I's *Moralia in Iob* was the most popular commentary on the book of Job. Compare this account with Taio's letter to Bishop Eugenius II of Toledo: MGH AA 14:287-90.

[41]Apparently Martin I (649-53), who was the only pope whose pontificate overlapped with both Chindasuinth's reign and Taio's tenure as bishop.

church was illuminated with an indescribable glow, such that the candelabra of the church were not needed to illuminate it. Along with the light shone multitudes of saints singing psalms and carrying lamps that radiated light. As Taio stood frozen in awe and wonder, two old men in white vestments slowly stepped forth from that company of saints, once they had completed their singing, and began to hover over that part of the church where the bishop was praying. Finding him almost dead from fright, they tenderly brought him back to his senses. They asked him why he had exerted such great effort and why he had undertaken such a long voyage from the west, and they listened to his answers as if they did not already know them. Then, with many eloquent words, they gave him his due reward: they showed him the exact place in which the very books he sought lay hidden. Taio then asked the holy men to identify that body of saints accompanying them with such brilliant light. They answered, saying that it contained Peter, Apostle of Christ, and Paul, holding each other's hand, along with all of Peter's successors in the church who lay resting in that place. Then, when Taio asked the names of the saints with whom he was having such a miraculous conversation, one of them replied that he was Gregory, whose book Taio was trying to find, and that he had come to reward his great labour and to give him even more than what he had desired for so long. When Taio asked if wise Augustine—whose books, like those of St Gregory himself, he had always, since childhood, read with passionate enthusiasm—was present in that multitude of saints, that most distinguished and gracious Gregory simply replied, 'Augustine, whom you seek, occupies a more elevated position than ours'. Then, when Taio tried to bow at their feet, the holy men vanished before his eyes, along with all the light, to the terror of the guards. From that day on, the venerable Taio, who previously had been looked down upon as somewhat indolent, was regarded as glorious by everyone in the apostolic see.[42]

---

[42]That is, in Rome.

24. In the era 684 (646), Constans, son of Constantine, became the fifty-ninth to be crowned emperor of the Romans, ruling for twenty-seven years, 5,871 years having elapsed since the beginning of the world.[43] He fought fiercely in a naval battle with the Arabs. After his twenty-seventh year as emperor had expired, he was killed in Syracuse, that renowned city in Sicily, as the result of a conspiracy.[44] During his reign as emperor, the sun darkened at midday and stars appeared in the sky.

25. In the time of Constans, in the era 685 (647), in the thirtieth year of the kingdom of the Saracens, with Uthman ruling over them in his seventh year, Chindasuinth established his loose-living but generous son Reccesuinth as king of the Goths, and he ruled for twenty-four years.[45]

26. Reccesuinth excellently organized a well-attended council in the pretorian basilica of the holy Apostles Peter and Paul, with the illustrious and pious Eugenius,[46] metropolitan bishop of the royal city of Toledo, along with forty-six bishops, countless clerics and vicars representing those absent, and the most worthy palace officials.[47] Eugenius enlightened the minds of the ignorant not only about secular affairs but also about the mystery of the Holy Trinity.

27. In the time of Reccesuinth, an eclipse of the sun, which made the stars visible at midday, terrified everyone in Spain and foreshadowed an invasion by the Basques that resulted in no small damage to the army.[48]

---

[43] Constans II (641-68).

[44] Constans II intended to establish a new imperial capital in Sicily. Ostrogorsky, pp. 121-2.

[45] Reccesuinth (649-72; with his father until 653).

[46] Eugenius II of Toledo (646-57).

[47] Toledo VIII (653). Vives, pp. 260-93.

[48] The Basques had allied themselves with the pretender Froia. They were ultimately defeated by Reccesuinth. Thompson, pp. 199-200.

28. In the time of Reccesuinth, in the era 690 (652), in the thirty-fifth year of the Arabs, Muawiyah received the throne of his predecessor, ruling for twenty-five years.[49] For five of these years, he waged wars against his own people,[50] but he brought his reign to a very successful conclusion and all the Ishmaelite people were obedient to him for twenty years. The emperor Constans, gathering together a thousand or more ships, struggled against the Arabs without success. In the end he barely escaped, fleeing with only a few of his ships.[51] Many victories were won in the west by a general named Abd Allah, who a short time before had taken command of the unfinished campaign.[52] He came to Tripoli and Cidamo and also advanced in war upon Lebida.[53] Having caused great devastation, conquered various lands, dominated vast provinces, and received the homage of many peoples, he reached Africa,[54] still thirsty for blood, with all of his bands of soldiers. After preparing for war, the battle line of the Moors immediately turned in flight and all of the nobility of Africa, including Count Gregory, was wiped out entirely.[55] Abd Allah, laden with great amounts of booty, returned with all his cohorts to Egypt at the end of the tenth year of Muawiyah's rule.

---

[49]Muawiya I (661-80).

[50]The first *fitnah* (civil war; literally, 'trial' or 'temptation') began with the assassination of Uthman (656) and ended with that of Ali (661). The Umayyad Muawiyah ultimately prevailed. Hodgson, 1:212-17.

[51]655. Muawiyah was the first caliph to devote serious attention to the construction of a navy. Ostrogorsky, p. 116.

[52]Abd Allah ibn Said, the governor of Egypt.

[53]Each of these cities is located within modern Libya.

[54]'Africa' here refers to the imperial exarchate of Africa, that is, the area around Carthage that had been reconquered from the Vandals during the reconquest orchestrated by Justinian.

[55]Gregory was the imperial exarch of Africa. He had revolted against Constantinople shortly before the battle with the Arabs (647). Ostrogorsky, p. 124.

29. Muawiya sent 100,000 men under the command of his son to Constantinople. They surrounded it with a siege that lasted all spring,[56] but because they could not bear the burden of hunger and disease, they left. They seized many other towns and, laden with booty, once again set their eyes on Damascus and the king who had sent them, safe and sound after a two-year absence. After twenty years of rule and another five years spent in civil war,[57] Muawiya paid his debt to human nature.

30. In the era 711 (673), Constantine, son of Constans, became the sixtieth to be crowned emperor of the Romans.[58] He ruled for fifteen years, 5,886 years having elapsed since the beginning of the world. Hearing at Syracuse that his father had been killed by a revolt of his own men, he headed for the palace with as large a fleet as he could muster and ascended the throne in glorious triumph.

31. In the time of Constantine, in the era 716 (678), in his fifth year as emperor and the sixty-first year of the Arabs, Yazid, the most pleasant son of Muawiyah, obtained power for three years and was very well liked

---

[56]The first siege of Constantinople lasted on and off from 674 to 678. The Greeks defended themselves, for the first time, with Greek fire. Ostrogorsky, p. 124.

[57]The author here used the adverb *civiliter*, which would normally be taken to mean 'peacefully' or 'in the manner of a private citizen'. But the fact that he just finished informing the reader (*Chr*754 28) that Muawiyah ruled for a total of twenty-five years, five of which he spent in *bella civilia*, strongly suggests that the author used *civiliter* as an adverbial way of reiterating that the caliph had spent part of his reign fighting domestic enemies. The chronicler also described the reigns of the emperors Philippicus and Anastasius II using *civiliter* (*Chr*754 60, 63) and we know that both were cut short by strong internal opposition. Ostrogorsky, pp. 152-5. Still, he was aware of standard usage, as evidenced by *Chr*754 31. It is very possible that the chronicler modelled his idiosyncratic use of *civiliter* on Augustine, *City of God 2.25: romani bellando civiliter.* (My thanks to Christopher Jones for drawing my attention to this passage). Compare López Pereira, *Crónica mozárabe*, p. 49, n. 13 and Du Cange, *Glossarium Mediae et Infimae Latinitatis* (Paris, 1937), 2:347, for opposite views on this matter.

[58]Constantine IV (668-85).

by all of the peoples subject to his rule.[59] He never, as is the habit of men, sought glory just because he was king, but lived like a private citizen together with everyone else.

32. After three years, Yazid left as his successor his son Muawiya, who was similar in his habits to his father.[60] When he had attained the peak of royal power, he remitted to everyone one third of the tribute that was due him. After remaining in power for half a year, Muawiya left this world.

33. In the time of Constantine, in the era 716 (678), in the beginning of his sixth year as emperor and the sixty-second year of the Arabs, Muawiya the younger having died, the army of the Arabs was divided between two princes for almost four years.[61] They remained in such great conflict that countless troops were devoured by the sword on both sides. One of these two princes, named Marwan, paid the emperor one thousand *solidi* of pure gold and of proven weight, as well as an Arabic mule laden with silk sheets, every day for nine years, so that he might receive military aid or at least not be attacked. In addition to the aforementioned items, he gave as tribute a beautiful girl and he released all the captives that he held from times past, regardless of the circumstances under which they had originally been captured.

34. In the time of Constantine, in the era 720 (682), in his tenth year as emperor and the sixty-sixth year of the Arabs, Abd al-Malik achieved the apex of the kingship and ruled for twenty years.[62] Pursuing his father's

---

[59]Yazid I (680-3).

[60]Muawiya II (683).

[61]The second *fitnah* (680-92) began with the death of Ali's son Husayn, and pitted Marwan, an Umayyad pretender, against Abd Allah ibn al-Zubayr, who was leading a revolt in Arabia. Marwan was proclaimed caliph (Marwan I) in 684 but died the following year, leaving his son Abd al-Malik to succeed him. Hodgson, 1:219-23.

[62]Abd al-Malik (685-705).

rival to Mecca[63]—the home of Abraham, as they assert, between Ur of the Chaldeans and Carrhae[64] of Mesopotamia—he had him killed by a general that he had sent there. He very wisely suppressed the civil wars with force.

35. In the time of Constantine, in the era 712 (674), in his first year as emperor, the fifty-seventh year of the Arabs, and the twenty-third of Muawiya's reign, Wamba had been placed over the Goths and was to rule for eight years.[65] In that year, as he wielded the royal sceptre in his third year, Wamba renovated the city of Toledo with wonderful and elegant workmanship. Versifying on the sculpted work, he completed it by inscribing epigrams on the bright and shining marble: 'The renowned king Wamba erected this city with the help of God, to increase the honour and fame of his people'. And in memory of the martyrs, whose names he set over the turrets on the gates, he inscribed, in the same manner: 'You, holy saints, whose presence shines here, protect this city and people with your accustomed favour'.

36. In the fourth year of Wamba's reign, in the era 713 (675), after eighteen years of uprisings and various misfortunes—like that bent woman in the gospel[66]—he organized a church council in the city of Toledo, in the sacristy of the church of the blessed mother of God, the Virgin Mary, and gathered all the bishops of Spain and Gallia Narbonensis, with whom he greatly deplored the amount of time that had passed without such councils.[67] In this council, he and many other men

---

[63]His father's rival was Abd Allah ibn al-Zubayr. The shrine of the Ka'bah was destroyed in the course of the struggle and had to be rebuilt. Hodgson, 1:223.

[64]Haran.

[65]Wamba (672-80). The chronicler did not mean to suggest that Wamba became king in the year 674 and ruled for eight more years; rather that he 'had been placed over the Goths' two years before and 'was to rule for eight years' in all.

[66]Luke 13:11.

[67]Toledo XI (675). Vives, pp. 344-69.

found solace in the fact that the most holy Ildephonsus, outshining everyone at that time, served as an anchor of the faith for the entire church. His golden mouth expressed itself sweetly in diverse books and expounded on the virginity of Our Lady, the eternally Virgin Mary, with brilliant and polished eloquence using a series of synonyms.[68] These little books that he wrote circulated throughout Iberia so that truly the minds of the faithful who attended the great council and studied them were refreshed while at the same time the ordinary people were greatly consoled by these rivulets of doctrine.

37. In the time of Constantine, in the era 718 (680), in his seventh year as emperor and the sixty-second of the Arabs, with Abd Allah and Marwan divided against each other and beginning to struggle for the kingship, Ervig was consecrated as king of the Goths.[69] He ruled for seven years. At this time a serious famine ravaged Spain.

38. In his first year, in the era 719 (681), Ervig splendidly convoked the twelfth Toledan council with thirty-five bishops, innumerable clerics and an assembly of Christians.[70] At this time, Bishop Julian, descended from Jewish stock like a rose blossom amidst the thorns, shone throughout the world for his understanding of Christian doctrine.[71] Born of Christian parents,[72] he was splendidly educated in all branches of knowledge in Toledo where he was later honoured with the office of bishop.

---

[68]Ildephonsus of Toledo (657-67). He was the author of the treatise *De viginitate perpetua Sanctae Mariae*, but he could not have attended Toledo XI since the council took place eight years after his death. Quiricus (667-80) signed the council proceedings as the metropolitan of Toledo. Vives, p. 367.

[69]Ervig (680-7).

[70]Toledo XII (681). Vives, pp. 380-410. The precise composition of the *collegium Christianorum* is unclear.

[71]Julian of Toledo (680-90). His parents were Jewish converts to Christianity.

[72]His parents apparently converted to Christianity prior to Julian's birth.

39. In the era 726 (688), Justinian became the sixty-first to be crowned emperor of the Romans.[73] He ruled for ten years before being deposed, 5,896 years having elapsed since the beginning of the world.

40. In the time of Justinian, in the era 726 (688), in his first year as emperor and the seventieth of the Arabs, Abd al-Malik retained the peak of dignity, having already ruled for four years.

41. In the time of Justinian, in the era 726 (688), in his first year as emperor and the seventieth of the Arabs, with Abd al-Malik ruling in his fifth year, Egica obtained the most lofty position of power for the protection of the kingdom of the Goths.[74] He ruled for fifteen years and oppressed the Goths with cruel death. Moreover bubonic plague spread mercilessly at this time. In his first year, the era 726 (688), he celebrated a council in the city of Toledo in the pretorian church of the holy Apostles Peter and Paul with all of the bishops of Spain and Gallia Narbonensis congregated there. The brilliant teacher Julian, of blessed memory, was present among the sixty bishops and the large assembly of Christians in attendance, with the clerics and all the populace gathered around.[75] In the course of this council, for various reasons, Egica asked the synod that he be released from the injurious oath that he had sworn to King Ervig.[76] Julian, the most holy metropolitan bishop of the royal city, had previously sent his book about the three substances[77] to Rome. After examining it superficially, the Roman pope[78] decreed that it should be censored because two years before Julian had written that 'the will begets the will'.

---

[73] Justinian II (685-95).

[74] Egica (687-702).

[75] Toledo XV (688). Vives, pp. 449-74.

[76] Specifically, an oath to protect his predecessor Ervig's children from harm. Vives, pp. 450-1. Thompson, pp. 242-3.

[77] In other words, a treatise on the Trinity.

[78] Benedict II (684-5) feared that Julian had erred in the direction of the Monothelete heresy.

Bishop Julian, proving in this council—to the honour of King Egica—on the basis of the truthful testimony of the authority of the Fathers, that what he had sent to Rome was correct, composed a defence[79] and sent it, along with acclamatory verses in praise of the emperor like those that he had sent before, to Rome through his ecclesiastical envoys: a priest, a deacon, and a subdeacon, most erudite servants in all things pertaining to God and imbued with knowledge of the divine scriptures. Rome worthily and piously received the defence, ordered everyone to read it, and made it known to the emperor with the acclamation: 'Your praise, Lord, to the ends of the earth'.[80] The pope honourably sent back to lord Julian, by means of the aforementioned envoys, a rescript thanking him and declaring everything that he had written to be true and pious.

42. In the era 736 (698), Leontius, as the result of a rebellion, became the sixty-second to be crowned emperor of the Romans and ruled lawlessly for three years, 5,899 years having elapsed since the beginning of the world.[81] He elevated himself after Justinian had been unlawfully removed from power.

43. In the time of Leontius, in the era 736, 737, and 738 (698, 699, and 700), the first, second, and third years of his reign, and the seventy-ninth, eightieth, and eighty-first years of the Arabs, Abd al-Malik completed the thirteenth, fourteenth, and fifteenth years of his rule.

44. In Leontius' time, in the era 736 (698), in his first year as emperor, the eightieth year of the Arabs, and the sixteenth of Abd al-Malik, Egica made his son, Witiza, his heir and held the kingship of the Goths jointly

---

[79] *Apologeticum de tribus capitulis* (686).
[80] Psalm 47:11.
[81] Leontius (695-8).

with him.[82] Although he succeeded to his father's throne petulantly, Witiza was most clement during the fifteen years that he remained in the kingship. He not only brought back to favour those whom his father had condemned to exile, but he did them service when they were restored. Indeed Witiza brought back to their former joy those whom his father had oppressed with a heavy yoke and he freely gave land back to those who had been deprived of it by his father. Finally he called everyone together and publicly and formally burned the pledges that his father had exacted by trickery. Not only did he release the innocent from, if you like, their unbreakable bonds, but he also returned from his own property, that which had long been alienated from the fisc, restoring it to the public domain.

45. At this time, Felix, bishop of the see of the royal city of Toledo, was a man of outstanding gravity and wisdom, who held important councils under both princes.[83]

46. In the era 738 (700), Apsimar became the sixty-third to be crowned emperor of the Romans and ruled for seven years, 5,905 years having elapsed since the beginning of the world.[84]

47. In Apsimar's time, in the era 738 (700), in his first year as emperor and the eighty-second of the Arabs—with the eighty-third having already begun—with Abd al-Malik in his seventeenth year, Witiza ruled jointly with his decrepit father. In the era 739 (701), unable to bear the destruction throughout Spain brought on by the aforementioned misfortune,[85] they vacated the palace. After this misfortune had passed,

---

[82]The traditional dates of Witiza's reign are 698-710 (alone from 702). But a recently discovered charter from his reign suggests that he joined his father as a co-ruler in 693 or 694. Collins, *Arab Conquest*, pp. 29-30.

[83]Felix of Toledo (693-700).

[84]Apsimar, also known as Tiberius II (698-705).

[85]Presumably a reference to the plague mentioned in *Chr754* 41.

Witiza's father Egica died a natural death and Witiza ruled prosperously for the aforementioned number of years. Everyone in Spain, confident in their great joy, eagerly rejoiced.

48. At this time, Gunderic, metropolitan bishop of the see of the royal city of Toledo, already renowned for his sancity, was even more highly honoured for his many miracles.[86]

49. In the era 745 (707), Justinian, the sixty-first emperor of the Romans, was restored with the assistance of a powerful force of Khazars,[87] as the sixty-fourth, ruling again for ten years, 5,915 years having elapsed since the beginning of the world.[88]

50. In Justinian's time, in the aforesaid year, the first year of his rule and the eighty-ninth of the Arabs, Walid held the kingship among the Arabs.[89] In Spain, Witiza continued to rule in his fifteenth year.

51. In Justinian's time, in the era 747 (709), in his fourth year as emperor and the ninety-first of the Arabs, Walid received the sceptre of the kingdom of the Saracens, as his father had arranged, and fought various peoples for four years. He was victorious and, endowed with great honours, exercised his rule for nine years. He was a man of great prudence in deploying his armies to the extent that, though lacking in divine favour, he crushed the forces of almost all neighbouring peoples. He weakened Romania[90] with constant raiding, nearly destroyed the islands,[91] raided and subdued the territory of India,[92] brought cities to

---

[86]Gunderic of Toledo (700-pre-711).
[87]A Turkish people residing between the Black and Caspian Seas.
[88]Justinian II (restored: 705-11).
[89]Walid I (705-15).
[90]A reference to Asia Minor.
[91]Apparently a reference to the Aegean Islands.
[92]The Indus Valley campaigns of 710-13.

utter destitution, besieged fortresses, and, from the twisted paths of Libya, subjugated all of Mauretania.[93] In the western regions, Walid, through a general of his army by the name of Musa,[94] attacked and conquered the kingdom of the Goths—which had been established with ancient solidity almost 350 years before, it having been founded in the era 400 (362),[95] and which had been extended peacefully throughout Spain from the time of Leovigild for almost 140 years up to the era 750 (712)—and having seized the kingdom, he made it pay tribute.

52. In Justinian's time, in the era 749 (711), in his fourth year as emperor and the ninety-second of the Arabs, with Walid retaining the sceptre of the kingdom for the fifth year, Roderic rebelliously seized the kingdom of the Goths at the instigation of the senate.[96] He ruled for only one year. Mustering his forces, he directed armies against the Arabs and the Moors sent by Musa, that is against Tariq ibn Ziyad[97] and the others, who had long been raiding the province consigned to them and simultaneously devastating many cities. In the fifth year of Justinian's rule, the ninety-third of the Arabs, and the sixth of Walid, in the era 750 (712), Roderic headed for the Transductine mountains[98] to fight them and in that battle the entire army of the Goths, which had come with him fraudulently and in rivalry out of ambition for the kingship, fled and he was killed. Thus Roderic wretchedly lost not only his rule but his

---

[93]Carthage fell in 698. The Arabs reached the Atlantic by 705.

[94]Musa ibn Nusayr, who was appointed governor of Ifriqiya (the Arab province of Africa, established in 670 and centered in Kairouan) in 707.

[95]According to Isidore, Athanaric was elected king in 369.

[96]Roderic (710-11). The term 'senate' probably refers to the palace officials.

[97]Tariq ibn Ziyad, governor of the newly-conquered city of Tangiers, was chosen by Musa to lead a predominately Berber force into Spain in 711. There appears to have been a reconnaissance mission the previous year.

[98]Precise location unknown, but thought to be in the vicinity of Medina Sidonia.

homeland, his rivals also being killed, as Walid was completing his sixth year of rule.[99]

53. At that time, Sindered of pious memory, metropolitan bishop of the royal city, was renowned for the zeal of his sanctity.[100] But motivated more by this zeal than by reason, he provoked the aged and honourable men whom he found in the church that had been committed to him and, at the instigation of the prince Witiza, he did not cease to vex them while he was bishop. A short time after the invasion of the Arabs, he lost his nerve and, like a hireling rather than a shepherd,[101] and contrary to the precepts of the ancients, he deserted Christ's flock and headed for his Roman homeland.

54. In Justinian's time, in the era 749 (711), in his fourth year as emperor, the ninety-second of the Arabs, and the fifth of Walid, while Spain was being devastated by the aforesaid forces and was greatly afflicted not only by the enemy but also by domestic strife, Musa himself, approaching this wretched land across the straits of Cádiz and pressing on to the pillars of Hercules—which reveal the entrance to the port like an index to a book, or like keys unlocking the path to Spain—entered the long plundered and godlessly invaded Spain, to destroy it.[102] After forcing his way up to Toledo, the royal city, he imposed on the adjacent regions an evil and fraudulent peace. He decapitated on a scaffold those noble lords who still remained, arresting them in their flight from Toledo

---

[99]All of the sources, Latin and Arabic alike, agree that the Visigoths were in the midst of a civil war at the time of the invasion. In some cases the Muslims are depicted as forming an alliance with disaffected Visigothic or imperial noblemen. There is no real consensus about the exact date of the invasion, the legitimacy of Roderic's election, or whether he was even the last Visigothic ruler. See: Abilio Barbero and Marcelo Vigil, *La formación del feudalismo en la península ibérica*, 3rd ed. (Barcelona, 1982), pp. 203-7.

[100]Sindered of Toledo (pre-711-711).

[101]John 10:12.

[102]Musa entered Spain in 712 and, after taking Seville and Mérida (the only city to offer prolonged resistance), met Tariq in Toledo in 713.

with the help of Oppa, King Egica's son. With Oppa's support, he killed them all with the sword. He devastated not only Hispania Ulterior, but Hispania Citerior up to and beyond the ancient and once flourishing city of Zaragoza, which was now, by the judgement of God, openly exposed to the sword, famine, and captivity. He ruined beautiful cities, burning them with fire; condemned lords and powerful men to the cross; and butchered youths and infants with swords. While he terrorized everyone in this way, some of the cities that remained sued for peace under duress and, after persuading and mocking them with a certain craftiness, the Saracens granted their requests without delay. When the citizens subsequently rejected what they had been forced to accept out of fear and terror, they tried to flee to the mountains where they risked hunger and various forms of death. The Saracens set up their savage kingdom in Spain, specifically in Córdoba, formerly a patrician see and always the most opulent of cities, a city accustomed to giving its first fruits to the kingdom of the Visigoths.

55. Who can relate such perils? Who can enumerate such grievous disasters? Even if every limb were transformed into a tongue, it would be beyond human capability to express the ruin of Spain and its many and great evils. But let me nevertheless try to summarize everything for the reader on one brief page. Leaving aside all of the innumerable disasters that this cruel, unclean world has brought to its countless regions and cities since the time of Adam—that which, historically, the city of Troy sustained when it fell; that which Jerusalem suffered, as foretold by the prophets; that which Babylon bore, according to the scriptures; that which finally Rome went through, martyrially graced with the nobility of the apostles—all this and more Spain, once so delightful and now rendered so miserable, endured as much to its honour as to its disgrace.[103]

---

[103]For the apocalyptic context of this concatenation of disasters, see: Collins, *Arab Conquest*, p. 63.

56. In the era 750 (712), in Justinian's sixth year as emperor and the ninety-fourth of the Arabs, Musa, after fifteen months had elapsed, was summoned by order of the princes and, leaving his son Abd al-Aziz in his place, he returned to his homeland and presented himself to the king Walid in the last year of his reign. Musa brought with him from Spain some noblemen who had escaped the sword; gold and silver, assayed with enthusiasm by the bankers; a large quantity of valuable ornaments, precious stones, and pearls; ointments to kindle women's desire; and many other things from all over Spain that would be tedious to record. But by God's will, Walid was angry at him.[104] Musa was ignominiously removed from the prince's presence and publicly paraded with a rope around his neck.[105]

57. In Justinian's time, in the aforesaid year, Walid, the *Amir Almuminin*—a term of royalty which in their language means: 'carrying out all things prosperously',[106]—despite having seen the resources of Spain and having been shown its riches and the beauty of its young girls, belittled Musa's great fame and condemned him to death by torture. But due to the entreaties on his behalf by leaders and powerful men, to whom Musa had offered many gifts from his enormous wealth, Walid opted to fine Musa 2,000,000 *solidi*. Shortly thereafter, Walid reached the end of his life and left this world. Musa, on the advice of Urban[107]—that most noble man of the African region, reared under the doctrine of the Catholic faith, who had accompanied him throughout Spain—opted to pay the fine as if it were nothing, deeming the imposed penalty to be slight in

---

[104]Actually, Walid was ill and died shortly after the return of Musa and Tariq (who left Spain in 714), leaving Sulayman, his successor, to deal with the conquerors of Spain.

[105]A punishment designed to humiliate him.

[106]More accurately, 'leader of the faithful'.

[107]Some identify this Urban with Julian, the supposed imperial exarch of Ceuta who, according to Arabic sources, capitulated to Musa and collaborated with him during the Spanish campaign. Evariste Lévi-Provençal, *Histoire de l'Espagne musulmane*. 3 vol., 2nd ed. (Paris, 1950), 1:12-15. Collins (*Arab Conquest*, p. 36) is sceptical.

proportion to his great wealth. So, giving sureties from among his freed men, he counted out a huge pile of coins. With wonderful speed he paid the required amount, which was assigned to the fisc in the time of Walid's successor.[108]

58. In Justinian's time, in the era 752 (714), in his eighth year as emperor and the ninety-sixth of the Arabs, upon the death of Walid, Sulayman, his brother by blood, succeeded him as king with honour, in accordance with his expressed wishes.[109] He ruled for three years. A scourge of Romania, he sent his brother, by the name of Maslama—child of a mother of similar rank—with 100,000 soldiers to destroy it. With both sword and fire, he brought destruction to war-torn Asia Minor. From there he moved on to Constantinople.[110] But realizing that supply problems were threatening his campaign, he returned, at the command of the new prince, having had little success.

59. At about the same time, in the era 753 (715), in Justinian's ninth year as emperor and the ninety-seventh of the Arabs, Abd al-Aziz pacified all of Spain for three years under the yoke of tribute.[111] He took for himself all the riches and honours of Seville, as well as the queen of Spain, whom he joined in marriage, and the daughters of kings and princes, whom he treated as concubines and then rashly repudiated. He was eventually killed on the advice of Ayub[112] by a revolt of his own men, while he was in prayer. After Ayub had held Spain for a month,

---

[108]Musa, already an old man by the time he entered Spain, died a few years after his return. Nothing is known of the fate of Tariq.

[109]Sulayman (715-17).

[110]This, the second major siege of Constantinople, occurred in 717. See: *Chr754* 72. Ostrogorsky, pp. 156-7.

[111]Abd al-Aziz (714-16), the son of Musa. Seville, the first city conquered by Musa, was the first 'capital' of Muslim-occupied Spain. Within a few years (under either al-Hurr or as-Samh), Córdoba became the seat of government.

[112]Ayyub ibn Habib al-Lakhmi (716).

al-Hurr[113] succeeded to the throne of Hesperia[114] by order of the prince,[115] to whom the death of Abd al-Aziz was reported in this way: that on the advice of queen Egilona, wife of the late king Roderic, whom he had joined to himself, he tried to throw off the Arab yoke from his neck and retain the conquered kingdom of Iberia for himself.

60. In the era 754 (716), Philippicus became the sixty-fourth to be crowned emperor of the Romans, ruling for a year and a quarter amidst civil war, 5,916 years having elapsed since the beginning of the world.[116]

61. In Philippicus' time, in the aforesaid era, the first year of Philippicus and the ninety-eighth of the Arabs, Sulayman held the kingship of the Saracens and ruled for three years. The Arabs cruelly ravaged Romania and destroyed Pergamum, that most ancient and flourishing city of Asia Minor, with avenging fire.

62. In Philippicus' time, al-Hurr extended the power of the judges throughout Spain.[117] For almost three years, by means of fighting and negotiating treaties, he sought control over Gallia Narbonensis. A short time later, after organizing Hispania Ulterior for the collection of taxes, he returned to Hispania Citerior, and ruled for the aforesaid number of years.

63. In the era 756 (718), Anastasius became the sixty-fifth to be crowned emperor of the Romans, ruling amidst civil war for a year and

---

[113] Al-Hurr ibn Abd ar-Rahman al-Thaqafi (716-18).

[114] A poetic term used to refer to the western parts of the Roman Empire.

[115] By 'prince' the chronicler would seem to be refering to the caliph in Damascus, though it would be customary for the governors of Ifriqiya, based in Kairouan, to select the governors of Spain on behalf of the caliph.

[116] Philippicus (711-13).

[117] A reference to the *qadis*, whose responsibility it was to interpret Islamic law. See also: *Chr754* 79, 81, 82, 84.

nine months, 5,918 years having elapsed since the beginning of the world.[118] In his time, Sulayman, who held the kingship over the Arabs, approved as his successors Umar, the son of his paternal uncle, and his brother Yazid.

64. In Spain al-Hurr retained his rule over the patrician city of Córdoba, deploying garrisons of Saracens. He restored to the Christians the small estates that had originally been confiscated for the sake of peace so as to bring in revenue to the public treasury.[119] He punished the Moors, who had long been dwelling in Spain, on account of the treasure they had hidden.[120] He imprisoned them in sack cloth, infested with worms and lice, and weighed them down with chains. He tortured them as he interrogated them.

65. At that time, in the beginning of the era 758 (720), in the one hundredth year of the Arabs, an eclipse of the sun, lasting from the seventh to the ninth hour of the day, was observed in Spain. A number of the witnesses even saw stars appear. Many contend that the eclipse occurred at the time of al-Hurr's successor, as-Samh.

66. In the era 757 (719), Artemius, also known as Theodosius, became the sixty-sixth to be crowned emperor of the Romans and ruled for two years, 5,920 years having elapsed since the beginning of the world.[121]

---

[118]Anastasius II (713-15).

[119]The use of *pacificus* in relation to property (as in this reference to *resculas pacificas*, as well as *pro pacificis rebus* in *Chr754* 75) suggests to me that the chronicler was referring to property surrendered to the Muslims by Christian landowners at the time of the conquest. They were 'pacific' in the sense that they were handed over as part of a capitulation agreement. Collins is probably right in interpreting this passage to mean that the governor restored confiscated estates to the Christians so that he would be able to tax them. Theoretically Muslim landholders were exempt from such taxes. *Arab Conquest*, p. 46.

[120]Perhaps a reference to booty that was not handed over to the commanders of the expedition at the time of the conquest.

[121]Artemius, also known as Theodosius III (715-17).

67. In Artemius' time, Umar, exercising tutelage over his brother[122] Yazid on account of his scrupulous observance of the law, assumed the government of the kingdom himself.[123] Ending all the fighting, Umar was so benign and patient in his rule that even today great honour and praise is bestowed upon him, so that he is extolled more than any of his predecessors not only by his own people but by foreigners. He was regarded as more conscientious in his government of the kingdom than anyone else from the people of the Arabs.

68. When his brother[124] Umar died and Yazid fully assumed the government of the Saracen kingdom by succession,[125] the army of his people, which had defended the kingdom against the Persians, rose in revolt and instigated a civil war. Yazid had just sent his brother, whom we mentioned above, by the name of Maslama,[126] with a huge army to the Babylonian plain near the Tigris River. Once the fighting had begun, the battle line of the rebels immediately broke into wondrous flight. Granting a pardon, Yazid spared the life of the instigator of this evil act, also named Yazid.

69. In the western regions the Arabs achieved many military victories under their leader, as-Samh.[127] Having held power in Spain for a little less than three years, he undertook, on his own initiative, a census of Hispania Ulterior and Hispania Citerior. He divided by lot among his allies the booty, arms, and whatever else in the way of plunder the Arab people in Spain had not yet divided, and added a portion of all the moveable and immoveable goods to the fisc. Afterwards he made Narbonne his own and harassed the people of the Franks with frequent attacks. He placed

---

[122]Actually, his cousin.
[123]Umar II (717-20).
[124]Cousin.
[125]Yazid II (720-4).
[126]*Chr754* 58.
[127]As-Samh ibn Malik al-Khaulani (718-21).

garrisons of Saracens in the city of Narbonne to oversee its defence more effectively. Assembling his forces, as-Samh came to attack Toulouse and surrounded it with a siege, trying to overcome it with slings and other types of machines. Informed of this turn of events, the Franks gathered together under Eudes, their commander.[128] There, at Toulouse, while the battle lines of both armies were engaged with one another in serious fighting, the Franks killed as-Samh, the leader of the Saracen forces, along with that portion of the army that accompanied him, and pursued the remaining part as it slipped away in flight. Abd ar-Rahman accepted the command of the Saracens for one month[129] until Anbasah, by order of the prince, came to serve as governor.[130]

70. At that time, Bishop Fredoarius of the see of Guadix, Urban, the aged chanter of the cathedral of the see of the royal city Toledo, and Archdeacon Evantius of the same see were regarded as brilliant in their teaching, wisdom and sanctity, strengthening the church of God with hope, faith, and charity, all in accordance with scripture.[131]

71. In the era 758 (720), Leo became the seventy-seventh to be crowned emperor of the Romans.[132] He ruled for twenty-four years, 5,944 years having elapsed since the beginning of the world. Leo was an expert in the art of war.

72. The Saracens captured nothing worthwhile during the short time that they spent under Umar, who diminished his brother's kingdom,[133] but they fought many battles under Yazid. Later, as they were beginning

---

[128]Eudes was the Duke of Aquitaine. The battle of Toulouse occurred in 721.

[129]Abd ar-Rahman ibn Abd Allah al-Ghafiqi (721).

[130]Anbasah ibn Sahim al-Kalbi (721-5).

[131]A letter written by Evantius (c. 730) to the Christian community in Zaragoza, reprimanding them for judaizing, has survived. *Corpus scriptorum muzarabicorum* 1:2-5.

[132]Leo III (717-41).

[133]That is, his cousin Sulayman's 'kingdom'.

to advance under their new king Hisham[134] toward the royal city[135] to conquer it, Leo received the sceptre of the empire, as we have said, with the acclamation of the entire imperial senate.

73. In Leo's time, in the aforesaid era, Yazid, king of the Saracens, assumed the government of the kingdom.[136] Among the Arabs, it is customary that the king's successor assume his title at the king's prerogative so that upon the king's death, the successor might take up the reins of government without difficulty.

74. At that time, in the era 759 (721), in the second year of the emperor Leo and the one hundred third year of the Arabs, Anbasah proudly held the rule of Spain for four and a half years. He planned campaigns against the Franks and implemented them using the satraps that he dispatched, but he fought without success. Nonetheless he harassed not a few cities and fortresses with his bands of soldiers, weakening them with surprise attacks. He burdened the Christians by doubling their taxes. He triumphed in Spain with the highest honour.

In his time, the Jews were tempted—as they had been under Theodosius the Younger[137]—and led astray by a certain Jew, who, having ironically assumed the name of Serenus,[138] assailed them with a murky error. Preaching that he was the Messiah, he announced to them that they were to hasten to the promised land and ordered them to get rid of everything that they possessed. Once they had done this, they remained empty-handed and penniless. When news of this came to Anbasah, he incorporated into the fisc everything that they had disposed of and called Serenus to him, to

---

[134]Hisham (724-43).

[135]Constantinople.

[136]Another reference to Yazid II. See: *Chr754* 67, 68, 72.

[137]Isidore, *Chronicle* 109.

[138]Ironic in the sense that there was nothing 'serene' about this 'false Messiah'.

ask whether, if he indeed was the Messiah, he thought that he was truly doing the work of God.[139]

Afterward Anbasah wanted to launch another expedition against the Franks, one that he would lead personally, and so he immediately planned to attack them with his entire army. But as he was setting out, raging against the enemy, he died a natural death. Just before he died, he ordained Udhrah as consul of the land committed to him and commander of the retreating and disorganized army.[140]

75. In the era 763 (725), in almost the sixth year of the emperor Leo and the one hundred seventh of the Arabs, a Saracen by the name of Yahya succeeded at once by order of the princes. He was a cruel and terrible despot who raged for almost three years.[141] With bitter deceit, he stirred up the Saracens and Moors of Spain by confiscating property that they were holding for the sake of peace and restoring many things to the Christians.[142]

76. In Leo's time, Yazid departed this world after completing the fourth year of his rule, leaving the kingdom to his brother, Hisham, and designating Walid, his own natural son, to succeed his uncle.[143] In the beginning of his rule in the era 761 (723), almost in Leo's fifth year as emperor and the one hundred sixth of the Arabs, Hisham showed sufficient moderation and won some victories through the commanders of his army which he sent against Romania by land and by sea. In the western regions he accomplished little worthy of note. But then he was seized with greed and a greater collection of money was made, east and

---

[139]This account was apparently added to the chronicle after its original composition. It does not appear in all of the manuscript versions.

[140]Udhrah ibn Abd Allah al-Fihri (725-6).

[141]Yahya ibn Salamah al-Qalbi (727).

[142]See the note to *Chr754* 64 above.

[143]Hisham (724-43) and Walid II (743-4).

west, by the generals he sent out than had been gathered by any king at any time before him. Realizing that there was in him a perverse cupidity, large numbers of people removed themselves from his dominion. For three, almost four, years, there was a civil war with no little slaughter, to the extent that Hisham had great difficulty restoring the lost provinces to his power.[144]

77. In Leo's time, in the era 766 (728), in his tenth year as emperor, the one hundred eleventh of the Arabs, and the sixth of Hisham, Hudjifah, a frivolous man, received authority from the African governor—whose privilege it was to confer power in Spain with the consent of the prince[145]—and held it for six months though without taking it seriously.[146] The brevity of his rule prevented him from accomplishing anything either beneficial or detrimental.

78. At that time, in the era 767 (729), in the eleventh year of the emperor Leo, the one hundred twelfth of the Arabs, and the seventh of Hisham, Uthman came secretly from Africa to rule Spain.[147] After Uthman had ruled for four months, substituting for Hudjifah with honour, Haytham openly revealed the seal or authorization of the prince, sent from the aforesaid region, indicating that he was to take control of Spain immediately.[148] After Haytham had ruled in a troubled state for ten months, he found out—I do not know by what craft—that some Arabs wished to remove him from power. He captured them and eventually extracted with whips the various details of the rebellion. After torturing them, he cut off their heads, as he had been secretly ordered to do by his counterparts on the other side of the sea. Among those decapitated was

---

[144]See below: *Chr754* 84.

[145]That is, the governor of Africa normally appointed the governor of Spain with the consent of the caliph in Damascus.

[146]Hudjifah ibn al-Ahwan al-Qaysi (728).

[147]Uthman ibn Abi Nasah al-Khathami (728).

[148]Haytham ibn Ubayd al-Kilabi (729-30).

Zaid, of full Saracen lineage, brilliant in his eloquence and a most wealthy lord with a great deal of property. He was tortured, scourged with whips, beaten with rods, and then decapitated with a sword. Not many days later, at the request of those people whose blood Haytham had spilled, Muhammad the Saracen was sent from Libya, by order of the prince, with a secret authorization that Abd ar-Rahman[149] be elevated in Haytham's place without delay. But when Muhammad came to the Cordoban palace, Abd ar-Rahman was not to be found right away, so Muhammad, confused, immediately captured Haytham by force. He would not allow Haytham to be placed in prison unpunished, so without delay, he had him fiercely beaten and shamefully judged. His head was then shaved and he was paraded through the streets placed backwards on an ass, with his hands tied behind his back, bound with iron chains. Not many days later, Muhammad sent Haytham under guard to be presented to the African governor who had, they say, secretly ordered the journey. They awaited word from the royal throne as to what should be done with Haytham, but impeded by multiple interrogations and conflicting accusations, nothing was decided about him for a long time. A month after he left for Africa, Muhammad al-Ashjai took his place.[150]

79. In the era 769 (731), in the twelfth and a half year of the emperor Leo, the one hundred thirteenth of the Arabs, and the ninth of Hisham, Abd ar-Rahman, a warlike man, quickly assumed power and stood out above all others for three years.[151] Although Abd ar-Rahman was pre-eminent in courage and fame, a Moor named Munnuza,[152] hearing that

---

[149]The same Abd ar-Rahman (*Chr754* 69) who had served as interim governor between as-Samh and Anbasah.

[150]Muhammad ibn Abd Allah al-Ashjai (730).

[151]Abd ar-Rahman ibn Abd Allah al Ghafiqi (730-2).

[152]The Berber Uthman ibn Abu Nisah, also known as Munnuza, attempted to set up an independent principality for himself just north of the Pyrenees at Cerdanya. He allied himself with Eudes, the duke of Aquitaine, and received his daughter in marriage. S. M. Imamuddin, *A Political History of Muslim Spain*, 4th ed. (Karachi, 1984), p. 41.

his people were being oppressed by the harsh temerity of the judges in the territory of Libya, quickly made peace with the Franks and organized a revolt against the Saracens of Spain. The palace was gravely disturbed once everyone had become aware of this because Munnuza was well-equipped for war. Not many days later, Abd ar-Rahman angrily prepared an army for battle and fiercely pursued the aforementioned rebel without mercy. When the warrior was found in the town of Cerdanya, he was surrounded by a siege. After being walled in for some time, he suddenly burst into flight, as a result of a judgement of God, and was deprived of his authority. He had made himself drunk on the blood of the Christians—the innocent blood that he had shed in that same place—and had burned to death the illustrious bishop Anambadus[153] in the flower of his youth. Already damned for these crimes, Munnuza was exhausted and hampered by thirst—due to the scarcity of water in the city despite its previous abundance—and did not know where to flee. He remained at large, on the verge of death, with the army following right behind along different paths. A commander of the Franks by the name of Eudes had once, in the interests of securing an alliance aimed at forestalling Arab attacks, given his daughter to Munnuza in marriage to satisfy his desires; but Munnuza did nothing to protect her from the band of pursuers. So Munnuza prepared his soul for death. Mocking the army in pursuit, he threw himself, already wounded, from a high pinnacle, onto the sharp edges of the rocks below, so as to avoid being captured alive, and thus gave up his soul. His pursuers found him and immediately cut off his head, presenting it along with the daughter of the general Eudes to the king. Abd ar-Rahman received her honourably, resolving to send her across the sea to the sublime prince.[154]

---

[153]Perhaps Bishop Nambaudus of nearby Urgel. Collins, *Arab Conquest*, p. 89.
[154]The governor Abd ar-Rahman sent Eudes' daughter to Damascus where she was married to one of the caliph Hisham's sons. Imamuddin, p. 41.

80. Then Abd ar-Rahman, seeing the land filled with the multitude of his army, cut through the rocky mountains of the Basques so that, crossing the plains, he might invade the lands of the Franks. He struck so far into Frankish territory that he joined battle with Eudes on the other side of the rivers Garonne and Dordogne. God only knows the number of those who died or fled, Eudes himself slipping away in flight. While Abd ar-Rahman was pursuing Eudes, he decided to despoil Tours by destroying its palaces and burning its churches. There he confronted the consul of Austrasia by the name of Charles,[155] a man who, having proved himself to be a warrior from his youth and an expert in things military, had been summoned by Eudes. After each side had tormented the other with raids for almost seven days, they finally prepared their battle lines and fought fiercely. The northern peoples remained as immobile as a wall, holding together like a glacier in the cold regions. In the blink of an eye, they annihilated the Arabs with the sword.[156] The people of Austrasia, greater in number of soldiers and formidably armed, killed the king, Abd ar-Rahman, when they found him, striking him on the chest. But suddenly, within sight of the countless tents of the Arabs, the Franks despicably sheathed their swords, postponing the fight until the next day since night had fallen during the battle. Rising from their own camp at dawn, the Europeans saw the tents and canopies of the Arabs all arranged just as they had appeared the day before. Not knowing that they were empty and thinking that inside them there were Saracen forces ready for battle, they sent officers to reconnoitre and discovered that all of the Ishmaelite troops had left. They had indeed fled silently by night in tight formation, returning to their own country. Worried that the Saracens might attempt to ambush them, the Europeans were slow to react and thus they searched in vain all around. Deciding against pursuing the Saracens,

---

[155]Charles Martel, mayor of the palace of Austrasia (714-41).

[156]The famous Battle of Poitiers (or Tours). The traditional date is 732, but in fact the battle probably took place in 733 or 734. Collins, *Arab Conquest*, pp. 90-1.

they took the spoils—which they divided fairly amongst themselves—back to their country and were overjoyed.

81. In the era 772 (734), in the fourteenth year of the emperor Leo, the one hundred sixteenth of the Arabs and the twelfth of Hisham, Abd al-Malik, from a noble family, was sent by order of the prince to be the governor of Spain.[157] He found it, despite all it had been through, to be abundant in every good thing and, even after all its suffering, to be filled with beauty, so that you could say that it was like a pomegranate in August. But he treated it so harshly for almost four years that little by little it was ruined, cut off from its neighbours. His judges, seized with cupidity, so defiled Spain with their deceit that not only did it begin to decline from that time on as if moribund, but it remained, deprived of all its best men, completely without hope of recovery. When the prince rebuked him for having won no military victories in the land of the Franks, Abd al-Malik immediately left Córdoba with the entire army and tried to subdue the inhabitants of the Pyrenean mountains. But leading the expedition through the narrow passes, he won no victories. After launching occasional attacks here and there in these remote places and losing many of his soldiers, he was convinced of the power of God, from whom the small band of Christians holding the pinnacles awaited mercy. He retreated to the plains and returned home through unfamiliar territory.

82. A little later, in the era 775 (737), in the seventeenth year of the emperor Leo, the one hundred nineteenth of the Arabs, and the fifteenth of Hisham, came a successor to Abd al-Malik by the name of Uqbah.[158] After he had attained the height of power, all Spain trembled before his lineage[159] and his enforcement of the law, as he bound his predecessor in chains and severely punished the judges appointed by him. After

---

[157] Abd al-Malik ibn Qatan (732-4).

[158] Uqbah ibn Hajjaj (734-40).

[159] His father, al-Hajjaj (d. 714), was the Umayyad governor of Iraq.

extending the ceremonies of the law, he ordered a census to be taken of the people and strenuously promoted the exaction of tribute. He sent Spanish malefactors and those implicated in crimes away in ships designated for this purpose. He very energetically enriched the fisc by various means and lived austerely on his private income. He condemned no one except according to the justice of his own law. He also undertook an expedition against the Franks with a large army. He left proudly with his great army, heading toward the city of Zaragoza. But when he learned, by means of letters sent from Africa, of a rebellion on the part of the Moors,[160] he returned to Córdoba without delay and as quickly as possible made his way through the Transductine mountains. Dispatching Arabs to the Moorish strongholds without success, he crossed the sea himself when the ships that he had been waiting for arrived. Whenever he encountered any rebels, traitors, evil-doers, or those heretics whom they call 'Arures',[161] he decapitated them with the sword. Thus, disposing everything as best he could and guarding the Trinacrian ports,[162] he clemently ascended his throne. After a short time, that is to say, five years later, Uqbah became ill and he restored the kingdom to Abd al-Malik. As soon as the disease reached his vital organs, Uqbah departed from the world.

---

[160]The Berber rebellion in North Africa lasted for nine years in North Africa (734-42) and spread to Spain in 740. The Berbers, who constituted the bulk of the invading force in 711, never received their share of the power in Muslim Spain, which was politically dominated by the Arabs. After the invasion, the Berbers tended to settle in the northern plateau region where they lived primarily as herders. With the revolt, many of the Berbers left Spain and returned to Morocco. Imamuddin, pp. 41-2. Hodgson, 1:216, 221-2.

[161]Most likely a reference to the Kharijites (a.k.a. al-Haruriya), the earliest sectarian movement within Islam, dating from the mid-seventh century. *Encyclopaedia of Islam*, 2nd ed., 4:1074.

[162]Precise location unknown.

83. At this time Urban and Evantius, learned men strengthened with the great zeal of their sanctity, passed joyfully to the Lord and rested in peace.[163]

84. In the era 780 (742), the twenty-second year of the emperor Leo, the one hundred twenty-fourth of the Arabs, and the twentieth of Hisham, Abd al-Malik was again elected king of the Arabs with everyone's consent.[164] At that time, Hisham, seized by an iniquitous rage, loosed the bridle of his cupidity, leaving it unrestrained, and all the peoples under his power immediately flung themselves into civil war.[165] All that vast desert, from which the Arab multitudes had arisen, was full of unrest, unable to tolerate the injustice of the judges. And in the western region, which extends to the southern zone and which is occupied more than any of the others by the Moors, the inhabitants openly shook their necks from the Arab yoke, unanimous and determined in their wrath.[166] When Hisham realized the scale of the rebellion, he immediately sent powerful reinforcements of 100,000 soldiers to the African governor. After Kultum[167] was given command over the armies of the east and the west, they made their way to African soil, organized into companies and phalanxes. They decided on their own initiative to hasten toward the sea, crossing the territory of the Moors to attack Tangiers with the sword. But the army of the Moors, realizing this, immediately burst forth from the mountains naked, girded only with loin-cloths over their shameful parts. When they joined with each other in battle at the Nava river, the Egyptian horses immediately recoiled in flight, as the Moors on their beautiful horses revealed their repulsive colour and gnashed their white teeth. The Arab cavalry launched another attack in despair but again recoiled instantly due to the colour of the Moors' skin. The horses fled in fear,

---

[163]See above: *Chr754* 70.
[164]Abd al-Malik ibn Qatan (restored: 740-1). See: *Chr754* 81.
[165]See above: *Chr754* 76.
[166]The Berber rebellion.
[167]The commander of the Syrian army.

resulting in their death as well as the death of their riders. Hastening without restraint or rest through rough and out-of-the-way places, many perished in the vast desert. In this manner, all the forces from the east as well as the west were dispersed, slipping away in flight. Kultum, the commander, was decapitated by his exhausted allies.[168] The whole army found itself divided into three groups: one part was held captive in the hands of the victors; another, like vagabonds, turned and fled, trying to return home. A third part, confused and not knowing where to go, headed for Spain—oh the pain!—with Balj,[169] a man of good lineage and an expert in military matters, as their leader.

85. At that time, as we said above, in the era 780 (742), in the twenty-second year of emperor Leo and the twentieth of Hisham, Abd al-Malik ruled Spain. When he discovered that the third part of the army under Balj had arrived at the port,[170] he denied them a crossing by withholding the ships. When the Moors of Spain realized this, they gathered for war, wanting to subject Abd al-Malik to themselves, cross over the sea in ships, and offer his conquered kingdom to their allies on the other side of the sea. Dividing themselves into three groups, they sent one to Toledo to attack the strong walls of the city; they directed another to kill Abd al-Malik at his residence in Córdoba; and they dispatched the third to the port of Ceuta to watch for the arrival of Balj's forces, which had fled after the battle with the Moors. But Abd al-Malik sent companies of soldiers against each of these groups of Moors. The first one he destroyed by means of a detachment under the command of his son Umayyah, sixteen miles from the city of Toledo, which had been under siege for twenty-seven days. The second one he assailed with forces under the command of the Arab al-Muzar, thus diverting it into another region, though not without losing al-Muzar and the army. The third one,

---

[168]G. Sumner, 'The Mozarabic Chronicle of 754 and the Location of the Berber victory over the army of Kultum', *Al-Qantara* I (1980), pp. 443-6.

[169]Balj ibn Bishr al-Qushayri, a nephew of Kultum.

[170]Ceuta.

which had come to the city of Algeciras to capture those responsible for
the naval defence, he destroyed with ships under the command of Balj,
whom a short time before he had denied passage to Spain.[171]

86. Having frightened the rebels, Abd al-Malik headed home and
admonished Balj by letter that he should return to his homeland. But Balj,
deceitful and troublesome, remembered what great torments of hunger
Abd al-Malik had inflicted on him. When Abd ar-Rahman launched an
attack against him, Balj forced his way into Córdoba, after it had resisted
him for some time. Finding Abd al-Malik abandoned by his sons as well
as by his army, Balj tortured him at length, cutting him with whips and
dissecting his entire body as if it were a fish,[172] before he finally
decapitated him with a sword. So great were the battles that ensued
between the armies gathered by the easterners with their leader Balj and
the westerners[173] under Abd al-Malik's son Umayyah—as the aforesaid
era expired, in the already noted year of emperor Leo and of Hisham the
Amir Almuminim—that the human tongue is scarcely able to express it.[174]
But because no one in all of Spain is ignorant of these events, this history
has only summarized these tragic wars. In a separate work, already
written by my own pen, all the events have been laid out clearly.[175]

87. At this time, in the era 781 (743), in the twenty-third year of the
emperor Leo and the one hundred twenty fifth of the Arabs, Walid 'the

---

[171]Though Abd al-Malik had hesitated to allow Balj to cross, he ultimately conceded
because he needed Balj's assistance against the rebelling Berbers.

[172]The Latin reads: *more sequati. Sequati* poses a problem. It could be either a form of
squatus, a type of fish (see Isidore's *Etymologies* 12.6.37), or a form of *sequax*, meaning a
'following'. López Pereira (p. 113) has opted for the latter, rendering the phrase, *more
sequati*, as 'in the customary manner'. But I find it difficult to get 'customary' out of the
basic meaning of *sequax*. López Pereira attributes the 'fish' interpretation to Juan Gil.

[173]That is, the Syrians led by Balj versus the Andalusians led by Umayyah.

[174]Though the Syrians ultimately prevailed, Balj himself died in the course of the decisive
battle near Córdoba in 742. Lévi-Provençal, p. 47.

[175]Unfortunately this work is no longer extant.

Fair' was unanimously placed on the throne as *Amir Almuminim* in the appropriate place.[176] The kingdom remained his for a year and nine months before it was suddenly taken away by Yazid.[177]

1. At that time, in the era 782 (744), a warlike man by the name of Theodemir died. He had brought no little destruction to the Arabs in various parts of Spain. But after maintaining this level of destruction for a long time, he ultimately negotiated peace with them. Under both Egica and Witiza, kings of the Goths, he had triumphed with the palm of victory over the Greek kings whose sailors had descended upon his land.[178] Great dignity and honour were conferred upon him and indeed, when questioned by the eastern Christians, such steadfastness regarding the true faith was found in him that everyone gave no small praise to God. He was a lover of the scriptures, marvellously eloquent, and ever ready in battle. The *Amir Almuminim* found him to be more prudent than the rest and treated him with honour. The pact that Theodemir had made with Abd al-Aziz some time before was firmly renewed.[179] Theodemir returned to Spain rejoicing and remained secure from then on, so that in no way were these powerful bonds dissolved by subsequent Arab rulers.[180]

2. After Theodemir's death, Athanagild[181] enjoyed great honour and authority. He was a most generous lord to everyone, dispensing no

---

[176]Walid II (743-4).

[177]Yazid III (744). See: *Chr754* 88.

[178]Presumably a reference to the imperial forces based in North Africa before the Muslim conquest.

[179]This pact, worked out between Theodemir, Count of Murcia, and Abd al-Aziz in the wake of the conquest, has survived in Arabic sources. Francisco X. Simonet. *Historia de los mozárabes de España* (Madrid, 1903), pp. 797-8.

[180]This paragraph and the one following are thought to be later interpolations. López Pereira, *Estudio*, pp. 40-3.

[181]Probably Theodemir's son.

little wealth. But after a time, the king al-Husam[182] came to Spain and, seized by I know not what madness, inflicted no little injury on Athanagild, fining him 27,000 *solidi*. Considering the armies which had come with the general Balj, Athanagild produced all of the money within the space of scarcely three days and was quickly restored to the grace of al-Husam—who bore the cognomen, Abu al-Khattar. Al-Husam exalted Athanagild and remunerated him with various gifts.

88. In the era 782 (744), the twenty-fourth year of emperor Leo, the first year of Walid's rule having expired, all of Spain was shaken by internal strife until Abu al-Khattar, sent by order of his prince, calmed all of these disorders. Abu al-Khattar, called al-Husam, solicitously took care to govern the land committed to him. Without delay he sent the army overseas under the pretext of war so as to bring the proud ones of Spain under control. In the era 782 (744)—the twenty-fourth year of the emperor Leo having come to an end along with the one hundred twenty-fifth of the Arabs, with the one hundred twenty-sixth just beginning, and Yazid Walid[183] having been in power for almost a year, having been placed there as a result of a rebellion, with the entire east embroiled in unheard of wars—all at once everyone,[184] informed of the death of Walid,[185] began to think that they should expel Abu al-Khattar from power. They plotted together with Sumayl,[186] a man endowed with authority over his people, to remove Abu al-Khattar from the city of Córdoba—at that time the royal residence—in an act of rebellion. After considering various options, they finally put one into action. In accordance with the plan, Sumayl feigned flight and without delay Abu al-Khattar pursued headlong with his palace guard. A number of those

---

[182] Abu al-Khattar Husam ibn Dhirar al-Khalbi (743-5).

[183] Yazid III. See: *Chr754* 87.

[184] That is, everyone in Spain.

[185] That is, Walid II (*Chr754* 87), whose death in 744, as the chronicler has just informed us, led to the accession of Yazid Walid or Yazid III.

[186] As-Sumayl ibn Hatim al-Kilabi, closely connected to Balj.

who pursued the rebel with him, however, had conspired with the enemy and eagerly sped off with the king according to the insidious plan. When they joined their vengeful swords in battle, these counts disengaged themselves from the fighting and the forces of Sumayl immediately overcame Abu al-Khattar, who was left all alone. After killing Abu al-Khattar's men, Sumayl's army pursued the king who fled in the company of three men who remained loyal to him.

1. At this time Cixila,[187] a most holy man, who had, from his very cradle, faithfully served God, occupied the see of Toledo...[188] and from the invasion of the Arabs into the aforementioned church...he was ordained metropolitan of the church. Erudite in holy things, he was a restorer of churches and, in accordance with the scriptures, was most firm in hope, faith, and charity,...he was known to all on account of his merits. One day a man seduced by the Sabellian heresy[189]...wanted to approach, he was asked by Cixila if he was conscious of such sin, and he, denying the sin.... Immediately, he was seized by a demon so that everyone congregated in the church was left in a daze. But the holy man gave himself to prayer and restored him safe and sound to the holy church. Having carried out his apostolate for nine years, in the same spirit of charity with which he had begun, he came to the end of his life.[190]

Then they elevated to the throne Thalabah, who had furnished strong auxiliary support to Sumayl.[191] Abu al-Khattar remained at large, hiding among his own people, hoping to renew the struggle. After spending

---

[187]Cixila authored an extant life of Ildephonsus of Toledo. *Corpus scriptorum muzarabicorum* 1:60-6.

[188]The ellipses indicate lacunae in the manuscript.

[189]One branch of the Monarchian form of Trinitarian heresy.

[190]This has traditionally been regarded as an interpolation. Collins has questioned whether this is justified. *Arab Conquest*, pp. 72-3.

[191]Thalabah ibn Salamah (745-7).

some time stirring up battles that contributed to his own demise as well as
to that of his people, he destroyed himself, as well as the army allied to
him, in an awful manner. Whosoever might wish to learn about these
events will find them all set out in a chronological summary which we
assembled a short time ago.[192] He will also find recorded there all the
battles that the Moors fought against Kultum and he will be able to read
accounts of the wars that threatened Spain at that time.

89. When the era 782 (744) had ended and the era 783 (745) had
begun, Constantine, son of Leo, became the sixty-eighth to be crowned
emperor of the Romans, succeeding his father, and ruled for "x" years,
5,954 years having elapsed from the beginning of the world up to the
completion of Constantine's tenth year.[193] When his father had reached
his last day and Constantine was crowned emperor, he discovered that
Ardabastus, who had joined himself to Constantine's family,[194] was about
to seize power. Ardabastus, who was one of Constantine's generals, had
secretly and gradually gathered all the soldiers of the palace on the
pretext of using them to fight against other peoples. Then, when he saw
Constantine alone and about to be abandoned by the senate, he advanced
in haste with the allies who were with him to frighten Constantine from
the palace and then do away with him. When Constantine found out that
Ardabastus was approaching with a wild band of soldiers, he left his
residence with his men to seek help from the neighbouring peoples. At
length, when he saw that he had the support of the army, he hastened
back to his former residence and warned Ardabastus to relinquish the
palace. But Ardabastus gave instructions to the people that they were not
to open the gates of the city to the approaching army. Finding the city

---

[192]The chronicler has already referred to this work in *Chr754* 86.

[193]Constantine V (741-75). Our author, writing in 754, could only indicate how many years
Constantine had ruled up to that time.

[194]Ardabastus, an imperial general in Armenia, was married to Constantine's sister. In 742,
he proclaimed himself emperor and occupied Constantinople. By 743, Constantine was
back in control. Ostrogorsky, 165-6.

was fortified against him, Constantine encircled it with his people and besieged it, preparing for a fierce war. After almost three years, the citizens had been rendered weak from hunger. Constantine negotiated peace with them through intermediaries and Ardabastus was handed over, bound in chains and greatly oppressed with the weight of the iron. He was sent into exile, after being tortured and having his eyes put out, without ever having been interrogated as to why he had committed so great a crime.

90. At this time, in the beginning of the era 783 (745), the first year of Constantine, with the one hundred twenty-seventh of the Arabs about to expire, everyone in the land quickly learned that Yazid Walid had died a natural death and that his brother Ibrahim[195] had been left as his replacement. But an Arab named Marwan,[196] approaching the doomed palace while Ibrahim was distracted by various domestic matters, ferociously sought war through rebellion. In the era 784 (746), the second year of the emperor Constantine and the one hundred twenty-eighth of the Arabs, Marwan, fighting along with his allies, came upon Ibrahim with very few of his men and, in his desire to obtain the palace, immediately struck him with his sword. As a result of this deed, Marwan was hindered by civil war and lived in rebellion for five years, waging various battles.[197] He was finally pursued from Damascus to the Babylonian plains by Zali, paternal uncle of Abd Allah, whom the great multitude of the Ishmaelites had elected to be their prince. After crossing the Nile, Marwan was decapitated.[198]

---

[195]Ibrahim (744).

[196]Marwan was the Umayyad governor of Armenia at the time of his rebellion against Ibrahim.

[197]Marwan II (744-50) was to be the last of the Umayyad caliphs in the east.

[198]The chronicler covers the pursuit and death of Marwan in more detail below: *Chr754* 94.

91. At this time, in the aforesaid era 784 (746), in the second year of the emperor Constantine, the one hundred twenty-eighth year of the Arabs, and the second of Marwan, Thalabah, a warlike man of noble lineage, was appointed in Spain with unanimous support. He ruled for one year, the kingdom having been previously taken away from Abu al-Khattar with the help of Sumayl. When Thalabah died a natural death in the era 785 (747)—the third year of the emperor Constantine, the end of the one hundred twenty-ninth and the beginning of the one hundred thirtieth year of the Arabs, and the third of Marwan—Yusuf, noble and aged, was wonderfully acclaimed by all the senate of the palace as king of the land.[199] After a few days, the Arabs stirred up various rebellions against him throughout Spain, but without success, and they surrendered their souls to hell. Yusuf ordered a census of the remaining people to be taken and, although it amounted to embezzlement, he solicitously ordered the scribes to erase from the public records the names of those Christian taxpayers who had been killed by the sword during the great slaughter.[200]

92. In the sixth year of Constantine's rule, in the era 788 (750), on Sunday, the nones of April, during the first, second, and part of the third hours, with all the citizens of Córdoba watching, three suns, shining in a wondrous manner and fading into a crescent of emerald fire, were seen. From the moment of their appearance, avenging angels laid low with an intolerable famine all those who by the grace of God lived in the land of Spain.

93. At that same time, Deacon Peter of the see of Toledo was known throughout Spain as a beautiful chanter and for being most learned in all the scriptures. He wrote a beautiful little book composed from the work

---

[199]Yusuf ibn Abd ar-Rahman al-Fihri (747-56).
[200]Presumably a reference to the civil war between Balj and Umayyah (*Chr754* 86).

of various patristic authors for the benefit of the inhabitants of Seville because of their errors in celebrating Easter.[201]

94. In Constantine's time, in the era 788 (750), in his sixth year as emperor, the one hundred thirty-third of the Arabs, and the first of Abd Allah Alescemi, Marwan was pursued, as we said, by the army and terrified by the rebellion of his people.[202] He fled from the palace with the public treasure intending to enter Libya and prepare to fight anew. Abd Allah, now fearing nothing, made for the royal palace at the instigation of the nobles. Immediately he sent his paternal uncle Zali after Marwan with a huge army of Persian soldiers, who still worshipped the sun and black demons.[203] They vehemently pursued Marwan, who was fleeing from city to city but who found no refuge on account of the evil things he had done and the various slaughters he had brought upon the Saracens. Coming to the Nile River in Egypt, he crossed it. When the two armies confronted each other in a place that they call in their tongue, Azunummin,[204] they attacked each other so forcefully that they mercilessly annihilated each other for two days, with many being slaughtered on both sides. At the beginning of the third day, Marwan was overcome and killed and the armies returned their swords to their sheaths and rested. Then, after sending the heads of the magnates to Abd Allah, Zali rewarded the soldiers handsomely from the booty, and effectively pacified all the original borders. But the remaining deeds—how both sides engaged in

---

[201] A letter from Peter to Felix, bishop of Córdoba, regarding this error is extant. *Corpus scriptorum muzarabicorum* 1:55-8.

[202] The chronicler is describing one of the episodes in the Abbasid revolution, which ended the Syrian-based rule of the Umayyad dynasty. The revolt culminated in the defeat of the Umayyad army at the Battle of the Greater Zab in Mesopotamia and Marwan II's flight to Egypt, where he was killed in 750. The Abbasid forces were led by Abd Allah ibn Ali (here identified as Zali), whose nephew, Abu al-Abbas as-Saffah (here identified as Abd Allah Alescemi) became the first Abbasid caliph (750-4). *Encyclopaedia of Islam* 1:103.

[203] A reference to Zoroastrianism.

[204] Ushmunayn, on the west bank of the Nile in Upper Egypt.

battle and how the wars in Spain under the princes Balj, Thalamah,[205] and Umayyah came about and were concluded under Abu al-Khattar, and in which order, under prince Yusuf, their rivals were killed—'were these not recorded in the book of the words of the days'[206] of this age, which we took upon ourselves to add to earlier chronicles?[207]

95. 5,954 years have passed from the beginning of the world to the era 792 (754), which has now begun, the tenth year of the emperor Constantine, the fourth of Abd Allah, the *Amir Almuminim*, the seventh of Yusuf in the land of Spain, and the one hundred thirty-sixth of the Arabs. If you wish, you may subtract four of these years in accordance with certain historians who diligently affirm that this should be done, computing the fifty-sixth year of the reign of Octavian to have expired in the 5,210th year of the world and asserting that Christ was born in Octavian's forty-second year. So it is in the sixth chapter of the first book of the *Ecclesiastical History* of lord Bishop Eusebius of Caesarea[208] as well as the *Chronicle* of the master Isidore[209] and all the scriptures, which also indicate the same year: subtracting fourteen years from Octavian's fifty-six, forty-two remain at the time of the birth of Christ. When the fifth year of Julius Caesar was completed, 5,154 years of the world had passed. Adding the forty-two of Octavian, 5,196 years had passed from Adam to the nativity of Christ, which, as we said above, is four years less than 5,200. If the 754 years since the Incarnation of the Lord—which is computed as the era 792—are added to the aforesaid 5,196 years, you get 5,950 years of the world, the four years having been subtracted.[210] But

---

[205]Probably a reference to Thala ibn Salama, one of Balj's successors. López Pereira, *Crónica mozárabe*, p. 127.

[206]I Kings 15:7, etc.

[207]This list of the contents suggests that it is the same as the 'epitome' cited by the author above (*Chr754* 86, 88).

[208]Eusebius, *Ecclesiastical History* 1.5.

[209]Isidore, *Chronicle* 66.

[210]In other words, if, as Isidore and Eusebius maintained, the last year of Octavian's fifty-six-year rule was the 5,210th year since the creation of the world, the forty-second year

because the years of the world have not been calculated sufficiently clearly by our predecessors so as to be numbered equally according to the same system or reckoned alike by all historians within a single sequence[211]—although with regard to this particular discrepancy in years the opinions are not so different from one another—we have added those four years in accordance with the many who contend that Christ was born in the year 5,200, lest we stray too far from the path that so many distinguished men have followed. Over such a large period of time, the addition or subtraction of four years would not seem to be damning, given the fact that in various other books of chronicles even more years are added or subtracted from the total which we have indicated. Because a part of a year is often counted as a whole or a whole as a part, or because the beginning or the end of a year of a given emperor is counted as one full year, you cannot easily decide, as we have said, between all those who affirm that the birth of Christ occurred in Octavian's forty-second year and those who show that he was born in Octavian's forty-first. Thus the most holy Julian, bishop of Toledo, in the book on the six ages of the world which he wrote against the Jews, says, 'Octavian Caesar ruled for fifty-six years. In his forty-first year, as Tertullian and Jerome bear witness, Christ the son of God was born from the perpetually virgin Mary'.[212] Is this in any way prejudiced by the fact that some reckon it to be the forty-second year and others the forty-first? Of course not. But the nativity of our Saviour has been calculated by the ancients— using two methods, too long to recount—as occurring in 5,200, so that through the generations and reigns, the 'fullness of time'[213] might be

---

of his rule (the year of Christ's birth) would be the 5,196th year. Adding the 754 years that had elapsed between Christ's birth and the time that the chronicle was written, the result would be 5,950, four short of the chronicler's choice of 5,954. The virtue of the latter figure, as the text indicates, is that it allows for placing Christ's birth in the year 5,200, a nicely rounded, 'beautiful' number.

[211]Compare John of Biclaro's calculation: Biclaro, Epilogue.

[212]Julian of Toledo, *De sextae aetatis comprobatione* 34.

[213]Galatians 4:4.

demonstrated, and through this perfect number, most full of beauty, that day that all should venerate might, by the perfect span of 5,200 years, be more clearly impressed even on those who treat it lightly. Thus it is right that the holy nativity be declared openly and that the number be not distorted with different numbers—whether more or less—of years. Julian, the most holy and learned with regard to this question, said, in the book that we mentioned above, 'If we want to determine the number of years from the beginning of the world to the nativity of Christ, according to the books of the seventy translators,[214] and according to certain national histories, we will find there to be 5,200 years from Adam to Christ; anything else is too much, according to those historians who have written about the chronology of the world'.[215]

---

[214]A reference to the Septuagint, the Greek Old Testament, which, according to tradition, was translated from the Hebrew simultaneously and identically by seventy different scholars in Alexandria in the third century B.C.E.

[215]Julian of Toledo, *De sextae aetatis comprobatione* 15.

THE CHRONICLE OF ALFONSO III

Here begins the chronicle of the Visigoths compiled from the time of King Wamba up to the present in the time of the glorious King Ordoño of holy memory, son of King Alfonso.[1]

1. Reccesuinth, king of the Goths,[2] left the city of Toledo and came to his own villa, the name of which was Gerticos—though it is now called Bamba by the people and is known to be near Mt. Caure[3]—and there he died a natural death. And after the king had come to the end of his life and was buried in that same place, Wamba was elected king by everyone in common, in the era 710 (672).[4] At first Wamba declined, not wanting to assume power, but he finally accepted against his will what the army requested. He was taken immediately to Toledo and was anointed king in the church of St Mary.[5] At that very hour in the presence of everyone, a bee was seen springing from Wamba's head and flying up into the heavens. This sign was made by the Lord so as to herald future victories, which actually came to pass.[6] Many times Wamba subdued the Asturians

---

[1]There is some ambiguity as to whether the Ordoño referred to in this *incipit* is the son of Alfonso III (Ordoño II) or his father (Ordoño I). Moralejo (*Crónicas Asturianas*, p. 194) has opted for the latter interpretation; Bonnaz (p. 31), the former. The parallel structure of the *incipit* of the Oviedo version of the chronicle, with its unambiguous reference to Alfonso's other son, García, leads me to agree with Bonnaz.

[2]Reccesuinth (649-72).

[3]Near Toledo.

[4]Wamba (672-80). The parenthetical dates in the text are simply 'translations' of the 'era' dates given by the chronicler. The notes provide the standard dates.

[5]Wamba's was the earliest anointment of a medieval king for which we have a reliable source: Julian of Toledo's *History of King Wamba*. Abilio Barbero, 'El pensamiento político visigódo y las primeras unciones regias en la Europa medieval', *Hispania* 30 (1970), pp. 314-16. The chronicler clearly relied on Julian for his information about Wamba.

[6]'Bees', observed Isidore (*Etymologies*, 12.8.1), 'have kings and armies', making them an appropriate symbol for royal power. Roger Collins, 'Julian of Toledo and the Royal Succession in Late Seventh-century Spain', in P. H. Sawyer and I. N. Wood, *Early Medieval Kingship* (Leeds, 1977), pp. 46-7.

and Basques, who rebelled frequently, and subjected them to his dominion. Paul, a certain general who was sent to the province of Gallia Narbonensis, immediately rebelled and threw all of that country into disorder. Assisted by the armies of the Franks, he prepared for battle against King Wamba. This was reported by messenger to the king in Vasconia and immediately he moved his army into the region of Gallia Narbonensis. The king pursued Paul, who fled from city to city, until he entered Nîmes, where Wamba besieged him. On the third day Wamba captured the city. He dealt with Paul judicially and ordered that his eyes be put out. He also killed many Frankish troops there and brought that province under his authority, returning in triumph to the city of Toledo.[7]

2. In Wamba's time, 270 Saracen ships attacked the coast of Spain and there all of them were destroyed and burned.[8] King Wamba arranged for synods to be held frequently in Toledo, just as he proclaimed most fully in his canonical decree.[9] Previously, in the time of King Chindasuinth,[10] a man by the name of Ardabastus came from Greece—after being expelled from his country by the emperor—crossed the sea, and arrived in Spain. King Chindasuinth received him magnificently and gave to him his niece in marriage. From this union was born a son by the name of Ervig. After Ervig had been reared in the palace and exalted with the rank of count, he became puffed up with pride, and cunningly plotted against King Wamba. He gave him an herb called *spartus* to drink and immediately Wamba's memory was taken away. When the bishop of the city and the nobles of the palace who were faithful to the king, ignorant of the workings of the potion, saw the king prostrate and without his memory, they were moved out of piety to administer immediately the order of confession and penance, lest the king die outside of the order of penance. When the king recovered from the potion and understood what had happened, he went straight to a monastery.[11] And there he remained in

---

[7]This episode (673) is the focal point of Julian's *History of King Wamba.* The incident is summarized by Thompson, pp. 219-28.

[8]There is no other record of this remarkably early Muslim raid.

[9]This is a reference to Toledo XI (675), which began with a formal expression of the king's regret that nineteen years had passed since the last Toledan council. Vives, p. 344.

[10]Chindasuinth (642-53).

[11]At this early stage, the ritual of penance was not repeatable, so it was necessary to protect the shriven Christian from committing another irremediable sin. This was one of the

the religious life the rest of his days. He had been king for nine years and one month and then lived in the monastery for seven years and three months. He died a natural death in the era 719 (681).

3. After Wamba, Ervig took up the kingship that he had obtained rebelliously.[12] He held many synods and removed in part the laws issued by his predecessor and ordered others to be recorded in his own name.[13] He was, they say, pious and moderate toward his subjects. He also gave his daughter Cixilo in marriage to the nobleman Egica, nephew of Wamba. Ervig died a natural death in Toledo. He had ruled for six years and four months.

4. In the era 725 (687), Ervig's son-in-law Egica succeeded him as king.[14] He was wise and patient. He held general synods. He subdued many rebellious peoples within the kingdom. He did battle with the Franks three times but won no victory. When he ascended to the kingship, his maternal uncle, King Wamba, ordered him to repudiate his wife Cixilo because her father Ervig had cunningly removed him from power. Egica followed his orders and dismissed her on some pretext. But before her repudiation, she had given Egica a son named Witiza whom the king made his partner in rule during his own lifetime. Egica ordered Witiza to live in the city of Tuy so that, while the father held the kingship of the Goths, the son would rule the Suevi. Egica ruled for ten years

---

functions of the the so-called 'order of penance', a semi-monastic regimen which the penitent sinner was expected to observe for the rest of his or her life. Not surprisingly, many waited until their deathbed to undergo the ritual. But the occasional penitent who recovered from his maladies was no less subject to the restraints of the order of penance, which included abstaining from sexual activity as well as from the exercise of political authority. Wamba fell into this category. Canon 17 of Toledo VI (638) specifically prohibited anyone who had been tonsured or who had assumed the religious habit—thereby including those who lived as penitents—from ruling. Vives, pp. 244-5.

   In the account of Ervig's succession recorded in the proceedings of Toledo XII (681)—over which Ervig presided—there is no mention of foul play; only that the king became ill, prematurely received penance, and instructed Julian of Toledo to anoint Ervig. Vives, p. 386. As Thompson observes (p. 231), it is Ervig's efforts to excuse himself at Toledo XII that add to the suspicion of foul play.

[12]Ervig (680-7).

[13]One of many official revisions of the Visigothic legal code. Thompson, pp. 238-9.

[14]Egica (687-702).

before the accession of his son and five more years with his son as co-ruler. He died a natural death in Toledo.

5. In the era 739 (701), after the death of Egica, Witiza returned to Toledo to the royal throne.[15] He was a reprobate and was disgraceful in his habits. He dissolved the councils. He sealed the canons. He took many wives and concubines. And to prevent any council from being convened against him, he ordered the bishops, priests, and deacons to take wives.[16] This, then, was the cause of Spain's ruin. Thus says the scripture, 'Because iniquity abounded, charity grew cold'.[17] And another passage from scripture says, 'If the people sin, the priest prays, but if the priests sin, there will be a plague upon the people'.[18] They withdrew from the Lord and did not walk in the paths of his precepts nor did they attentively observe how the Lord prohibited priests from acting evilly when he said to Moses in Exodus, 'Let the priests who come to the Lord God be sanctified lest the Lord foresake them'.[19] And again: 'When they approach to serve at the holy altar, let them not bring along any sin within them lest perchance they die'.[20] And because the kings and priests forsook the Lord, all of the armies of Spain perished. Meanwhile, after the tenth year of his reign, Witiza died a natural death in Toledo, in the era 749 (711).

6. With Witiza dead, Roderic was elected king by the Goths.[21] Before we relate his rise to the kingship, we shall report on his family. Roderic was the son of Theodefred. Theodefred was the son of King Chindasuinth, his father abandoning him at a young age. When Theodefred reached maturity, King Egica feared that he might be elected king in his place. Thinking that Theodefred might conspire with the Goths and force him from his father's[22] throne, Egica commanded that he be blinded. After being expelled from the royal city, Theodefred went to

---

[15]Witiza (698-710).

[16]See p. 50 above.

[17]Matthew 24:12.

[18]Numbers 8:19, 16, 46-8.

[19]Exodus 19:22.

[20]Leviticus 21:33; Matthew 5:23.

[21]Roderic (710-11).

[22]That is, Theodefred's father, Chindasuinth.

live in Córdoba. There he chose a wife by the name of Ricilo, from a noble family, and she gave birth to their son Roderic. When Roderic grew up and reached maturity, he was a warlike man. Before he became king, he built a palace in the city of Córdoba which is now called 'uallat Ruderici' by the Chaldeans.[23] Now let us return to the events of his reign.

7. After Witiza died, Roderic was anointed as king. In his time Spain grew even worse in its iniquity. In the third year of his rule, the Saracens entered Spain on account of the treachery of the sons of Witiza.[24] When the king became aware of their invasion, he immediately went out with his army to fight against them. But, weighed down by the quantity of their sins and exposed by the treachery of the sons of Witiza, the Goths were put to flight. The army, fleeing to its destruction, was almost annihilated. Because they forsook the Lord and did not serve him in justice and truth, they were forsaken by the Lord so that they could no longer inhabit the land that they desired. Concerning the aforementioned King Roderic, we know nothing certain about his death. But in our own unrefined times, when the city of Viseo and its suburbs were being settled by our order,[25] a monument was found in a certain basilica there, upon which was inscribed an epitaph in this manner: 'Here lies Roderic, the last king of the Goths'. But let us return to that time when the Saracens entered Spain on the third day before the Ides of November, era 752 (November 11, 714).

8. The Arabs, after oppressing the region along with the kingdom, killed many with the sword and subjugated the rest to themselves by mollifying them with a covenant of peace. The city of Toledo, victor over all peoples, succumbed, vanquished by the victories of the Ishmaelites; subjected, it served them. They placed prefects throughout all the

---

[23]'Vallat' would appear to be a Latin transliteration of the Arabic *balat* or palace. 'Vallat Ruderici' would be 'Roderic's palace'. Bonnaz, p. 132. The 'Chaldeans'—in this chronicler's lexicon, anyway—are the Muslims.

[24]As Collins points out, Witiza could not have been more than thirty at the time, meaning that his sons could not have played much of a role in these events. *Arab Conquest*, pp. 144-5.

[25]The reference to *iussum nostrum* is the keystone of the traditional argument that Alfonso himself authored the chronicle.

provinces of Spain and paid tribute to the Babylonian king[26] for many years until they elected their own king and established for themselves a kingdom in the patrician city of Córdoba.[27] At almost the same time, in the region of the Asturians, there was in the city of Gijón a prefect by the name of Munnuza,[28] a companion of Tariq. While he held the prefecture, a certain Pelayo, the swordbearer of the kings Witiza and Roderic, oppressed by the dominion of the Ishmaelites, had come to Asturias along with his sister. On account of her, Munnuza sent Pelayo to Córdoba as his envoy.[29] Before Pelayo returned, Munnuza married his sister through some strategem. When Pelayo returned he by no means approved of it. Since he had already been thinking about the salvation of the church, he hastened to bring this about with all of his courage. The evil Tariq sent soldiers to Munnuza, who were to apprehend Pelayo and lead him back to Córdoba, bound in chains. But when they came to Asturias, seeking to apprehend him treacherously in a village called Brece,[30] the plan of the Chaldeans was made known to Pelayo by a friend. Seeing that it would be impossible for him to resist the Saracens given their great number, Pelayo escaped from their midst, rushed off and came to the banks of the river Piloña.[31] He found it overflowing, but by swimming with the help of the horse upon which he sat, he crossed to the opposite side and made his way into the mountaines. The Saracens stopped pursuing him. As he headed into the mountains, Pelayo joined himself to the many people that he found hastening to assemble. He climbed a high mountain called Auseva and headed for a cave on the side of the mountain which he knew to be very safe.[32] From this great cave flows a stream called the Enna.

---

[26]That is, the caliph in Damascus.

[27]After the Abbasid revolution of 750 (described at the end of the *Chronicle of 754*), an Umayyad refugee, Abd ar-Rahman (I), made his way to Spain where he established an independent Umayyad emirate in 756.

[28]To be distinguished from the Munnuza of *Chr754* 79, who led a Berber uprising against the Cordoban governor Abd ar-Rahman ibn Abd Allah (730-2).

[29]That is, as the text subsequently clarifies, on account of Munnuza's romantic interest in Pelayo's sister. Arab sources claim that Pelayo was sent to Córdoba as a hostage in an effort to forestall unrest in Asturias.

[30]Precise location unknown.

[31]Near Cangas de Onís.

[32]Covadonga, which lies a few miles east of Cangas de Onís. The chronicler will refer to it below (*ChrAlf* 9) as 'coba dominica' (from which the modern name has evolved). In the

After Pelayo sent an order to all of the Asturians, they gathered together in one group and elected him their leader.[33] Hearing this, the soldiers who had come to apprehend him returned to Córdoba and related everything to their king, saying that Pelayo, as Munnuza had suggested, was clearly a rebel. Hearing this, the king, moved by an insane fury, ordered a very large army drawn from all over Spain to set out for Asturias and he placed Alqamah, his companion, in charge of it. He ordered Oppa, a certain bishop of the see of Toledo and son of King Witiza[34]—on account of whose treachery the Goths had perished—to go with Alqamah and the army to Asturias. Alqamah was advised by his colleague Tariq that if Pelayo refused to come to terms with the bishop, he should be taken by force in battle and brought to Córdoba. Coming with an army of almost 187,000 soldiers, they entered Asturias.

9. Pelayo was on Mt. Auseva with his allies. The enemy army advanced to him and set up countless tents before the mouth of the cave. Bishop Oppa ascended the hill in front of Covadonga and spoke to Pelayo, saying,[35] 'Pelayo, Pelayo, where are you'?

Pelayo, responding from an opening, said, 'I am here'.

The bishop said to him, 'I suppose you are not unaware, my brother and son, how all of Spain a short time ago was organized according to one order under the rule of the Goths, and that it outshone all other lands in learning and knowledge. If when the entire army of the Goths was assembled, it proved incapable of withstanding the attack of the Ishmaelites, how much more effectively do you expect to defend yourself on this mountain top? To me it seems difficult. Rather, heed my warning and recall your soul from this decision, so that you may enjoy the partnership of the Chaldeans and take advantage of many benefits.

Oviedo version, it is called, 'cova sancte Marie' (*Crónicas Asturianas*, p. 125). Both names reflect the presence of a shrine to the Virgin Mary in the cave.

[33] Pelayo (718-37).

[34] According to the *Chronicle of 754* (54), Oppa was the son of Egica, thus the brother of Witiza. The Oviedo version of the chronicle refers to him as the bishop of Seville rather than Toledo.

[35] The dialogue between Pelayo and Oppa is so distinct in style from the rest of the chronicle that it would appear to have been a popular legend incorporated into the account. The Oviedo version is much less elaborate.

To this Pelayo responded, 'Have you not read in the divine scriptures how the church of God is compared to a mustard seed and that it will be raised up again through divine mercy'?[36]

The bishop responded, 'It is indeed written thus'.

Pelayo said, 'Christ is our hope that through this little mountain, which you see, the well-being of Spain and the army of the Gothic people will be restored. I have faith that the promise of the Lord which was spoken through David will be fulfilled in us: "I will visit their iniquities with the rod and their sins with scourges; but I will not remove my mercy from them".[37] Now, therefore, trusting in the mercy of Jesus Christ, I despise this multitude and am not afraid of it. As for the battle with which you threaten us, we have for ourselves an advocate in the presence of the Father, that is, the Lord Jesus Christ, who is capable of liberating us from these few'.

The bishop then turned to the army and said, 'Go forth and fight. You heard how he responded to me. I can see by his determination that you will never have a covenant of peace with him unless it be achieved by means of a vengeful sword'.

10. Then Alqamah ordered his men to engage in battle. They took up arms. The catapults were set up. The slings were prepared. Swords flashed. Spears were brandished. Arrows were shot incessantly. But on this occasion the power of the Lord was not absent. For when stones were launched from the catapults and they neared the shrine of the holy virgin Mary, which is inside the cave, they turned back on those who shot them and violently cut down the Chaldeans. And because the Lord does not count spears, but offers the palm of victory to whomsoever he will, when the Asturians came out of the cave to fight, the Chaldeans turned in flight, dividing into two groups. There Bishop Oppa was immediately captured and Alqamah was killed. In that same place 124,000 of the Chaldeans were killed. But the 63,000 who were left alive ascended to the summit of Mt. Auseva and then descended to Liébana through Amuesa.[38] But they

---

[36]Matthew 17:20.

[37]Psalms 89:32-3.

[38]The Muslims apparently fled through the heart of the mountainous Picos de Europa region of eastern Asturias and western Cantabria. For a reconstruction of this route, see: *Crónicas Asturianas*, plate 1.

could not escape the vengeance of the Lord. For when they had reached the summit of the mountain—which is over the bank of a river called the Deva, next to a village called Cosgaya—it happened, by a judgement of God, that the mountain, quaking from its very base, hurled the 63,000 men into the river and crushed them all. There even now, when this river fills beyond its limit,[39] it reveals many visible signs of these events. Do not think this to be unfounded or fictitious. Keep in mind that he who once parted the waters of the Red Sea so that the children of Israel might cross,[40] has now crushed, with an immense mass of mountain, the Arabs who were persecuting the church of God.

11. When Munnuza learned what had happened, he quickly left the coastal city of Gijón and fled. In a certain village called Olalies he was captured and killed along with his men. Then the country was populated and the church was restored. Everyone together gave thanks to God, saying, 'Blessed be the name of the Lord who strengthens those who believe in him and destroys wicked peoples'. Within a short time, Alfonso, the son of Peter, who was the leader of the Cantabrians and was from the royal line, came to Asturias. He received in marriage the daughter of Pelayo, named Ermesinda, and enjoyed many victories alongside his father-in-law as well as after Pelayo's death. Finally peace was restored to the land. To the extent that the dignity of Christ's name grew, the derisive calamity of the Chaldeans wasted away. Pelayo lived as king for nineteen years. His life ended with a natural death at Cangas de Onís in the era 775 (737).

12. Afterwards, Favila, Pelayo's son, succeeded in the place of his father.[41] He constructed, with marvellous workmanship, a basilica in honor of the Holy Cross.[42] He lived only a short time. He is reported to have been killed by a bear during a moment of levity in the second year of his reign, in the era 777 (739).

---

[39]The meaning of this passage (*Ubi nunc ipse fluvius dum limites suos sequitur...*) is elucidated by the corresponding passage in the Oviedo version, which specifically states, 'When in winter it fills its channels and dissolves its banks.' *Crónicas Asturianas*, p. 129.

[40]Exodus 14:21-2.

[41]Favila (737-9).

[42]Presumably in Cangas de Onís.

13. After the death of Favila, Alfonso was elected king by all the people, receiving the royal sceptre with divine grace.[43] He always crushed the audacity of his enemies. Together with his brother, Fruela, he took many cities in battle, deploying his army frequently. Specifically, he took: Lugo, Tuy, Oporto, Anegia, the metropolitan city of Braga, Viseo, Chaves, Ledesma, Salamanca, Numancia, which is now called Zamora, Avila, Astorga, León, Simancas, Saldaña, Amaya, Segovia, Osma, Sepúlveda, Arganza, Clunia, Mave, Oca, Miranda, Revenga, Carbonárica, Abeica, Cenicero, and Alesanco, with their fortresses, villas and villages.[44] Killing all the Arabs with the sword, he led the Christians back with him to his country.[45]

14. At that time Asturias, Primorias, Liébana, Trasmiera, Sopuerta, Carranza, Vardulias, which is now called Castile, and the coastal region of Galicia were settled. Alava, Viscaya, Aizone, and Orduña were found to have been continuously occupied by their inhabitants just like Pamplona, Degio, and Berrueza. Alfonso was a great man. He was loved by God and by everyone alike. He built many basilicas. He lived as king for eighteen years and died a natural death.

15. I will not be silent about the miracle which I know truly to have occurred. When Alfonso gave up his spirit in the silence of the dead of night, his body was being guarded by palace officials. Suddenly the voices of angels on high singing psalms were heard by everyone: 'Behold how the just man is uplifted and no one reflects, and behold how the just men are uplifted and no one understands with the heart: the just man is borne up from the face of iniquity and he will be at peace in his sepulchre'. Know this to be the truth, and do not think it fabulous. I would prefer to say nothing than to pass on a falsehood.

---

[43]Alfonso I (739-57).

[44]This list of towns in the Duero and upper Ebro valleys reflects the geographical range of Asturian raids in the wake of the Berber rebellion and exodus from northern Spain (740-1). Actual Asturian control over these areas probably dates from the next century when the chronicle was written. Barbero, 219-20.

[45]This 'depopulation' of the Duero valley has been the focus of much discussion. Salvador de Moxó, *Repoblación y sociedad en la España cristiana medieval* (Madrid, 1979), pp. 21-45.

16. In the era 795 (757), after the death of Alfonso, his son Fruela succeeded him as king.[46] He was a man of very ardent temperament. He won many victories. He fought a battle with the Cordoban host at Pontubio in the province of Galicia and there he killed 54,000 Chaldeans. He also captured alive the leader of the cavalry by the name of Umar and in that very same place cut off his head. He overcame the rebellious Basques and took for himself a wife from their territory named Munia and she bore a son named Alfonso. Fruela overcame the peoples of Galicia who were rebelling against him and violently laid waste the entire province. He put an end to that crime whereby priests since the time of Witiza had become accustomed to taking wives.[47] Applying whips to the many who remained in sin, he confined them to monasteries. Thus from then on it was forbidden for priests to take wives. Observing canonical doctrine once again, the church grew great. In Fruela's time, Galicia was settled up to the river Miño. He was harsh in his conduct. He killed his brother by the name of Vimarano with his own hands. Not long after— the Lord giving him what he had given his brother—he was killed by his own men. He had ruled for eleven years, three months. Era 806 (768).

17. After his death, his cousin Aurelio succeeded him as king.[48] In his time, the slaves rose up in rebellion against their own masters. But overcome by the industry of the king, all were reduced to their former servitude.[49] Aurelio fought no battles. He remained at peace with the Chaldeans. He ruled for six years. In the seventh year his life came to an end as the result of a natural illness, in the era 811 (773).

18. After Aurelio's death, Silo received Adosinda, daughter of Alfonso, in marriage, on account of which he also obtained the kingship.[50] He remained at peace with the Ishmaelites. He overcame and subjected to his dominion Galicia, which had rebelled against him, the conflict beginning at Mt. Cuperio. While he ruled, Alfonso, the son of

---

[46]Fruela I (757-68).

[47]*ChrAlf* 5.

[48]Aurelio (768-74). He was the son of the older Fruela (brother of Alfonso I) mentioned in *ChrAlf* 13.

[49]The nature of this rebellion remains unclear.

[50]Silo (774-83).

Fruela and grandson of the older Alfonso, governed the palace because Silo had no son from his wife Adosinda. After the ninth year of his rule, Silo departed from this world as the result of a natural death, in the era 821 (783).

19. With Silo dead, all of the magnates of the palace along with the queen Adosinda, placed Alfonso on the throne of his father, Fruela. But his uncle Mauregato, son of the older prince Alfonso,[51] though born of a slave, swelled with pride and removed King Alfonso from power. Fleeing, Alfonso made for Alava[52] and was received by his mother's relatives. Mauregato appropriated for six years the kingship that he had rebelliously usurped.[53] He died a natural death in the era 826 (788).

20. With Mauregato dead, Vermudo, the son of Fruela—of whom we first made mention in the account of the older Alfonso[54] because he was his brother—was elected king.[55] This Vermudo was a very great man. He ruled for three years and then voluntarily gave up his rule because he was a deacon.[56] He installed his nephew Alfonso, whom Mauregato had removed from power, as his successor and lived with him most lovingly for many years. He died a natural death and departed from this world in the era 829 (791).

21. King Alfonso the great was anointed as king on the eighteenth day before the kalends of October in the era mentioned above.[57] In the third year of his reign, an army of Arabs entered Asturias under the command of a certain general named Mugait.[58] Headed off by the Asturians at

---

[51]That is, Alfonso I. Fruela I and the illegitimate Mauregato were half-brothers.

[52]In Vasconia.

[53]Mauregato (783-8).

[54]*ChrAlf* 13.

[55]Vermudo (788-91). Vermudo was Aurelio's younger brother.

[56]Vermudo seems to have been drafted to serve as king after he had already entered the church. Technically, this was a violation of ecclesiastical law. As Bonnaz suggests (p. 188), Vermudo was probably elevated as the result of a compromise between the contending parties within the Asturian elite. Alfonso (II) was forced to wait one more time.

[57]September 14, 791. Alfonso II (791-842).

[58]Abd al-Malik ibn Mugait.

Lodos,[59] 70,000 of the Arabs were killed along with their commander. Alfonso established his throne in Oviedo,[60] adding a basilica in honour of our Lord and Saviour Jesus Christ, with twelve altars in accordance with the number of the apostles. He also built a church in honour of the holy, ever-virgin Mary, with individual altars of wonderful workmanship and strong construction placed here and there. He also founded another church dedicated to the most blessed martyr Tirsus near the church of the Holy Saviour. And some distance from the palace he built a church in honour of Sts Julian and Baselissa with a pair of altars of wonderful workmanship and set up in a marvelous arrangement. He also directed and ordered to be built a royal palace, baths, and storehouses for all types of provisions.

22. In the thirtieth year of Alfonso's reign, two armies of Chaldeans entered Galicia, led by two brothers of the Quraysh[61] named Al-Abbas and Malik, who were prefects. But they were annihilated at the same time, one in a place called Narón and the other at the river Anceo. In Alfonso's time, a certain man by the name of Muhammad, a citizen of Mérida and a muwallad[62] by birth, rebelled against King Abd ar-Rahman[63] and fought many battles with him, putting his armies to flight. When he was no longer able to inhabit his country, Muhammad turned to Alfonso and the king received him with honour. For seven years he lived in the province of Galicia with all of his followers. Then, puffed up with pride, he vainly conspired against the king and the country. He gathered his allies, assembled his army, and pillaged the land. When Alfonso learned what had happened, he assembled his army and hastened to Galicia. When Muhammad heard that the king was coming, he made for a certain strong fortress with his allies. The king and his army pursued Muhammad and surrounded him in the fortress. What more shall I say? On that same day Alfonso's army attacked, killed Muhammad, and

---

[59] Southwest of Oviedo.

[60] Alfonso II set himself up in Oviedo where, in the 760s, the priests Maximus and Fromistanus had established a monastery dedicated to St. Vincent. *Crónicas Asturianas*, pp. 13-14.

[61] A powerful Arab tribe that controlled Mecca during Muhammad's rise to power.

[62] *Mollitus* (modern Castilian: *muladí*) refers to a Christian convert to Islam. The Arabic word, used as a technical term by historians of Spain writing in English, is muwallad.

[63] Abd ar-Rahman II, emir of Córdoba (822-52).

brought his decapitated head to the king. As soon as they broke the battleline they entered the fortress, where they killed more than 50,000 Saracens who had come to assist Muhammad from the provinces of Spain.[64] The king returned to Oviedo with a great victory.[65] King Alfonso led a glorious, chaste, continent, sober, and immaculate life for many years, and in ripe old age, after ruling for fifty-two years, sent his most holy spirit to heaven. He who led a holy life in this world came to rest in a tomb in Oviedo.

23. In the era 881 (843), after the death of Alfonso, Ramiro, son of the prince Vermudo, was elected king.[66] At that time he was away from the throne because he had travelled to the province of Vardulias[67] to take a wife. When King Alfonso departed from this world, Nepotianus, count of the palace, rebelled and seized power. When he heard what had happened, King Ramiro made for the region of Galicia and assembled his army in the city of Lugo. After a short period of time, he invaded Asturias. When Nepotianus learned of his arrival, he went with his army to meet him at the bridge over the river Narcea. But when the battle began, Nepotianus was deserted by all of his men and was quickly put to flight. He was captured in the province of Primorias[68] by the two counts Scipio and Sonna and his eyes were put out. Ramiro ordered him confined to a monastery and he lived out his life in the habit of a monk. At the same time the Northmen, a pagan and extremely cruel people previously unknown to us, arrived in our region with their naval forces.[69] Ramiro, who had by then been made king, gathered a great army and fought against them at a place called Farum Brecantium.[70] There he

---

[64] That is, Muslim Spain.
[65] Carolingian sources report that Alfonso also plundered Lisbon. *Royal Frankish Annals*, a. 798.
[66] Ramiro I (842-50).
[67] Castile.
[68] In Asturias.
[69] The ninth century marked the hey-day of Viking raids. England and northern France and Germany suffered the most, but Spain was not immune from the threat, as evidenced by the two references in this chronicle: 844 (*ChrAlf* 23) and 859 (*ChrAlf* 27). See: A. A. El-Hajji, 'The Andalusian Diplomatic Relations with the Vikings during the Umayyad Period', *Hespéris Tamuda* 8 (1967), pp. 67-110.
[70] Probably La Coruña in Galicia.

destroyed many bands of Northmen and burned their ships with fire. The others, those who were left, took to the sea and went to the province of Baetica. They entered the city of Seville and annihilated many bands of Chaldeans there, partly by the sword and partly by fire. After the year had passed and the city of Seville had been invaded, they returned to their own country. But let us return to our subject.

24. The oft-mentioned King Ramiro was shaken frequently by civil war. Two magnates, one a nobleman, the other a count of the palace, became puffed up with pride against the king. When the king learned of their conspiracy he ordered one of the two by the name of Aldroitus to be blinded and decapitated the other one, named Piniolus, along with his seven sons. After Ramiro quieted the civil wars, he built many arched buildings of granite and marble—without using any wood—on the side of Mt. Naranco two miles from Oviedo. He did battle with the Saracens twice and with the help of God emerged victorious. After the seventh year of his reign he died as the result of a natural illness and rested in a tomb in Oviedo.

25. In the era 888 (850), with Ramiro dead, his son Ordoño succeeded him as king.[71] He was a modest and patient man. He built walls around cities that had been long ago deserted, namely: León, Astorga, Tuy, and Amaya. He built their gates on high ground. He filled them partly with people from his own kingdom and partly with those coming up out of Spain.[72] He did battle with the Chaldeans frequently and always emerged the victor. At the outset of his reign, the province of the Basques rebelled against him. When he and his army invaded, the Saracen host suddenly advanced against him from the other side. But with God's help, he put the Chaldeans to flight and brought the Basques under his jurisdiction. I will not be silent about what I know to have occurred. A certain man by the name of Musa[73]—a Goth by birth but deceived by the Muhammadan rite

---

[71]Ordoño I (850-66).
[72]That is, Muslim Spain. A reference to the migration of Andalusian Christians (Mozarabs) to the north.
[73]Musa ibn Musa ibn Fortun.

along with all of his family, which the Chaldeans call the Banu Qasi[74]—
rebelled against the Cordoban king and took control of many cities partly
by the sword and partly by treachery. First he took Zaragoza, and then
from there Tudela and Huesca, and after that, Toledo, where Musa
installed his son by the name of Lupe as prefect. Later, Musa turned his
arms against the Franks and the Gauls and brought about great slaughter
and pillage. He captured two great Frankish commanders, Sanctio and
Epulo, partly through battle, partly through treachery, and bound them in
chains.[75] Two great rebels from the Chaldeans—one from the tribe of the
Quraysh by the name of Ibn Hamza and the other a muwallad by the
name of Alporz along with his son Azet—were captured in battle, partly
by the father Musa and partly by his son Lupe. On account of these
victories, Musa swelled so much in pride that he demanded that his men
call him the third king of Spain.

   26. King Ordoño moved his army against him and came to the city
called Albelda that Musa had just recently built with wonderful
workmanship. The king arrived with his army and surrounded it with
fortifications. Musa, then arrived with a countless multitude and set up
tents on the mountain which is called Laturce. King Ordoño divided his
army into two units, one to besiege the city, the other to fight against
Musa. They immediately engaged in battle and Musa and his army were
put to flight. 'Meeting them, they made such a slaughter of them'[76] that
more than 10,000 of Musa's best soldiers, along with his son-in-law by
the name of García, were killed, not counting the footsoldiers. Musa
himself, struck by a sword three times, escaped only half alive, losing
many of the battle supplies and gifts that Charles, king of the Franks,[77]
had sent. Never, from then on, did he win a victory. King Ordoño then
sent the army to the city of Albelda and stormed it on the seventh day of
fighting. He killed all of the soldiers with the sword. He destroyed the

---

[74]The Banu Qasi was a family of converts of Islam who controlled the Ebro Valley. 'Banu
Qasi' literally means 'sons of Cassius', who was probably a Visigothic count at the time of
the invasion.

[75]This Frankish defeat probably corresponds to the one recorded in the *Royal Frankish
Annals* (a. 824) involving counts Aeblus and Asinarius.

[76]Judges 20:25.

[77]Charles the Bald (840-77).

city itself down to its foundations and returned to his own city with a great victory.[78] Lupe, the son of the same Musa, who served as consul of Toledo, upon hearing that his father had been overcome, subjected himself and all of his followers to King Ordoño and remained subject to him for as long as he lived. Later he fought many battles against the Chaldeans alongside the king.

27. King Ordoño took many other cities in battle: specifically, the city of Coria with its king, Zaid, and the city of Talamanca with its king, Murzuk, and his wife. He killed all of the soldiers. The rest of the people, with their wives and children, were sold into slavery. At this time the Northmen pirates again came to our shores. They then spread out all over Spain, ravaging its coasts with sword and fire. From there, crossing the sea, they invaded the city of Naacor in Maurctania and killed a multitude of Chaldeans with the sword. Then, heading toward the islands of Mallorca and Menorca, they depopulated them with the sword. They then sailed to Greece and finally returned to their own country three years later.

28. Ordoño, after completing the sixteenth year of his reign, was afflicted with gout and died in Oviedo. He was placed in a tomb in the church of St Mary alongside the previous kings. He who ushered in happy times during his reign is now himself happy in heaven. He who was so loved here by the people is now rejoicing with the holy angels in the celestial kingdom.

29. In the era 904 (866), with Ordoño dead, his son Alfonso succeeded him as king.[79]

---

[78] In 859.
[79] Alfonso III (866-910).

LISTS OF RULERS

BYZANTINE (ROMAN) EMPERORS[1]

Justinian I (527-65)
Justin II (565-78)
Tiberius I Constantine (578-82)
Maurice (582-602)
Phocas (602-10)
Heraclius (610-41)
Constantine III (641)
Constans II (641-68)
Constantine IV (668-85)
Justinian II (685-95)
Leontius (695-8)
Apsimar, also known as Tiberius II (698-705)
Justinian II (restored: 705-11)
Philippicus (711-13)
Anastasius II (713-15)
Artemius, also known as Theodosius III (715-17)
Leo III (717-41)
Constantine V (741-75)

VISIGOTHIC KINGS[2]

Athanaric
Alaric I (395-410)
Athaulf (410-16)
Sigeric (416)
Wallia (416-19)

---

[1]Based on: Deno John Geanakoplos, Byzantium (Chicago, 1984), pp. 449-50.
[2]Based on: Collins, *Early Medieval Spain*, pp. 299-300, and Thompson.

Theoderid, also known as Theodoric I (419-51)
Thorismund (451-3)
Theodoric II (453-66)
Euric (466-84)
Alaric II (484-507)
Gesalic (507-11)
Amalric (511-31)
Theudis, also known as Theodoric III (531-48)
Theudigisel, also known as Theodisclus (548-9)
Agila I (549-54)
Athanagild (554-68)
Liuva I (568-73)
Leovigild (569-86)
Reccared I (586-601)
Liuva II (601-3)
Witteric (603-10)
Gundemar (610-12)
Sisebut (612-21)
Reccared II (621)
Suinthila (621-31)
Sisenand (631-6)
Chintila (636-9)
Tulga (639-42)
Chindasuinth (642-53)
Reccesuinth (649-72)
Wamba (672-80)
Ervig (680-7)
Egica (687-702)
Witiza (698-710)
Roderic (710-11)

ASTURIAN KINGS[3]

Pelayo (718-737)
Favila (737-9)
Alfonso I (739-57)
Fruela I (757-68)
Aurelio (768-74)
Silo (774-83)
Mauregato (783-8)
Vermudo I (788-91)
Alfonso II (791-842)
Ramiro I (842-50)
Ordoño I (850-66)
Alfonso III (866-910)

MUSLIM CALIPHS[4]

Abu Bakr (632-4)
Umar (634-44)
Uthman (644-56)
Ali (656-61)
Muawiya I (661-80)
Yazid I (680-3)
Muawiya II (683)
Marwan I (684-5)
Abd al-Malik (685-705)
Walid I (705-15)
Sulayman (715-17)
Umar II (717-20)

---

[3]Based on: Collins, *Early Medieval Spain*, p. 301. I have chosen to use the Castilian forms of the names of the Asturian kings.
[4]Based on: *The Cambridge History of Islam*, ed. P. M. Holt. et al., 2 vol. (Cambridge, 1970), 1:57-103, 231.

Yazid II (720-4)
Hisham (724-43)
Walid II (743-4)
Yazid III (744)
Ibrahim (744)
Marwan II (744-50)

MUSLIM GOVERNORS OF AL-ANDALUS[5]

Musa ibn Nusayr (711-14)
Abd al-Aziz (714-16)
Ayyub ibn Habib al-Lakhmi (716)
Al-Hurr ibn Abd ar-Rahman al-Thaqafi (716-18)
As-Samh ibn Malik al-Khaulani (718-21)
Abd ar-Rahman ibn Abd Allah al-Ghafiqi (721)
Anbasah ibn Sahim al-Kalbi (721-5)
Udhrah ibn Abd Allah al-Fihri (725-6)
Yahya ibn Salamah al-Qalbi (727)
Hudjifah ibn al-Ahwan al-Qaysi (728)
Uthman ibn Abi Nasah al-Khathami (728).
Haytham ibn Ubayd al-Kilabi (729-30).
Muhammad ibn Abd Allah al-Ashjai (730)
Abd ar-Rahman ibn Abd Allah al Ghafiqi (730-2)
Abd al-Malik ibn Qatan (732-4)
Uqbah ibn Hajjaj (734-40)
Abd al-Malik ibn Qatan (restored: 740-1)
Balj ibn Bashr al-Qushayri (741-2)
Abu al-Khattar Husam ibn Dhirar al-Khalbi (743-5)
Thalabah ibn Salamah (745-7)
Yusuf ibn Abd ar-Rahman al-Fihri (747-56).

---

[5]Based on: Imamuddin, pp. 32-46.

SELECT BIBLIOGRAPHY

Alvarez Rubiano, P. 'La crónica de Juan Biclarense: versión castellana y notas para su estudio'. *Analecta Sacra Tarraconensia* 16 (1943), pp. 7-44.

Arjona Castro, Antonio. *El reino de Córdoba durante la dominación musulmana*. Córdoba: 1982.

Barbero, Abilio, and Marcelo Vigil. *La formación del feudalismo en la península ibérica*. 3rd ed. Barcelona: 1982.

Barbero, Abilio. 'El pensamiento político visigodo y las primeras unciones regias en la Europa medieval'. *Hispania* 30 (1970), pp. 245-326.

Barbero, Abilio, and Marcelo Vigil. *Sobre los orígenes sociales de la reconquista*. Barcelona: 1974.

Barkai, Ron. *Cristianos y musulmanes en la España medieval: el enemigo en el espejo*. Madrid: 1984.

Barker, John W. *Justinian and the Later Roman Empire*. Madison: 1966.

Bassett, P. M. 'The Use if History in the "Chronicon" of Isidore of Seville'. *History and Theory* 15 (1976), pp. 278-92.

Benito Ruano, Eloy, and Francisco Javier Fernández Conde. *Historia de Asturias*. vol. 4: *La Alta Edad Media*. Vitoria: 1979.

Bury, J.B. *A History of the Later Roman Empire from Arcadius to Irene (395 A.D. to 800 A.D.)*. 2 vol. London: 1889.

Cambridge History of Islam. ed. P. M. Holt. 2 vol. Cambridge: 1970.

Chejne, Anwar G. *Muslim Spain: Its History and Culture*. Minneapolis: 1974.

Collins, Roger. *The Arab Conquest of Spain, 710-797*. Oxford: 1989.

Collins, Roger. *Early Medieval Spain: Unity in Diversity, 400-1000*. New York: 1983.

Collins, Roger. 'Julian of Toledo and the Royal Succession in Seventh-century Spain'. *Early Medieval Kingship*. ed. P. H. Sawyer and I. N. Wood. Leeds: 1977, pp. 30-49.

Courcelle, Pierre. *Histoire littéraire des grandes invasions germaniques*. 3rd ed. Paris: 1964.

Díaz y Díaz, Manuel C. *La cultura española de Isidoro al siglo XI*. Barcelona: 1976.

Díaz y Díaz, Manuel C. 'La historiografía hispana desde la invasión árabe hasta el año 1000'. *La storiografia altomedievale*. Settimane di studio del centro italiano di studi sull'alto medioevo. Spoleto: 1970.

Diehl, Charles. *L'Afrique Byzantine: Histoire de la domination Byzantine en Afrique (533-709)*. 2 vol. Paris: 1896.

Domínguez, Ursicino. *Leandro de Sevilla y la lucha contra el arrianismo*. Madrid: 1981.

Donner, Fred McGraw. *The Early Islamic Conquests*. Princeton: 1981.

Dubler, César E. 'Sobre la crónica arábigo-bizantina de 741 y la influencia bizantina en la península ibérica'. *Al-Andalus* 11 (1946), pp. 283-349.

SELECT BIBLIOGRAPHY 185

Encyclopaedia of Islam. 2nd ed. Leiden: 1960-.

Estudios sobre la monarquía asturiana. Instituto de estudios asturianos. Oviedo: 1971.

Ferreiro, Alberto. *The Visigoths in Gaul and Spain, A.D. 418-711: A Bibliography.* Leiden: 1988.

Floriano, Antonio Cristino. ed. *Diplomático español del periódo Astur: estudio de las fuentes documentales del reino de Asturias (718-910).* Oviedo: 1949.

Fontaine, Jacques. 'Conversion et culture chez les wisigoths d'Espagne'. *La conversione al cristianismo dell'Europa dell'alto medioevo.* Settimane di studio del centro italiano di studi sull'alto medioevo. vol. 14. Spoleto: 1967, pp. 87-147.

Fontaine, Jacques. *Isidore de Seville et la culture classique dans l'Espagne wisigothe.* 2 vol. Paris: 1959.

Gárcia Moreno, Luís A. *Historia de España visigoda.* Madrid: 1989.

García Toraño, Paulino. *El reino de Asturias (718-910).* Oviedo: 1986.

Glick, Thomas. *Islamic and Christian Spain in the Early Middle Ages.* Princeton: 1979.

Goffart, Walter. *The Narrators of Barbarian History (A.D. 550-800): Jordanes, Gregory of Tours, Bede, and Paul the Deacon.* Princeton: 1988.

Gómez-Moreno, Manuel. 'Las primeras crónicas de la Reconquista: el ciclo de Alfonso III'. *Boletín de la Real Academia de la Historia* 100 (1932), pp. 562-99.

Goubert, Paul. *Byzance avant l'Islam*. 2 vol. Paris: 1965.

Guichard, Pierre. *Al-Andalus: estructura antropológica de una sociedad islámica en occidente*. Barcelona: 1970.

Hammond, Nicholas G. L. *Atlas of the Greek and Roman World in Antiquity*. Parkridge, NJ: 1981.

Herrin, Judith, *The Formation of Christendom*. Oxford: 1987.

Hillgarth, J. N. 'Coins and Chronicles: Propaganda in Sixth-Century Spain and the Byzantine Background'. *Historia* 15 (1966), pp. 483-508.

Hillgarth, J. N. 'Historiography in Visigothic Spain'. *La storiografia altomedievale*. Settimane de studio del centro italiano di studi sull'alto medioevo. vol. 17. Spoleto: 1970.

Hodgson, Marshall G. S. *The Venture of Islam: Conscience and History in a World Civilization*. 3 vols. vol. 1: *The Classical Age of Islam*. New York: 1972.

Imamuddin, S. M. *A Political History of Muslim Spain*. 4th ed. Karachi: 1984.

Jones, A. H. M. *The Later Roman Empire, 284-602*. 3 vol. Oxford: 1964.

Julien, Charles-André. *History of North Africa from the Arab Conquest to 1830*. tr. John Petrie. New York: 1970.

Kedar, Benjamin Z. *Crusade and Mission: European Attitudes toward the Muslims*. Princeton: 1984.

Lévi-Provençal, Evariste. *Histoire de l'Espagne musulmane*. 3 vol. 2nd ed. Paris: 1950.

Lòpez Pereira, José Eduardo. *Estudio crítico sobre la crónica mozárabe de 754*. Valencia: 1980.

Moxó, Salvador de. *Repoblación y sociedad en la España cristiana medieval*. Madrid: 1979.

Millet-Gérard, D. *Chrétiens mozarabes et culture islamique dans l'Espagne des VIIIe-IXe siècles*. Paris: 1984.

O'Callaghan, Joseph F. *A History of Medieval Spain*. Ithaca, New York: 1975.

Ostrogorsky, George. *History of the Byzantine State*. rev. ed. tr. Joan Hussey. New Brunswick, New Jersey: 1969.

Pérez de Urbel, Justo, and Ricardo Del Arco y Garay. *España cristiana: comienzo de la reconquista (711-1038)*. 4th ed. Historia de España. vol. 4. ed. Ramón Menéndez Pidal. Madrid 1982.

Pérez de Urbel, Justo. *San Isidro de Sevilla: su vida, su obra, y su tiempo*. Barcelona: 1940. Reydellet, Marc. 'La conception du sovereign chez Isidore de Seville'. Isidoriana. León: 1961, pp. 457-66.

Reydellet, Marc. 'La conception du souverain chez Isidore de Seville'. *Isidoriana*. León: 1961, pp. 457-66.

Reydellet, Marc. 'Les intentions idéologiques et politiques dans la "chronique" d'Isidore de Seville'. *Mélanges d'archéologie et d'histoire* 82 (1970), pp. 363-400.

Reydellet, Marc. *La royauté dans la littérature latine de Sidoine Apollinaire à Isidore de Seville*. Rome: 1981.

Romero, José Luís. 'San Isidore de Sevilla: su pensamiento histórico-político y sus relaciones con la historia visigoda'. *Cuadernos de historia de España* 8 (1947), pp. 5-71.

Sánchez Albornoz, Claudio. *Investigaciones sobre historiografía hispana medieval (s. VIII al XII)*. Buenos Aires: 1967.

Sánchez Albornoz, Claudio. *El reino de Asturias*. 3 vol. Oviedo: 1974.

Simonet, Francisco X. *Historia de los mozárabes de España*. Madrid: 1903.

Stratos, Andreas N. *Byzantium in the Seventh Century*. Amsterdam: 1975.

Sumner, G. V. 'The Mozarabic Chronicle of 754 and the Location of the Berber Victory over the Army of Kultum'. *Al-Qantara* 1 (1980), pp. 443-6.

Teillet, Suzanne. *Des Goths à la nation gothique. Les origines de l'idée de nation en occident du Ve siècle au VIIe siècle*. Paris: 1984.

Thompson, E. A. *The Goths in Spain*. Oxford: 1969.

White, Hayden. 'The Value of Narrativity in the Representation of Reality'. *The Content of the Form: Narrative Discourse and Historical Representation*. Baltimore: 1987.

Wolf, Kenneth Baxter. *Christian Martyrs in Muslim Spain*. Cambridge: 1988.

Wolf, Kenneth Baxter. 'The Earliest Latin Lives of Muhammad'. *Conversion and Continuity: Indigenous Christian Communities in Islamic Lands, Eighth to Eighteenth Centuries*. ed. Michael Gervers and Ramzi Jibran Bikhazi. Toronto: 1990, pp. 89-100.

Wolf, Kenneth Baxter. 'The Earliest Spanish Christian Views of Islam', *Church History* 55 (1986), pp. 281-93.

Wolfram, Herwig. *History of the Goths*. tr. Thomas J. Dunlap. Berkeley: 1988.

Ye'or, Bat. *The Dhimmi Jews and Christians under Islam*. rev. ed. tr. David Maisel, Paul Fenton, David Littman. East Rutherford, NJ: 1985.

INDEX

Abd al-Aziz 27, 134-6, 151
Abd Allah (Abbasid) 155, 157-8
Abd Allah (general) 122, 126
Abd al-Malik (caliph) 124, 127-9
Abd al-Malik (governor) 34, 37, 49, 146-50
Abd ar-Rahman II 173
Abd ar-Rahman (governor) 34, 139, 143-5
Abd ar-Rahman (general) 150
Abeica 170
Abu al-Khattar 152-3, 156, 158
Abu Bakr 114-5
Acephali 116
Addaeus 59
Adosinda 172
Adrianople 3-4, 11, 15, 16
Aegidius 94
Aetherius 59
Aëtius 90-1
Africa xv, 24, 37, 57, 60-1, 67, 90, 96, 111, 122, 134, 142-3, 147-8, 151
Agila 99-100
Agrippinus 94
Aizone 170
Al-Abbas 173
Al-Andalus xvi, 25-42 *passim*, 45, 53-5
Alans 19, 90, 108
Alaric I 4, 14, 16-17, 21, 24, 48, 86, 88, 90
Alaric II 95-6
Al-Ashjai 143
Alava 170, 172
Albelda 176
Alboin 62
Aldroitus 175
Alesanco 170
Alexander the Great 81
Alexander (bishop) 75
Alexandria 5, 59, 75, 115

Alfonso I 49, 52, 169-72
Alfonso II 44-5, 52, 54, 171-4
Alfonso III xvi-xvii, 43-4, 53, 161, 177
Algeciras 150
Al-Hurr 136-7
Al-Muzar 149
Alporz 176
Alps 19, 108
Alqamah 167-8
Amabilis 61
Amalric 97
Amaya 64, 170, 175
Ambrose 15, 19
Amuesa 168
Anagastus 65
Anambadus 144
Anastasius I 96-7
Anastasius II 136-7
Anbasah 139-41
Anceo R. 173
Anegia 170
Antioch 5
Apsimar 129
Aquitaine 11, 17, 90, 93, 96
Arabia 29, 37, 111, 113
Arabs 25-56 *passim*, 111-60 *passim*
Aramundarus 65
Arcadius 5, 88-90
Ardabastus 154-5
Ardabastus (Spain) 162
Aregia, Aregensian Mts. 65, 101
Arganza 170
Argimund 76
Arians, Arianism 1, 4, 7-10, 12, 20-2. 27, 62, 68, 73, 75-6, 83, 101-2
Arius 75, 84, 103
Arles 17, 90, 95
Armenians 58, 61
Artemius 137-8
Asia Minor (Romania) 82, 135-6, 141

Aspidius 65
As-Samh 137-9
Astorga 93, 170, 175
Asturias xv-xvi, 43-56 *passim*, 105, 161, 166-70, 172, 174
Atax 90
Athanagild (king) 59-60, 100
Athanagild (son of Theodemir) 151-2
Athanaric 4, 16, 20, 83-5, 107
Athaulf 4, 17, 88-9
Attila 92
Audeca 70-1
Augustine 14, 120
Aurelio 52, 171
Auseva, Mt. 166, 168
Austrasia 145
Authari 69, 72
Avars 60, 66-7
Avila 170
Avitus 93
Ayub 135
Azet 176

Babylon 54, 133, 138, 155, 166
Baduarius 65
Baetica 89, 94, 175
Baetis R. 70
Balj 33-4, 149-50, 158
Banu Qasi 53-5, 176
Barcelona 1, 89, 96
Basques 31, 103, 105-6, 121, 145, 162, 171
Bastetania 60
Baza 6
Beja 71
Benedict I (pope) 63, 66
Berbers 25, 27, 37
Berrueza 170
Boso 74
Braga 170
Braulio 117

Brece 166
Burgundy, Burgundians xv, 95-6

Cádiz, Straits of 90, 98, 132
Cangas de Onís 169
Cantabria 62, 101, 169
Carbonárica 170
Carcasonne 74
Carranza 170
Cartagena 12-13
Castile (Vardulias) 170, 174
Catalaunian Fields 91
Caure, Mt. 161
Celtiberia 67, 102
Cenicero 170
Cerdanya 35, 143
Ceurila 94
Ceuta 98, 149
Chalcedon 5, 9, 58, 75
Chaldeans 51-5, 165, 168-9, 171, 173, 175-7
Charles the Bald 176
Charles Martel 38, 145
Chaves 170
Childebert 97
Chindasuinth 46, 118-19, 121, 162, 164
Chinthila 117
Chosroes I 58, 64
Chosroes II 28-9, 112
Cidamo 122
Cixila 153
Cixilo 46, 163
Claudius (emperor) 16, 82
Claudius (general) 8, 22, 74, 103
Clovis 95
Clunia 170
Complutum 68
Constans II 121-3
Constantine I 2-3, 9-10, 16, 75, 82
Constantine III 118, 121

Constantine IV 123-6
Constantine V 154-8
Constantinople 1, 4-5, 7, 29, 58-60, 62-5, 85, 111, 113, 122, 135
Constantius 89
Córdoba 6, 26-7, 33, 37-8, 49, 62, 70, 99, 135, 137, 143, 146-7, 149-50, 152, 156, 165-7, 171, 176
Coria 177
Cosgaya 169
Covadonga 52, 167
Cunimund 61-2
Cuperio, Mt. 171

Damascus 34, 38, 123, 155
Danube R. 82, 84, 97, 108
Dara 64
Degio 170
Desiderius 73
Deva R. 169
Dioscorus 75
Domninus 62
Donatus 61, 71
Dordogne R. 145
Durance R. 96

Ebba 96
Eboric 70-1
Egica 33, 46, 127-8, 130, 151, 163-4
Egilona 136
Egypt 111, 115, 118, 122, 148
Enna R. 166
Epulo 176
Ermesinda 169
Ervig 46, 127, 162-3
Ethiopia 81, 118
Eudes 139, 144
Eugenius II 121
Euric 23, 94-5, 102
Europe xv, 108, 145
Eusebius 1-4, 10-11, 13, 26, 40, 57, 158

Eutropius 71, 75
Eutyches 75
Evantius 139, 148

Farum Brecantium 174
Favila 52, 169-70
Felix 129
Flavia 111
Florentina 12
Framidaneus 61
France xv
Franks 7-9, 22-3, 26, 38, 67, 70-4, 95-8, 103, 138-41, 144-7, 163, 176
Fredoarius 139
Frideric 93
Fritigern 83
Fruela I 52, 171-2
Fruela (brother of Alfonso I) 170

Gabata 114
Galicia 54, 61, 65, 70-4, 90, 94, 170-1, 173-4
Galla Placidia 5, 17, 88-9
Gallia Narbonensis 62, 71, 74, 100-2, 117, 125, 136, 162
Gallienus 82
Garamantes 59
García (king) 43
García (Musa ibn Musa's son-in-law) 176
Garmul 67
Garonne R. 145
Gaul 88-96, 108
Gazania 118
Geiseric 4, 7, 10
Gennadius 67
Gepids 61
Germanus 59
Gerona 1
Gerticos 161
Gesalic 23, 96-7
Getae 15-16, 79, 81, 107-9
Gijón 166, 169

Gog 15, 81
Gosuintha 60, 68, 73-4
Goths *passim*
Greece 2, 67, 82, 162, 177
Gregory I (pope) 8, 72, 120
Gregory (Africa) 122
Guadix 139
Gundemar 23, 105
Gunderic (Vandal) 90
Gunderic (bishop) 130
Gundobad 96
Gunthchramn 74

Haytham 142-3
Helna 62
Helladius 116
Heraclius 25, 27-9, 31, 33, 40, 105-6, 111-18
Herinan 64
Hermenegild 7-8, 12, 63, 67-8, 70-1, 101
Herodotus 15
Hesperia 136
Hisham 140-4, 146, 148-50
Honorius 5, 86, 88-90
Honoulf 97
Hudjifah 142
Huesca 176
Huns 4-5, 17, 19-20, 84, 91-2, 107
Hydatius 13

Iberia (Caucasi) 58, 61
Ibn Hamza 176
Ibrahim 155
Ildephonsus 126
Illyricum 69, 82
India 81, 130
Ingundis 7
Ishmaelites 36, 48-9, 54, 122, 145, 155, 167, 171
Isidore of Seville xvi-xvii, 1, 7, 11-24, 25, 27-8, 31, 41, 43-6, 48, 52, 116, 158
Islam xv, 36, 39, 53, 55-6

Istria 83
Italica 70
Italy 65, 67, 69, 72, 86, 88, 92, 97, 108

Jerome 2-4, 15-16, 57, 159
Jerusalem 5, 33, 133
Jews 23, 37, 55, 105, 115, 126, 140, 159
John of Biclaro xvi-xvii, 1-10, 14, 16, 21-2, 24-6, 28, 31, 38-9
John III (pope) 63
John of Médrida 67
Judaea 111
Julian of Toledo 46, 126-8, 159
Julius Caesar 81, 158
Justin (son of Germanus) 59
Justin II 5, 57-66, 100-1
Justinian I 6, 30, 57, 97-100
Justinian II 127, 130-2, 134-5
Justinian (general) 64

Kairouan 38
Khazars 130
Kultum 148, 154

Laturce, Mt. 176
Leander of Seville 7, 12, 72, 75, 119
Lebida 122
Ledesma 170
Leo I (emp) 94-5
Leo I (pope) 3
Leo III (emp) 139-43, 146, 148-50, 152, 154
León 170, 175
Leovigild 1-2, 6-8, 10, 12, 14, 16, 21-4, 49, 60-72, 100-2, 131
Libya 111, 118, 131, 143-4, 157
Liébana 168, 170
Litorius 21, 91
Liuva I 59-60, 62, 100-1
Liuva II 23, 25, 104
Lodos 173
Lugo 94, 170, 174

Lupe 55, 176-7
Lusitania 1, 74, 94-5
Lombards 4, 61, 65, 67, 69-70, 72

Maccuritae 60, 63
Macedonia 82
Magog 15, 80-1, 107
Málaga 6, 60
Malaric 72
Maldras 94
Malik 173
Mallorca 177
Marcian 9-10, 75, 93
Marmorica 118
Marseilles 95
Marwan I 124
Marwan II 39, 155-7
Maslama 135
Masona 63
Massila 94
Mauregato 52, 172
Mauretania 37, 131, 177
Maurice 67-74, 76-7, 102, 104
Mave 170
Mecca 36, 125
Medes 81
Menorca 177
Mérida 21, 44, 54, 63, 67, 94, 100, 173
Mesopotamia 29, 111, 113, 125
Miño R. 171
Miranda 170
Miro 61-2, 65, 70-1
Moors 36, 59-61, 67, 122, 131, 141, 143, 147-9, 154
Morocco 21, 27
Mozarabs 45
Muawiya I 122-3, 125
Muawiya II 124
Mugait 172
Muhammad (prophet) xv, 29, 36, 54-5, 113-6, 175

Muhammad (muwallad rebel) 54, 173-4
Muhammad the Saracen 143
Munia 171
Munnuza (Berber rebel) 35, 143-4
Munnuza (Gijón commander) 166-7, 169
Murzuk 177
Muslims xv-xvii, 25-42 *passim*, 45, 49, 54-5
Musa ibn Musa 54, 175-7
Musa ibn Nusayr 32-4, 37, 131-2, 134

Naacor 177
Naranco, Mt. 175
Narbonne 5, 17, 94, 96-7, 100
Narcea R. 174
Narón 173
Nava R. 148
Nepotianus (Asturian rebel) 174
Nepotianus (Visigothic general) 94
Nestor 75
Nicaea 9, 75
Nicetas I 111
Nile R. 155, 157
Nîmes 162
Nisibis 64
Northmen 53-4, 174-5, 177
Novellus 68

Oca 170
Octavian Caesar 158-9
Odoacer 97
Olalies 169
Ologicus 106
Oporto 93, 170
Oppa 33, 50, 167-8
Orbigo R. 93
Ordoño I 43, 53, 161, 175-7
Ordoño II 43, 161
Orduña 170
Orespeda 66

Orosius, Paul 14-16, 20-1, 24
Osma 170
Ostrogoths 97
Oviedo 44, 52-3, 173-5, 177
Oxifer, Mt. 44

Pamplona 95, 170
Pannonia 67
Paul 162
Pelagius II (pope) 66, 72
Pelayo 49-53, 166-9
Pentapolis 118
Pergamum 136
Persians 25, 28, 30, 39, 58, 61, 63-5, 68, 76, 81, 92, 112-15, 118, 138, 157
Peter of Cantabria 49, 169
Peter of Toledo 156
Philippicus 136
Phocas 25, 105, 111
Piloña R. 166
Piniolus 175
Pliny 15
Poitiers 38, 96
Pompey 81
Pontubio 171
Pontus 82
Primorias 170, 174
Prosper of Aquitaine 2-5, 7, 13-14, 57
Pyrenees 38, 49, 108, 146
Pyrrhus 81

Quraysh 173, 176

Radagaisus 14, 21, 86
Ramiro I 53, 174-5
Reccared 1-2, 8-10, 12, 14, 22-3, 25, 40, 45, 49, 63, 71-7, 102-4, 117
Reccared II 106, 116
Reccesuinth 32, 46, 121-2, 161
Rechiarius 93-4
Recopolis 7, 67, 102

Red Sea 51, 169
Remismund 94
Reptila 62
Revenga 170
Rhone R. 71
Riccimir 13, 107
Ricilo 165
Roderic 25, 31, 33, 48, 50, 131, 136, 164-5
Roman (Byzantine) empire *passim*
Romans *passim*
Romanus 65
Rome (city) 3-5, 11-12, 14, 17, 48, 63, 87-90, 97, 108, 117, 119, 127-8
Ruccones 62, 105

Sabaria 63, 101
Sabellians 153
Saguntum 104
Salamanca 170
Saldaña 170
Salla 94
Sanctio 176
Sappi 63
Saracens 25-56 *passim*, 65, 111-59 *passim*, 162, 165-77 *passim*
Sarmatians 82
Scipio 174
Sclaveni 66, 69
Scythians 16, 81, 86, 107
Segga 73
Segovia 170
Sepúlveda 170
Serenus 140
Servitanum 61, 71, 75
Severianus 12
Seville 12, 31, 53, 68, 70, 72, 75, 99-100, 116-7, 119, 135, 157, 175
Sextus Julius Africanus 2
Sicily 24, 88, 121
Sidonia 6, 61
Sigeric 89
Sigibert 67

Silo 52, 171-2
Simancas 170
Sindered 33, 132
Sisbert 71-2
Sisebut 1-13, 23, 25, 27, 30, 46, 105-6, 109, 115-6
Siseguntia 70
Sisenand 13, 116
Slavs 113
Sonna 174
Sophia 59
Sopuerta 170
Spain *passim*
Stilicho 86
Suani 65
Suevi 8, 19, 61-2, 65, 70-1, 73, 90, 93-4, 101, 108, 163
Suinthila 11-13, 23, 25, 30, 45-6, 106-7, 116
Sulayman 134, 136
Sumayl 152-3, 156
Sumeric 94
Sunna 73
Susa 112
Syracuse 121, 123
Syria 29, 33, 111, 113-4, 116

Taio 119-20
Talamanca 177
Tangiers 148
Tariq ibn Ziyad 25, 31-2, 131, 166-7
Tarraconensis 95, 98, 106
Tarragona 71
Tertullian 159
Thalabah 153, 156
Thalamah 158
Theodefred 164
Theodemir of Murcia 27, 151
Theodemir (Suevi) 61
Theoderid 17, 21, 90-1, 93
Theodore (Africa) 59
Theodore (general under Heraclius) 114

Theodoric the Great 17, 96-7
Theodoric II 21, 93-4
Theodosius I 4, 16, 85-6, 88
Theodosius II 140
Theodosius (son of Maurice) 72-3
Theudigisel 23, 98-9
Theudis 21, 23, 97-9
Thessaly 81
Thorismund 91, 93
Thrace 60, 66-7, 69, 85, 108
Tiberius I Constantine 60, 64-9, 72
Tigris R. 138
Toledo *passim*
Toulouse 95, 139
Tours 26, 145
Trasaric 62
Transductine Mountains 131, 147
Trasmiera 170
Trinacrian ports 147
Tripoli 122
Troy 33, 133
Tudela 176
Tulga 118
Tuscany 86
Tuy 163, 170, 175

Udhrah 141
Ugernum 71
Uldida 73-4
Ulfilas 84
Umar I 27, 36, 115-8
Umar II 34, 137-9
Umar (general) 171
Umayyad 39
Umayyah 149, 157
Uqbah 34, 39, 146-7
Urban (ally of Musa) 37, 134
Urban (chanter) 139, 148
Ushmunayn 157

Uthman (caliph) 118, 121
Uthman (governor) 142

Valencia 70
Valens 2, 15, 20, 83-5
Valentinian 91
Valerian 82
Vandals 4-5, 13, 19, 89-90, 96, 108
Vasconia 69, 162
Vermudo 52, 172
Victor 2, 5, 7, 57
Victoriacum 69
Vimarano 171
Vincent of Zaragoza 102
Viscaya 170
Viseo 44, 165, 170
Visigoths *passim*
Vouillé 23

Walid I 26, 32
Walid II 141, 150-1
Wallia 17, 24, 89-90
Wamba 33, 43, 46, 52, 125, 161-3
Witiza 32, 46-52, 128-30, 132, 151, 163-7, 171
Witteric 23, 25, 104-5

Yahya 35, 141
Yazid I 34, 123-4
Yazid II 137-41
Yazid III 151-2, 155
Yazid (rebel) 138
Yusuf 34, 39, 156, 158

Zaid of Coria 177
Zaid (conspirator) 143
Zali 157
Zamora 170
Zaragoza 32, 95, 102, 117, 147, 176
Zeno 95, 97